AURORA CENTRAL H.S.

THE Unexplained

STAFF CREDITS

CONSULTANTS TO THE UNEXPLAINED	Professor A. J. Ellison Dr J. Allen Hynek Brian Inglis Colin Wilson
EDITORIAL DIRECTOR	Brian Innes
EDITOR	Peter Brookesmith
DEPUTY EDITORS	Lynn Picknett Jean Elgie
EXECUTIVE EDITOR	Lesley Riley
CHIEF SUB EDITOR	Nigel Flynn
SUB EDITORS	Chris Cooper Hildi Hawkins Jenny Dawson
PICTURE RESEARCHERS	Anne Horton Paul Snelgrove Frances Vargo
EDITORIAL MANAGER	Clare Byatt
ART EDITOR	Stephen Westcott
DESIGNER	Richard Burgess
ART BUYER	Jean Hardy
PRODUCTION CO-ORDINATOR	Nicky Bowden

REFERENCE EDITION

MARKETING MANAGER	Robert Paulley
PRODUCTION DIRECTOR	Barry Roberts
EDITOR	Mary Lambert
INDEX	Moira McIlroy

Cataloging in Publication Data

The Unexplained, the mysteries of mind, space
 and time.
 1. Curiosities and wonders
 I. Brookesmith, Peter
 001.9′4.   AG243

ISBN 0-86307-098-1 (set)

Reference Edition Published 1984

© Marshall Cavendish Limited MCMLXXXIII
© Orbis Publishing Limited MCMLXXXI

Published by Marshall Cavendish Corporation,
147 West Merrick Road,
Freeport, Long Island
N.Y. 11520

Printed and bound in Great Britain

ISBN 0-86307-098-1 (set)
ISBN 0-86307-097-3 (vol. 1)

PICTURE ACKNOWLEDGEMENTS

1: Barnaby's Picture Library; 2–3: Robert Estall; 2: ZEFA (cl); Fortean Picture Library (bl); Robert Harding Associates (r); 3: John Cutten (bl); Syndication International/Academy of Applied Science, Massachusetts (tr); Topham (br); 4: ZEFA (t); Mary Evans Picture Library (b); 5: ZEFA (l); Mary Evans Picture Library (r); 6: Arnold Desser (t); Fortean Picture Library (b); 7: illustration by Robert Hunt; 8: illustrations by Robert Hunt (t and c); Fortean Picture Library (b); 9: map by Richard Burgess; Fortean Picture Library; 10: Mary Evans Picture Library (t, c and b); 11: Fortean Picture Library (t and b); 12: John Cutten (t); Mary Evans Picture Library (b); 13: Topham (t and c); John Cutten (b); 14: Leif Geiges (t); Mary Evans Picture Library (b); 15: artwork by Hayward Art Group; John Cutten (l); 16–17: John Cleare; 16: map by Bob Bonner, key by Ed Stuart; 17: Royal Geographical Society (l); Associated Press (r); 18: Colin and Janet Bord (tr); Topham (b); 19: artwork by Hayward Art Group; 20: Fortean Picture Library (t and b); 21: Mary Evans Picture Library; 22: Ronald Grant; Syndication International (b); 23: Mary Evans Picture Library (t); Press Association (c and b); 26: Brooke Bond Oxo Ltd (t); 27: Fortean Picture Library; 28: Popperfoto; Photri (l and r); 29: Fortean Picture Library (t); Martin Aircraft Co (c); Mary Evans Picture Library (b); 30: Space Frontiers (t); 30/31: Spectrum Colour Library (b); 31: Kitt Peak National Observatory (t); Topham/Lick Observatory (b); 32: Spectrum Colour Library (t); Space Frontiers (NASA) (b); 33: Royal Greenwich Observatory (t and b); 34: Colorific (t); Mary Evans Picture Library (b); 35: Mary Evans Picture Library (t); Topham (b); 36/37 MARS; 36: Leif Geiges (t); Topham/Leif Geiges (b); 37: S. Ostrander; 38: Fortean Picture Library © Dahinden (tl and tr); Fortean Picture Library (b); 39: Fortean Picture Library © Dahinden (c); 40: Fortean Picture Library; 42: Martin Schwarzschild (tl); artwork by Ed Stuart (tr); artwork by Studio Briggs (b); 43: artwork by Ed Stuart (t); Popperfoto (c); artwork by Studio Briggs (b); 44: artwork by Ed Stuart (t and b); 45: Hale Observatories, USA (tl); artwork by Ed Stuart (tr and b); 47: Fortean Picture Library (b); 48: Fortean Picture Library (b); 49: Topham; 50: Photri (t); Novosti (b); 50–51: J. Cutten (t and c); 51: Brian Snellgrove; 52: Brian Snellgrove (t); Roy Stemman (cl); Brian Snellgrove (cr and b); 53: J. Cutten (t and b); 54: Robert Harding Associates (t and c); Mary Evans Picture Library (b); 55: Mary Evans Picture Library (t); Popperfoto; 56: Mary Evans Picture Library; 57: Mansell Collection (t); Giraudon (c); J. Cutten (b); 58: Rex Features; 59: Space Frontiers (t); Space Frontiers/NASA/Lunar and Planetary Laboratory, University of Arizona (c); Rex Features (bl, bc and br); 60: Rex Features (cl, cr and b); 61: Sonia Halliday Photographs; 62: Sonia Halliday Photographs/F. H. C. Birch; 63: Robert Estall; 64: Sonia Halliday Photographs (t and b); 65: Mary Evans Picture Library (t and b); 66: Fate Magazine (t, c and b); 67: ZEFA (t); Michael Holford (b); 68: Mary Evans Picture Library (t and b); 69: Mary Evans Picture Library (tl); John Cutten (tr, c and b); 70: Mary Evans Picture Library (l); 70–71: Fortean Picture Library (t); Anwar Hussein (b); 71: Photri (t); 72: artwork by Space Frontiers/Don Dixon (tl); Space Frontiers (tr); Robert Hunt Picture Library (b); 73: Institute of Advanced Study, Princeton (tl); Popperfoto (b); 74: John Cleare (t); Fortean Picture Library (b); 75: John Cleare; 76: Musée de l'Homme (tl); Fortean Picture Library (tr and b); 77: Topham (t and b); 78: British Library/Department of Manuscripts; 78–79: Mansell Collection; 79: Associated Press (t); 80: Mary Evans Picture Library (t); George E. Crouter (c); 81: Association of Universities for Research in Astronomy, Inc., The Kitt Peak National Observatory; Spectrum Colour Library (inset c); artwork by Space Frontiers/Don Dixon (inset b); 82: artwork by Hayward Art Group (t and b); 82–83: artwork by Studio Briggs; 84: Topham (t); Press Association (b); 85: Mary Evans Picture Library (t); Colorific! (b); 86: Contrad Research Library (t and b); 87: artwork by Stephen Westcott; 88: Robert Hunt Picture Library (t); Syndication International (b); 89: artwork by Hayward Art Group/Crown Copyright HMSO; 90–91: Camera Press/Mike Wells (b); 91: Fortean Picture Library (t); 91: Michael Holford/Parham Place Collection (c); Mary Evans Picture Library (tr); 92: Popperfoto; Fortean Picture Library (c and b); 93: Bettmann Archive (t); Frank W. Lane/Photo Erling Sivertsen (b); 94: Brian Snellgrove (l); 94–95: Rex Features; 95: Brian Snellgrove; 96: John Cutten (tl, tr and c); Brian Snellgrove (b); 97: John Cutten (t); Brian Snellgrove (c); 98: Michael Taylor (t); illustration by Richard Burgess (b); 99: illustration by Richard Burgess (t); Neville Spearman Ltd/Photo Jacques Vainstain (c); 100: illustration and map by Richard Burgess (t); 101: Michael Holford; 102: Sonia Halliday (t); British Museum Dept of Prints and Drawings (b); 103: Cooper-Bridgeman Library (t); 104: Mary Evans Picture Library; 105: Robert Estall (t); Mike Duffy/York Archaeological Trust (c); Picturepoint (b); 106: Mary Evans Picture Library (t and c); 107: Mansell Collection (t); National Portrait Gallery, London (b); 108: Ground Saucer Watch Inc (t and b); 109: Ground Saucer Watch Inc (t, c and b); 110: Topham (t); 110–111: Popperfoto (c); 111: Mary Evans Picture Library (t and b); National Maritime Museum (br); 112: Robert Hunt Picture Library (t); Lauros-Giraudon (tr); Topham (c); Photri (b); 113: Mary Evans Picture Library (t); John Hillelson Agency/Sygma (c and b); 114: Polish Institute and Sikorski Museum; 115: Giraudon (t); William MacQuitty (bl); Michael Holford (br); 116: M. Vautier (t); Mansell Collection (b); 117: Scala (t); National Gallery, London (b); 118: illustration by Tony Roberts/Young Artists; 119: artwork by Ed Stuart; 120: artwork by Ed Stuart (t); Hale Observatories (b); 121: Fortean Picture Library (c and b); 122: Mary Evans Picture Library (t); Fortean Picture Library (c and b); 123: Michael Holford (t); map by Colin Edwards, key by Ed Stuart; 124: artwork by Linden Artists (tr); Press Association (c and b); 125: artwork by Linden Artists; 126: National Maritime Museum (t); *More lives than One?* by Jeffrey Iverson (Souvenir Press) (b); 127: National Portrait Gallery, London (l); Robert Harding Associates (r); 128: Michael Holford (t); Mary Evans Picture Library/Society for Psychical Research (b); 129: Scala (r); 130: Center for UFO Studies (t); Photri (b); 130–131: artwork by Linden Artists (t); 132: Photri; 133: Robert Harding Associates (t); Spectrum Colour Library (cl); Photri (cr); 134: map by Colin Edwards (t); Vincent Mercie–Explorer (c); John Cutten (b); 135: News and Publications Service, Stanford University (tl); John Cutten (bl); Carl Sargent (br); 136: Cambridge Evening News (t); Mary Evans Picture Library/Society for Psychical Research (tr); British Museum Dept of Prints and Drawings (bl); Mary Evans Picture Library (br); 137: John Cutten (t); Associated Newspapers (c); 138: BBC Hulton Picture Library (t); Mansell Collection (bl); 138–139: Mansell Collection (b); 139: Mary Evans Picture Library; 140: Mansell Collection (t); Mary Evans Picture Library (c); Inter-Photo (b).

THE Unexplained

MYSTERIES OF MIND, SPACE AND TIME

Volume 1

Aurora Central High School

Marshall Cavendish · New York & London

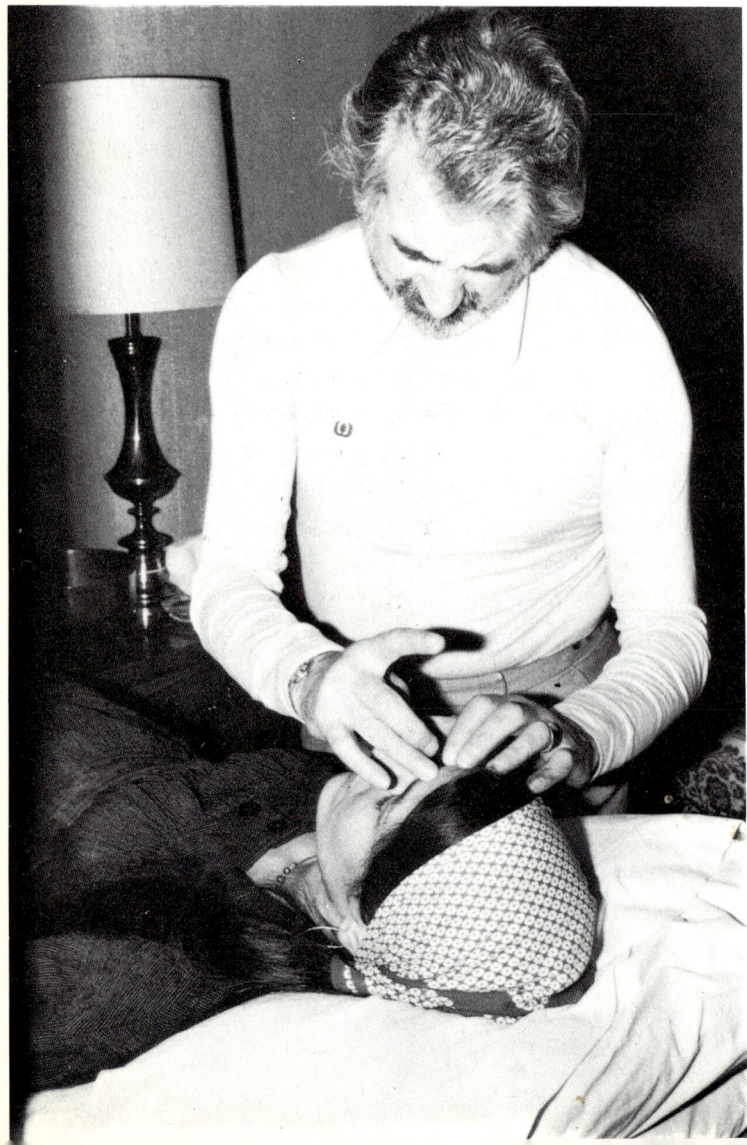

Introduction

As the sun rises over Salisbury Plain in England on the morning of 21 June, it lights up the tip of the so-called Hele Stone, throwing its long black shadow forward into the great sarsen circle that we know as Stonehenge. At this dramatic signal a group of men and women dressed in the flowing white robes of the Druids begin to chant; while beyond the wire fence that encloses the ancient site a crowd of many thousands end their night-long vigil to press forward in curiosity and awe.

For a few minutes, all are united in a celebration that transcends time: the Druids, sustained by their conviction that their rites are drawn from a tradition lost in the mists of antiquity; the crowd, drawn to the place as if by atavistic instinct; and the ancient stones themselves, shrouded in mystery.

We all respond in some measure to such occasions, feeling the deep-down tug of emotions older than human memory, the sense of communion with other minds, the excitement and the magic of a world that will not submit to the physical laws we try to impose upon it. In everyday circumstances, too, we can be made uneasily aware that the Universe is not a simple one of cause and effect. How often the images of friends or relatives come unsummoned into the mind only minutes before we receive news of them; how often we exclaim 'I know this place!' when we have never previously visited it.

And so, in spite of all the efforts of the scientists, our world remains a place full of mysteries. Many of these mysteries manifest themselves almost daily – everybody knows someone who has seen a UFO, or visited a 'healer', or successfully prophesied some coming event – yet few people can agree on any kind of explanation for them. Other mysterious phenomena are rarer: showers of extraordinary objects from the skies; surviving prehistoric monsters on land and in the sea; unknown forces in the Earth that can be detected by dowsers' rods and migrating animals. And the remarkable powers of human beings themselves: the influence that can move things at a distance, the healing touch, the ability of the mind in trance to explore both the past and the future, and even tune in to events taking place miles away.

There are those who must develop powers such as these by study and exercise, but others, more fortunate, appear to be born with them. Indeed, many people believe that once all human beings practised what we now call extra-sensory perception, that even today children are born with these abilities, but that through education and training we lose them.

In the pages that follow, we shall be exploring all the great unexplained mysteries of our world, seeking some common factor linking them together, and subjecting every phenomenon to critical analysis in depth. Where a plausible scientific explanation exists, we shall give it; but where (as too often happens) scientists deny the occurrence of a phenomenon because they are unable to explain it, we shall bring together all the available evidence and all the theories, and try to present a balanced view. Space, and time, and the enigmas of the human mind – the unexplained universe lies before us!

THE EDITOR

Contents

VOLUME ONE

Major Contributors

Professor A. J. Ellison, who has been engaged in research into the paranormal for many years, was President of the Society for Psychical Research from 1976 to 1979

Dr J. Allen Hynek is Professor of Astronomy at Northwestern University, Illinois, USA. He is Director of the Center for UFO Studies and author of *The UFO Experience*

Brian Inglis has worked as journalist and broadcaster for many years and has an absorbing interest in the paranormal. His books include *Natural and supernatural* and *Natural medicine*

Colin Wilson is well known as author and broadcaster. His encyclopedic knowledge of unexplained phenomena is reflected in many of his books, which include *The occult, They had strange powers* and *Mysteries*

The Earl of Clancarty, better known as author Brinsley le Poer Trench, is President of the international UFO organisation Contact, and since 1979 has been Chairman of the House of Lords UFO Committee

Adrian Berry, science correspondent of the *Daily Telegraph*, is a Fellow of the Royal Astronomical Society, a senior member of the British Interplanetary Society, and author of *The iron sun*

Janet and Colin Bord are long-established writers and photographers of the unexplained. They have recently published a major investigation of mysterious man-like animals around the world, *Alien animals*

Charles Bowen is editor of *Flying Saucer Review* and has been gathering and collating data on UFOs for many years

David Christie-Murray was Assistant Master of Harrow School until his retirement in 1973. He is ex-Chairman of the Society for Psychical Research, and author of *Voices from the gods*

Hilary Evans is a member of the council of the Society for Psychical Research, recently published a paper on UFO sources, and is book editor of the magazine *Alpha*

Andrew Green is one of the foremost authorities on the subject of ghosts and poltergeists. He has written a number of books on the subject, including *Ghost hunter's guide*

Brian Innes has written and broadcast on many topics associated with the paranormal. His books include *Horoscopes* and *The Tarot*

Richard Leigh and **Michael Baigent** have worked for many years as researchers into the paranormal, particularly with Henry Lincoln and the BBC

John Michell has spent many years researching the knowledge of ancient civilisations. He is well known for his theories on ley lines and standing stones, and his books include *The flying saucer vision, The view over Atlantis,* and *A little history of astro-archaeology*

Tony Morrison is a zoologist, film-maker and writer. His numerous television films include *Mystery on the desert* and *Pathways to the gods*

Tony Osman is science editor of the *Sunday Times Magazine*

Jenny Randles has been involved in UFO investigation for about fifteen years, and has had many articles published in Britain, Europe and the USA. She co-ordinates the UFO Investigators's Network

Bob Rickard is editor and founder of *Fortean Times*. With John Michell he wrote *Phenomena*

Frank Smyth is a journalist and broadcaster who has been concerned with the paranormal and crime for many years. His books include *Modern witchcraft, Ghosts and poltergeists,* and *Cause of death*

Brian Snellgrove is Britain's leading exponent of Kirlian photography, and author (with his wife Marita) of *The unseen self*

A to Z Quick Reference

The UFO paradox

Only the most hardened sceptic can still pretend that UFOs do not exist. But in what way are they real? HILARY EVANS examines this vexed question – and finds that there may be more than one answer

'THEY FLEW LIKE A SAUCER would if you skipped it across the water.' This is how, on 24 June 1947, American airman Kenneth Arnold, an experienced pilot, described some unusual flying craft he had seen over the mountains of America's west coast. Newspapermen applied his phrase to the craft themselves, and the misleading label 'flying saucer' has followed the UFO ever since, like a tin can tied to a cat's tail.

This fanciful name has deepened the reluctance of professional scientists to take the UFO seriously. Only a few have taken the trouble to investigate this bizarre phenomenon, which surely qualifies as the strangest of our time. Even that phrase, 'of our time', is a subject of controversy: many people claim that the UFO has been with mankind throughout history. But the evidence they offer is meagre and their case far from proven. There seems little doubt that our earliest ancestors were considerably more advanced than has generally been supposed, but that is a long way from the theory that our planet was long ago visited by extraterrestrial voyagers.

Whether or not UFOs existed in the past, there is no doubt that UFO sightings have proliferated in astonishing numbers over the past 30 years. This fact seems to be in some way linked with man's first steps towards exploring space, and this connection is undoubtedly an important clue in trying to explain the UFO.

Estimates of the total number of UFO sightings vary so widely as to be meaningless; more helpful figures are provided by the catalogues of reported sightings prepared by individual investigative organisations. Recently a French team catalogued more than 600 encounter cases in France alone, each vouched for by responsible investigators; how many more were not reported or investigated? In the early 1970s UFO investigators made lists of all reported landing cases for particular countries: 923 were recorded in the United States, 200 in Spain.

Are UFOs real in the sense that, say, spacecraft are real? The surest proof would be actually to get hold of one, and there are persistent rumours that certain governments, notably that of the United States, have indeed obtained a UFO, which is kept in total secrecy. However this remains mere conjecture, despite the sworn affidavits of alleged witnesses. Indeed, the whole matter of governmental involvement – or the lack of it – is a further and fascinating aspect of the UFO controversy.

In the absence of a real UFO that we can touch and examine, there is a great deal of evidence of the phenomenon in the form of a

The COMING of the SAUCERS

By Kenneth Arnold & Ray Palmer

Above: Kenneth Arnold's book, first published in 1952, was the first full study of UFOs. Arnold began collecting accounts of UFO sightings after he saw several disc-shaped objects in the sky in June 1947

mass of photographs and a handful of movies. The majority are undoubtedly fakes. Those with good credentials are so blurred, so distant or so ambiguous that they simply add a further dimension to the problem: why, if UFOs exist, and in an age when many people carry cameras with them most of the time, have we not obtained better photographic evidence?

Perhaps the strongest evidence we have is from the effects caused by UFOs on surrounding objects, particularly machinery. In November 1967 a truck and a car approaching each other on a Hampshire road in the early hours of the morning simultaneously suffered engine failure when a large egg-shaped object crossed the road between them. The police, and subsequently the Ministry of Defence, investigated the incident, but no official explanation was ever issued. Such a case may leave investigators puzzled, but it makes one thing certain: if they can cause physical effects, UFOs must be physically real.

If they are physical objects, UFOs must originate from somewhere. When the first UFOs of the current era were seen, back in the 1940s, it was assumed they came from somewhere on Earth. The Americans suspected they were a Russian secret device, perhaps developed using the expertise of German scientists captured at the end of the Second World War.

But as more reports came in it became clear that no nation on Earth could be responsible. Nor was there sufficient evidence to support other ingenious theories – that they came from the Himalayas, long a favoured source of secret wisdom, or Antarctica, where unexplored tracts of land and climatic anomalies provide a shaky foundation for speculation. Instead, ufologists began to look beyond the Earth, encouraged by the fact that our own space exploration programme was just beginning. We were starting to take an active interest in worlds beyond, and it seemed reasonable that other civilizations might have a similar interest in us.

However, although the number of potential sources of life in the Universe is virtually infinite, the probability of any civilisation being at a stage of development appropriate for space travel is very small. The fact that no solid evidence has been found for the extra-terrestrial hypothesis is discouraging. Although it is the best available explanation, it remains no more than speculation.

Messages from outer space?

Today it is recognised that the UFO poses a problem not only for the astronomer and the engineer, but also for the behavioural scientist. The psychologist confirms that an individual's response to a sighting is conditioned by his psychological make-up, while the sociologist places such responses in a wider social context and relates them to cultural patterns. The anthropologist detects parallels with myth and traditional belief, while the parapsychologist notes how frequently sightings are accompanied by such psychic manifestations as precognition and poltergeist phenomena.

This is particularly true of 'encounter' cases in which the observer claims to have had actual meetings with UFO occupants. The entities are generally described as extra-terrestrial aliens, often ambassadors from an inter-galactic power; their purpose is to examine human beings, to warn us of misuse of resources and to bring reassuring messages from some cosmic brotherhood. With only one or two such cases on record they could be dismissed as fantasy, but there are hundreds of such cases on file.

If a single one of these cases could be shown to be based on fact, the UFO problem would be established on solid foundations and serious scientific interest assured. But in every instance it remains an open question whether the incident actually occurred or is simply a fabrication – deliberate, unconscious, or perhaps induced by some external force. Hypotheses range from brainwashing by extraterrestrial invaders, to deliberate invention by the CIA.

Almost certainly, UFOs exist on both the physical and the psychological level. Somehow we have got to recognise that, although they are real, they are not what they seem. This is the paradox that lies at the heart of the UFO mystery, which we examine in the classic UFO case histories that follow.

Right: this photograph was taken at Taormina, Sicily, in 1954. Sceptics claim the 'objects' are nothing more than lenticular clouds, or even the result of lens flare

Below: a shot taken from Skylab III in 1973. The object rotated for several minutes before disappearing. UFOs have been reported by almost all astronauts

Strange encounters of many kinds

ESTABLISHED SCIENCE has always tended to view the UFO phenomenon with scepticism. In his book, *The UFO experience*, Dr J. Allen Hynek, who was astronomical consultant to Project Blue Book (the US Air Force investigation into UFOS), tells the story of an event at an evening reception held in 1968 in Victoria, British Columbia, at which a number of astronomers were present. During the evening it was announced that strange lights – possibly UFOS – had been spotted outside. Dr Hynek continues: 'The news was met by casual banter and the giggling sound that often accompanies an embarrassing situation.' And, he reports, not a single astronomer went outside to look.

Even Project Blue Book attempted to explain away every reported sighting in terms of conventional science. It soon began to earn itself a bad name because many of its explanations were impossible to believe. In 1966 the US Air Force set up a two-year research project – to investigate, in effect, its own investigations!

The Condon Report, as it was unofficially known, was published in 1969 and stated,

Unidentified flying objects have intrigued the world for decades, but objective reports by experienced investigators rarely reach the mass media. CHARLES BOWEN begins a major series of carefully authenticated cases

broadly, that since nothing valuable to science had come out of the study of UFOS, further research was not justified. This conclusion was reached despite the fact that about one in three of the 87 case histories studied by the commission remained unexplained in the report. After this the US Air Force relinquished responsibility for the monitoring of UFO reports and Project Blue Book was disbanded in December 1969. Since 1969 research has been largely left to private organisations, such as Ground Saucer Watch and Project Starlight International in the USA, and UFOIN (UFO Investigators' Network) and BUFORA (British UFO Research Association) in Britain.

From UFO reports made over the past 30 years it has been observed that they occur in distinct waves, often called 'flaps'. The flaps of 1954 and 1965, when reports reached vast numbers, were particularly interesting. Featured below are two incidents from the 1954 flap. The third incident we describe, at Socorro, New Mexico, belongs to the smaller flap of 1964; it is a classic early example of an encounter involving humanoids.

What kind of sighting?

Astronomer Dr J. Allen Hynek, Director of the Centre for UFO Studies, USA. Dr Hynek has spent many years in applying the techniques of science to the study of UFOS

Dr J. Allen Hynek, while acting as a consultant to Project Blue Book, developed a system of classification of UFO 'types' which has become standard. He divided UFO reports according to the distance, greater or less than 500 feet (150 metres), at which the UFO was observed, and subdivided each of these two sections into three, giving six categories altogether.

The commonest sightings are of the 'distant' type.
Nocturnal lights Strange lights seen at a distance in the night sky, often with unusual features such as variations in the intensity of light or colour and sudden, remarkable changes of speed and direction of movement.
Daylight discs Distant objects seen against the sky during the daytime. The shapes vary considerably: cigars, spheres, eggs, ovals and pinpoints as well as discs are often reported.
Radar-visuals Distant UFOS recorded simultaneously on radar and visually with good agreement between the two reports. Dr Hynek excluded 'sightings' made solely by radar since false traces can result from a number of natural factors such as ground scatter – the signal is reflected from high ground – temperature inversions and even thick banks of cloud or flocks of birds. Radar-visual sightings are the most important

category of UFO reports as they give independent instrumental evidence of the sighting; unfortunately, they are very rare.

Reports of UFOS seen at close range are the most interesting and often spectacular; these are the famous 'close encounters'.
Close encounters of the first kind Simple observations of phenomena where there is no physical interaction between the phenomena and the environment.
Close encounters of the second kind Similar to the first kind except that physical effects on both animate and inanimate matter are observed. Vegetation may be scorched or flattened, tree branches broken, animals frightened or car headlights, engines and radios doused. In cases of electrical failure the equipment usually begins to work normally again once the UFO has disappeared.
Close encounters of the third kind 'Occupants' are reported in or around the UFO. Dr Hynek generally ruled out so-called 'contactee' cases in which the reporter claimed to have had intelligent communication with the 'occupants', arguing that such reports were almost invariably made by pseudo-religious fanatics and never by 'ostensibly sensible, rational and reputable persons.' But even these cases occasionally have to be taken seriously by scientists.

'We are not alone'

Radar-visual: Atlantic Ocean off Labrador, 29 June 1954

The UFO seen by Captain James Howard and the crew and passengers of BOAC Strato-cruiser *Centaurus* on 29 June 1954 was not a saucer or a disc; it was, astonishingly, a shape that kept changing shape. The airliner had taken off from Idlewild, New York, bound for Newfoundland before making the Atlantic crossing to Shannon, then London.

The airliner was making its way steadily northeastwards when the radio crackled an order from ground control to 'hold' – a manoeuvre adopted when there is a hazard ahead. After half an hour's circling the skipper advised control that if he couldn't proceed he would have to return to Idlewild, as his fuel was low. After some delay permission was given to proceed and *Centaurus* went on automatic pilot at 19,000 feet (6000 metres), just below a broken layer of cloud and with a solid mass of cloud beneath it at 200 feet (60 metres). After some 20 minutes a glint of light suddenly caught Captain Howard's eye. On the port side of the aircraft he saw a large object of metallic appearance emerge from a gap in the clouds. Moving around this main shape were six much smaller objects, not unlike a screen of small destroyers escorting an enormous aircraft carrier.

A bizarre aspect of this remarkable apparition was that it seemed to be changing shape all the time. Captain Howard sketched on his knee pad the different forms he saw: they were a 'delta wing', a telephone handset, a pear. He has since said that, with its continual changes in shape, the object reminded him of a swarm of bees in flight. It was an estimated 4 miles (6 kilometres) from *Centaurus* and it maintained that position.

When Captain Howard turned to speak to his first officer, Lee Boyd, he found him already out of his seat, standing to watch the display. Captain Howard called up control:

'We are not alone.'

'We know.'

'What is it?'

'We don't know, but we've scrambled a Sabre from Goose Bay to investigate.'

'Good. Give me his frequency and I'll vector him in.'

A few minutes later the captain was in touch with the pilot of the Sabre jet fighter who, once he was in range, announced he had two images on his radar scope – one for *Centaurus* and the other, presumably, for the UFO. Then the unexpected happened: the six small objects manoeuvred into single file, bore down on the main object and appeared to merge into one end of it. Thereafter the size of the large UFO began to diminish until the Sabre's pilot announced he was overhead, at which point the object finally disappeared from the radar scope '. . . like a TV picture going off'.

Since about 1953, airline pilots have been required not to disclose to the public information about UFO sightings. In the case of *Centaurus*, however, many of the passengers had watched the display with amazement and the incident received wide press coverage. Researchers were fortunate in this, for this sighting falls into the important category of radar/visual cases. In this instance two separate radar sets were involved (at control and in the Sabre) plus visual observation by experienced pilots, air crew and some 30 or more passengers – only one of whom had a camera, and he was asleep!

'Luminous, silent and eerily still'

Nocturnal lights: Vernon, France, 23 August 1954

Vernon lies on the River Seine some 50 miles (80 kilometres) downstream from Paris; it is the point at which the Allied forces first crossed the river in pursuit of the German armies in 1944. Ten years later, and barely eight weeks after the Idlewild affair, the town was the scene of another significant event, which was witnessed by four people but received little attention in the press.

The sky was clear at 1 a.m. on 23 August 1954, with the moon in its third quarter and due to appear later that night and give only a faint light. M. Bernard Miserey had just returned home and was closing his garage door when he saw a giant cigar-shaped object hanging vertically over the north bank of the

river about 300 yards (275 metres) from him. This object, which he estimated to be some 300 feet (90 metres) long, was luminous, silent and eerily still. While the witness gaped at the phenomenon, a horizontal, disc-shaped object dropped from the bottom of the giant 'cigar', halted its free-fall, wobbled, turned a luminous red with a brilliant white halo and shot towards M. Miserey, passing silently over his house heading south-west.

This remarkable happening was repeated three times, then, after an interval, a fifth disc dropped almost to the level of the river bank before wobbling and disappearing at great speed to the north. While this last manoeuvre was under way the glow of the giant cigar began to fade and soon it was lost in darkness.

M. Miserey reported the incident to the police and was informed that two policemen on their rounds had also observed the happenings, as had an army engineer who was driving on Route Nationale 181 south-west of the town.

What was the meaning of the apparition M. Miserey saw? Was the large cigar-shaped object the 'carrier' of the smaller ones? Other UFO sightings have led many people to think this may be the case – including the Idlewild incident. The significant difference is that, whereas at Idlewild the smaller objects were assimilated by the larger one, at Vernon the small objects were ejected. But no conclusive evidence exists to establish what these objects in the sky actually are.

'Humanoids . . . and strange insignia'

Close encounter of the third kind: Socorro, New Mexico, USA, 24 April 1964

Below: Patrolman Lonnie Zamora whose close encounter is one of the best authenticated cases on record

At about 5.50 p.m. on 24 April 1964 Patrolman Lonnie Zamora of the Police Department in Socorro, New Mexico, was alone in his Pontiac giving chase to a speeding motorist who was heading out of town. Suddenly he heard a roar and at the same time saw a 'flame' in the sky, bluish and orange and strangely static as it descended some distance away. Fearful that a nearby dynamite shack might blow up, the patrolman gave up chasing the motorist and headed off over rough ground towards the point where the flame had come down.

After three attempts he forced his car to the top of a ridge and drove slowly westwards. He stopped when, suddenly, he saw a shiny, aluminium-like object below him, about 150–200 yards (140–185 metres) south of his position. Zamora said it looked like a car on end, perhaps 'turned over by some kids'. Then he saw two humanoid figures in white 'coveralls' close to the object. He estimated later that they were about 4 feet (1.2 metres) tall. One of them looked straight at him and seemed to jump. Zamora was wearing clip-on sunglasses over his prescription spectacles and couldn't distinguish any features or headgear at that distance.

The patrolman now accelerated thinking that, whoever the strangers were, they might be in need of help. The shape he'd seen was a

sort of vertical oval, and looking down he could see it was supported on girderlike legs. When the terrain became too rough for the car to go any further he radioed his headquarters to say that he was near the scene of a possible accident and would proceed on foot.

As Zamora left the car he heard two or three loud thumps, like someone hammering or slamming a door. These thumps were a second or two apart. When he was about 50 paces from the object there was a loud roar, which rose gradually in pitch. The humanoid figures were nowhere to be seen. At the same time he could see a blue and orange flame rise from the ground leaving a cloud of dust. Zamora beat a hasty retreat towards his car and as he reached it turned to see the oval shape, now horizontal, rising towards the level of the car. Frightened by the continuing roar, he ran on and dived for shelter over the edge of the ridge. When he realised the noise had ceased he raised his head from his hands and saw the UFO still in the air and moving away from him about 15 feet (4.5 metres) above the ground. It safely cleared the dynamite shack and continued to rise gradually, watched by the policeman, who was retracing his steps to the car. As he called up the radio officer he watched it accelerate away to clear a mountain range and disappear.

Zamora had seen a kind of strange insignia about 18 inches (45 centimetres) high on the side of the object and while he was waiting for his sergeant to arrive he decided to make a sketch of it.

Sergeant Sam Chavez was soon on the scene. Had he not taken a wrong turning he would have arrived in time to see the craft.

'What's the matter, Lonnie?' he asked. 'You look like you've seen the devil.'

'Maybe I have,' replied Zamora.

Zamora pointed out to Sergeant Chavez the fire that was still burning in the brush where the UFO had stood. When they descended to the site they found four separate burn marks and four depressions – all of similar shape – made, they assumed, by the legs of the landing gear. On three of the marks the dense soil had been pushed down about 2 inches (50 millimetres) and dirt had been squeezed up at the sides. The fourth pad mark, less well defined, was only 1 inch (25 millimetres) deep. When engineer W. T. Powers investigated the case he estimated that the force that produced the marks was 'equivalent to a gentle settling of at least a ton on each mark.' He also pointed out an interesting fact about the positions of the marks. Measurements show that the diagonals of a quadrilateral intersect at right angles, then the midpoints of the sides all lie on the circumference of a circle. Mr Powers noted that one of the burn marks occurred on the intersection of the diagonals and speculated that, assuming the linkage among the legs was flexible, this would mean the burn was immediately below the centre of gravity of the craft and might indicate the position of the blue and orange flame seen by Patrolman Zamora. Four small round marks were found within the quadrilateral on the side farthest from where Patrolman Zamora had stood; these were described as 'footprints'.

The Socorro incident was widely reported in the press and generated immense excitement throughout the world. The US Air Force's Project Blue Book usually ruled out UFO sightings with only one witness, but at Socorro Patrolman Zamora's story was so plausible that it was decided to carry out intensive on-the-spot investigations. This was one case in which Project Blue Book was forced to admit defeat: the apparition could

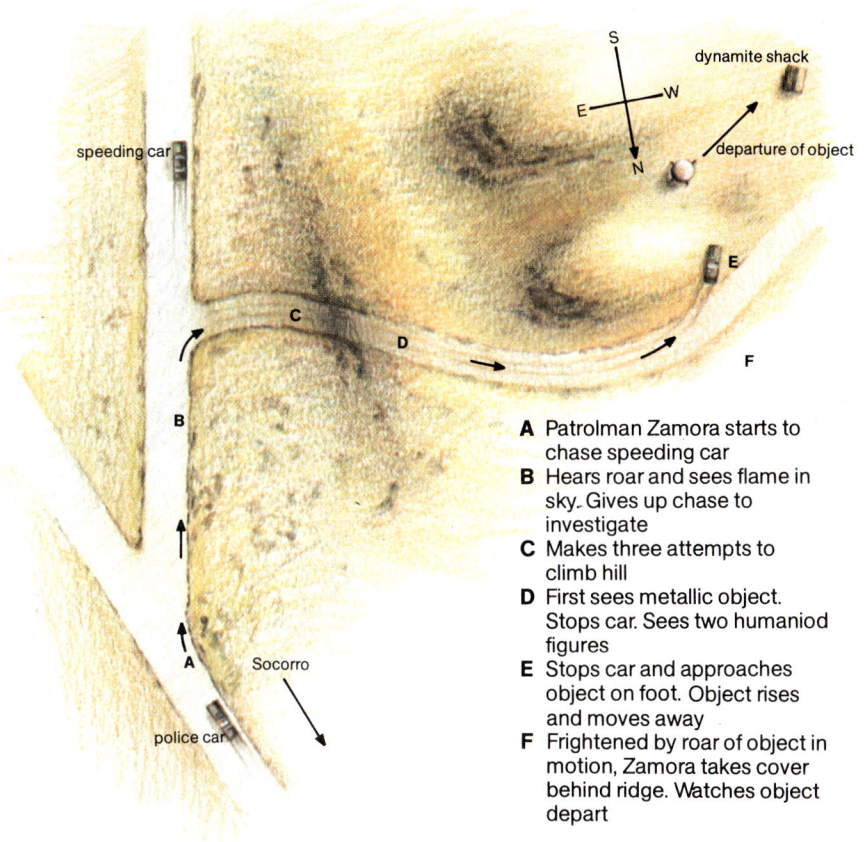

A Patrolman Zamora starts to chase speeding car
B Hears roar and sees flame in sky. Gives up chase to investigate
C Makes three attempts to climb hill
D First sees metallic object. Stops car. Sees two humaniod figures
E Stops car and approaches object on foot. Object rises and moves away
F Frightened by roar of object in motion, Zamora takes cover behind ridge. Watches object depart

not be explained as any known device or phenomenon. Dr J. Allen Hynek admitted that he was more puzzled after completing the investigation than when he had arrived in Socorro. He commented, 'Maybe there *is* a simple, natural explanation for the Socorro incident, but having made a complete study of the events, I do not think so.'

Below: one of the four impressions left by the UFO which landed at Sorocco, New Mexico on 24 April 1964. An engineer said pressure of 1 ton would have been needed to make the holes

him for 90 minutes.

Dr J. Allen Hynek is very wary of all so-called 'contactee' cases. And Allen Hendry, author of *The UFO handbook*, points out a suspicious feature of 'contactee' reports: until the late 1950s, when it was still believed that planets in our solar system were likely to be able to support intelligent life, most of the reported visitors came from Mars, Jupiter and Venus – but once scientists had proved that this was unlikely, the visitors began to hail from planets outside our own solar system.

Paul Villa's photographs have been subjected to very detailed analysis by Ground Saucer Watch Inc., a UFO organization in Phoenix, Arizona. Using advanced computer techniques, they can establish the exact shape of an

THE BEST UFO pictures usually turn out to be hoaxes; pictures of well-documented sightings are usually blurs on under- or over-exposed film.

These spectacular photographs, taken by Paul Villa in Albuquerque, New Mexico, are almost certainly fakes. The top photograph shows an object Villa claims to have seen on 18 April 1965; its three occupants, he says, talked to him. The other two pictures are views of a UFO he photographed on 16 June 1963. It contained nine beings from the constellation of Coma Berenices, who conversed with

alleged UFO, its distance from the camera, and even estimate its true size. Paul Villa's photographs failed GSW's tests: comparison between the photographic images of the UFOs and surrounding objects revealed that the alleged UFOs were in fact small objects seen at close range – not, as Villa had claimed, large ones at a distance. GSW have been known to be wrong – but ufologists the world over agree that Villa's pictures are just too *good* to be true!

Right: at about 6 p.m. on 19 November 1974, Christophe Fernandez, aged 16, was alone at home near Uzès in southern France. Suddenly he noticed a bright light outside. Forty yards (35 metres) from the house was a luminous sphere 2.5 yards (2.2 metres) wide. It was standing still on the ground or just above it.

Christophe could hear a faint 'glug-glug' sound like a bottle being emptied. On the surface of the sphere three circular shapes were moving about. Trembling, Christophe managed to photograph them.

Next, the globe rose slowly to a height of 5 or 6 yards (4 or 5 metres). A dazzlingly bright cylinder, about 1 yard (1 metre) long emerged from the underside of the sphere. Then the UFO suddenly shot upwards and out of sight

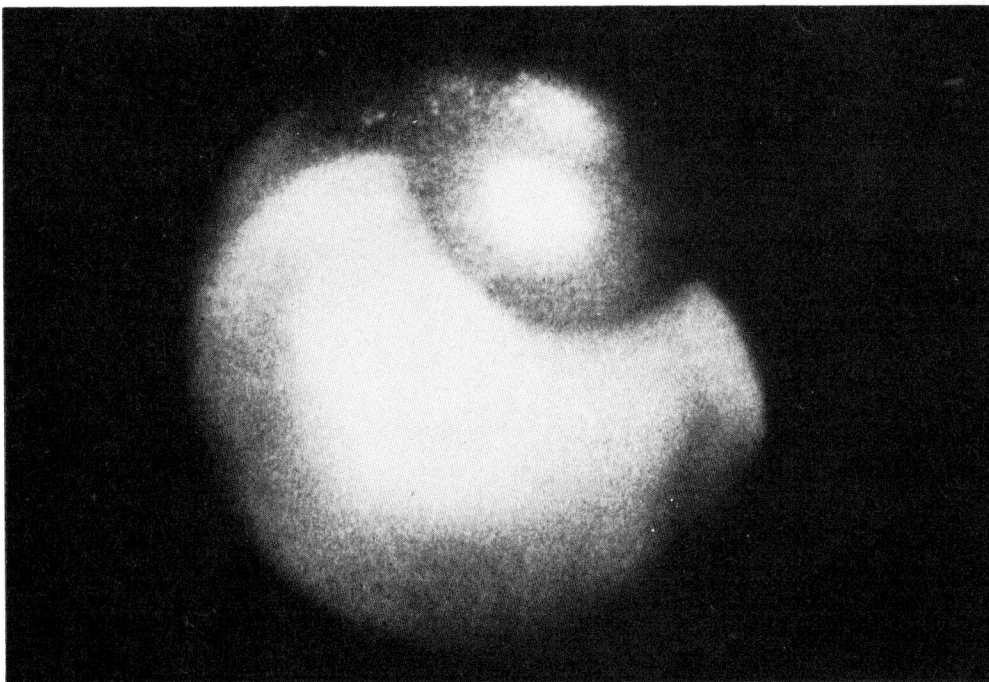

Left: 15-year-old Stephen Pratt and his mother were returning from a visit to the local fish-and-chip shop to their home in Conisbrough, Yorkshire, on the evening of 28 March 1966. At about 8.30 p.m. they saw an orange-coloured light in the twilit sky.

The light, they said, was 'throbbing'. Stephen went indoors to fetch his Instamatic camera, which was loaded with black and white film and set for 'cloudy'. Stephen took one shot of the light, which was travelling westwards.

Stephen claimed to have watched the light for 10 minutes – a long time for a UFO sighting. The film was taken to a local chemist's shop for processing, but when the negatives and prints were collected it was discovered that no print had been made of the 'UFO' negative.

Later Stephen sent his film to Granada TV asking them if they could explain the strange objects on the negative. Granada made the first prints and broadcast the photograph on 12 April 1966.

The negative did not appear to have been tampered with. The strangest feature of the story, however, is that, although Stephen told investigators he had seen only one light, the photograph shows three objects – and they appear to be solid, shaped like flying saucers, not lights.

In search of the sixth sense

The human mind has powers of understanding that are beyond the reach of the five senses. As ROY STEMMAN shows, extra-sensory perception is a fact – but one still shrouded in mystery

FOURTEEN-YEAR-OLD Stanley Krippner wanted an encyclopedia very badly. His parents had to refuse his request; they were apple farmers and a bad harvest had left them very short of money. Stanley went to his room and cried. After a while he began thinking of ways of raising the money himself and his thoughts turned to his rich Uncle Max. How could he best approach him for funds?

Suddenly the teenager sat bolt upright in bed as a horrible thought flooded his mind: 'Uncle Max can't help me because he's dead.' Many years later, Krippner – now one of America's leading psychic investigators – recalled: 'At that moment I heard the telephone ring. My mother answered the phone, then began sobbing as my cousin told her that Max had unexpectedly taken ill, was rushed to hospital, and had just died.'

Thousands of people have had similar experiences. Somehow information reaches them in a way that bypasses their 'normal' senses. During the past 50 years investigators have used the term *extra-sensory perception* (ESP) to describe the phenomenon and hundreds of experiments have been conducted around the world in an attempt to confirm its existence scientifically and understand how it works.

What is clear from this research, and from a study of spontaneous cases, is that ESP is not an isolated phenomenon. Take Krippner's experience, for example. There are three 'psychic' ways, all classified as types of ESP, in which he might have found out about his uncle's unexpected death:

Telepathy It is possible that the teenager's mind 'tuned in' to his cousin's mind and read his thoughts just as he was about to telephone with the bad news.

Clairvoyance It is just as likely that young Krippner had an awareness of his uncle's death – he sensed it had happened – without having any mind-to-mind communication.

Precognition Yet another possibility is that his knowledge came not from past or present events but from the future. Somehow he jumped fractionally ahead in time and knew what his mother was about to learn from the telephone call.

There is a fourth possibility: the dead uncle could have been communicating with his nephew. If that were the case, Krippner would have needed extra-sensory powers of some kind to be aware of the dead man's presence. Such communication is usually called mediumship and is outside the province of scientific research into ESP.

The strange case of Mrs Luther

People who investigate ESP – parapsychologists – are dealing with a very complex subject where many alternative explanations (including those in terms of conventional science) must be considered. At times it is difficult to determine where telepathy ends and clairvoyance begins.

The early investigators in the late 19th century began by collecting and collating an impressive range of cases. Books appeared, full of testimonies from reliable men and women – judges, doctors, lawyers – who had had unusual experiences. One example is Professor F. S. Luther, a mathematician of Trinity College, Cambridge, whose wife was asked by a friend if she had a book about the poet Ralph Waldo Emerson. She said she did not, but that night she dreamed she was giving such a book to her friend. The friend also had a dream in which she received the book from Mrs Luther. Next day the professor saw his wife suddenly turn to the bookshelves, prompted by an unexplained compulsion. She reached down a copy of *Century Magazine* and it opened immediately at an article entitled 'The homes and haunts of Emerson'.

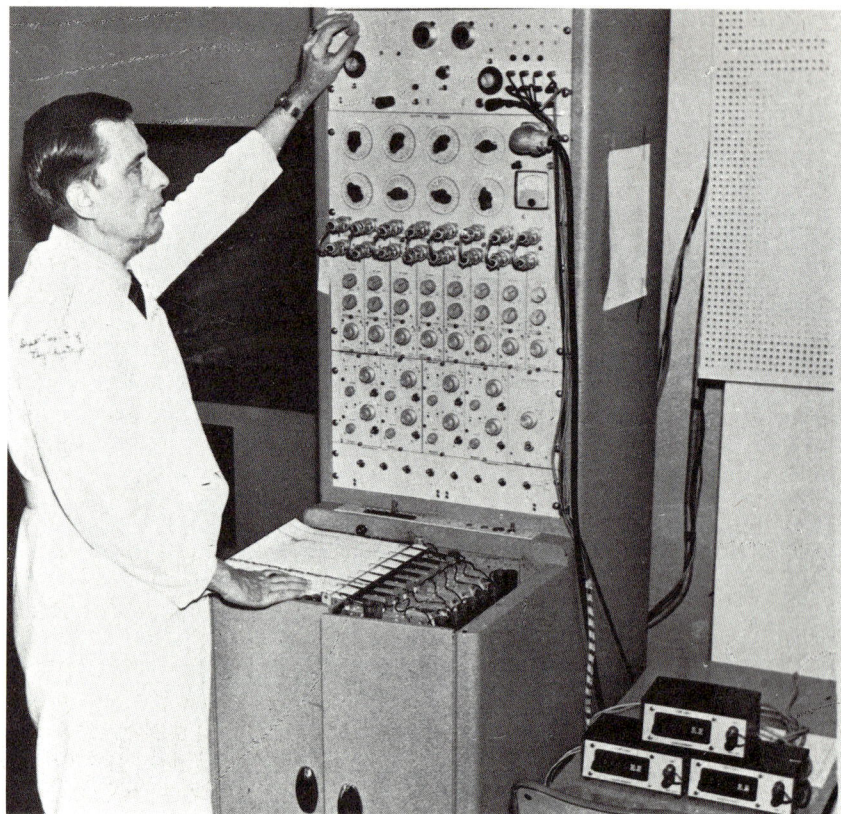

Above: Dr Stanley Krippner conducting an ESP experiment with an electro-encephalograph – a device for measuring brain waves. ESP research now uses the latest micro-chip technology

Below: Cambridge scholar F. W. Myers, author of the pioneer work, *Human personality and its survival of bodily death*. First published in 1903, Myers' book documents hundreds of ESP cases

Top: a set of Zener cards (*top row*) used to test ESP in individual subjects. Each of the five symbols is designed to make a distinct impression on the memory. Below are some of the cards used by Dr Soal, who devised these after becoming bored with Zener cards

Above: Dr Joseph Rhine, who with his wife Louisa began the first major scientific investigation into ESP in 1927

Such spontaneous cases occur when people least expect them, so they cannot be studied objectively. Waiting for ESP to manifest itself in a laboratory is as futile as waiting for ball lightning to strike your house or for a meteorite to land in your garden. But early spontaneous cases were easily dismissed by sceptics as coincidence and something had to be done to put the study of ESP on a scientific basis.

Dr Rhine deals the cards

It became apparent that there were people to whom psychic experiences were relatively common, and psychical researchers began to conduct controlled tests with them, aiming principally to prove the existence of telepathy. The pioneer of this work was Dr Joseph Banks Rhine who, together with his wife Louisa, ran the first large-scale ESP research project at Duke University, North Carolina, USA, under the sponsorship of Professor William McDougall, head of the psychology department. The Rhines were originally biologists until, in the mid-1920s, their interest in the paranormal became their chief concern. Through Professor McDougall's initiative they were able to start a full-time investigation of ESP in 1927 and with their work the science of parapsychology was born. Dr Rhine coined the term 'ESP', and he devoted over 50 years to its study before his death early in 1980.

The Rhines' method of researching ESP was to give their subjects guessing tasks. They used a pack of 25 cards, which was divided into five sets of five cards, each set carrying a different symbol: star, circle, cross, wavy lines, rectangle. These cards, called Zener cards after one of the researchers at Duke University, were shuffled, then looked at one at a time by the sender, or agent. In another part of the university the receiver, or subject, would point to the symbol he thought the agent was looking at. According to the laws of chance, a subject would get 5 out of 25 right if only guesswork was involved. Occasionally, luck might enable him to guess more than five correctly, but on other occasions he would do less well so that, in an extended series of tests, the results would even out. If, on the other hand, the subject had ESP abilities, the results should be above average. And that is precisely what Rhine found.

One of Rhine's early 'star' subjects was a man named Linzmayer, who liked to be provided with some means of distraction while making his guesses. Rhine would sometimes arrange for him to do this by taking him on country drives and stopping the car to carry out impromptu tests. On one occasion, using this procedure, Linzmayer correctly named all 15 cards Rhine looked at. Under better controlled conditions in Rhine's laboratory Linzmayer continued to record above-average scores, but his ESP subsequently declined and then vanished.

In the card-guessing experiment in Rhine's car, Linzmayer appears to have read the researcher's mind. But he also took part in tests in which he was asked to name a card before it was turned over. Since no one knew what the card would be, Linzmayer had to use clairvoyance to make his guesses. Again, his scores were significantly above average, and there were other subjects who were just as good at 'seeing through' the cards. Rhine's work soon demonstrated that there was much more to ESP than pure telepathy. Within 10 years he was exploring the possibility of looking into the future, or precognition. Subjects were asked to guess *in advance* what the order of Zener cards would be when shuffled. The results were just as impressive as his other ESP laboratory work.

The struggle for the truth

There was, unexpectedly, tremendous public interest in Dr Rhine's work when it was first published in 1934. Not surprisingly, there were sceptics among his scientific colleagues who endeavoured to find fault with his laboratory techniques and conditions. Rhine provided satisfactory answers to all these criticisms. If these were not at fault, the sceptics continued, then Rhine's statistical analysis might be wrong. Perhaps the above-average results he was recording were not a manifestation of ESP but a statistical quirk. That argument was silenced in 1937 when the American Institute of Mathematical Statistics issued a statement, following its own investigation of the Duke University results, which said that the statistical methods used to evaluate ESP phenomena in Rhine's tests were completely valid.

If the subjects were not allowed to cheat, if the conditions made it impossible for the information to be transmitted to the subject by 'normal' means, and if the statistical methods used to analyse the results were correct, then surely the critics *had* to believe that ESP did exist? But there was still one other possibility that had to be taken seriously: experimenter fraud. Perhaps Rhine had 'cooked the books'. This suggestion was put forward in 1955 by a medical researcher, G. R. Price, in an article for *Science*, the prestigious official journal of the American Association for the Advancement of Science. He argued that experimenter fraud was 'the one explanation that is simplest and most in accord with everyday experiment'. Most of his criticisms were aimed at Rhine and Dr S. G. Soal, an eminent British parapsychologist.

Many people regarded Price's attack as an 'exposure' of parapsychology, but Rhine took it very calmly. He entered into correspondence with Price, answering his various allegations and discussing in depth the procedures used in his work. The result, many years later in 1972, was the publication

Above: a practical demonstration of Dr Rhine's techniques. An agent outside the laboratory is given a set of Zener cards to look at. The subject inside the laboratory is asked to 'guess' which of the five symbols the agent is looking at and to indicate her choice on the display panel

Below: Dr S. G. Soal, the mathematician whose research into ESP has been seriously questioned

by Price of another article in *Science*. The headline tells its own story: 'Apology to Rhine and Soal'.

Although the apology to Rhine was well deserved and long overdue, later discoveries indicated that Price's suspicions were right as far as Soal was concerned, Soal's is a strange case, and one that sounds a warning to those who are tempted to put their trust in a single set of ESP experiments. Many researchers regarded Soal's results as a cornerstone of ESP and the new evidence means that the history of parapsychology will have to be rewritten.

Soal, who was a mathematician, originally became interested in psychical research when he conducted a lengthy series of ESP tests, hoping to provide independent corroboration of Rhine's work. He tested 160 people over a five-year period and analysed the total of 128,350 guesses against the targets (symbols on the cards) they were attempting to 'see'. He found nothing but chance results and promptly stopped his ESP research, criticising Rhine for what he considered must be errors in the methods he used to produce positive results.

That might have been the end of the story, had it not been for the influence of another English researcher, Whately Carington. In his own ESP tests, using drawings as targets, Carington had discovered a strange displacement effect. Sometimes a subject would miss

Random numbers

Consider the sequence: 1 2 3 4 . . . If Dr Soal had used a sequence like this one in his ESP experiments, Basil Shackleton – or anyone else – could have scored a 100 per cent success rate simply by working out what the pattern was and calculating the next number. To ensure that Shackleton could not cheat – that he was really using ESP and not arithmetic to score his 'hits' – Soal should have made sure that, at any point in the sequence, the chance of any one of the card symbols being next in line was the same as that of any other symbol.

This is, in fact, the idea behind the mathematical definition of a random number: a string of digits in which each digit is selected according to a procedure in which all the numbers from 0 to 9 have an equal chance of being selected.

The strange thing about random numbers is that they are very difficult to come by: you cannot simply ask someone to think of a random number since, however randomly he thinks he is selecting the digits, you will always be able to find some kind of pattern in the sequence. The mathematical definition demands that you use a mechanical method, independent of human bias. The easiest way is to throw a die repeatedly and to record the number on the uppermost face each time.

But this is a slow and laborious method and, besides, a die has only six sides. In laboratory experiments standard lists of random numbers, generated on computers by a variety of methods, are often used; ERNIE, for instance, selects Premium Bond numbers by ingeniously translating the haphazard motion of electrons in a diode into random numbers. In the days before it was possible to use computers to generate long sequences of random numbers, logarithmic tables were used to obtain 'pseudo-random' sequences.

Below: Dr R. G. Medhurst, a parapsychologist, who appeared in a dream to Betty Markwick. It was after her dream that Miss Markwick began analysing Dr Soal's research methods. She found that he may have manipulated the results and that his work was generally unreliable. Later, however, Miss Markwick came to recognise that had it not been for the appearance of Dr Medhurst in her dream she would never have begun work on Dr Soal

the target he was trying to guess and instead reproduce the previous day's target or even the one to be selected at random the next day. Carington urged Soal to re-examine his statistics and look for such a 'psychic displacement'. The mathematician did this, and sure enough the effect was found in the results produced by two subjects, Basil Shackleton and Gloria Stewart. Both showed positive and negative displacements at times, and Soal continued his ESP work using Shackleton and Stewart as his subjects.

Real evidence?

The results of experiments conducted with Shackleton between 1941 and 1943 were extremely impressive and were taken up by parapsychologists as evidence of the existence of ESP. But 20 years later Mrs Gretl Albert, who had been involved in the tests as an agent, claimed she had several times seen Soal altering the figures. A recent re-examination of the Soal statistics suggests that this is exactly what he did.

In order to ensure that the cards used in the experiments were picked at random, Soal used the standard laboratory technique of referring to Chambers' logarithmic tables and Tippett's random number tables (although he did not indicate exactly how he used them). What has been discovered is that the random lists Soal used in his experiments do not match the standard published ones. A study by Betty Markwick, published in 1978, has revealed that certain long sequences of numbers are repeated many times. This need only mean that Soal was using a small pool of random numbers and would not necessarily affect the validity of the experiment. However, Miss Markwick has discovered that the long repeated sequences are in fact not identical; they are sometimes interrupted by extra numbers, and that these, where they occur, show a remarkable correspondence with the ESP 'hits' recorded by Soal. Remove them and the scores fall to chance levels.

Summing up this evidence, Miss Markwick states that 'all the experimental series in card-guessing carried out by Dr Soal must, as the evidence stands, be discredited.'

The Soal case is a sad chapter in the chequered history of parapsychology. But the evidence for ESP does not depend on a single set of experiments. Over the last half century, as we will see in future articles, the evidence for extra-sensory perception has grown stronger. Although researchers cannot yet produce telepathy, clairvoyance and precognition to order in their laboratories, their investigations show that ESP *is* a very real phenomenon. The latest research even holds out the hope that we may all, one day, be able to use our psychic powers at will.

Next, we examine telepathy – seeing into the minds of others. How does it work? See page 34

Everyone has heard tales of the 'abominable snowman'
– or yeti – of the Himalayas. But sightings of mysterious
animals, neither man nor beast, have been reported from
all over the world: from North America, China, Australia,
Africa, the wastes of Siberia and the Amazon jungle.
JANET and COLIN BORD sift the evidence, and present the
case for the reality of these elusive creatures

Man, myth or monster?

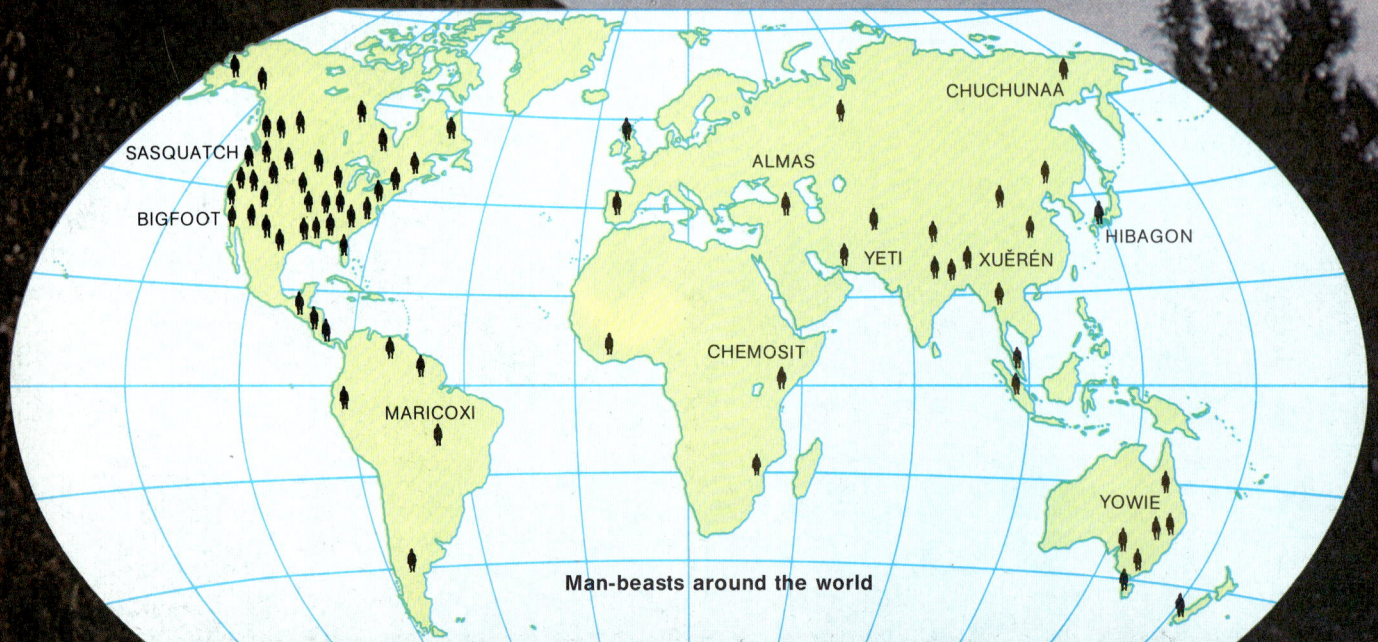

'WILD MEN OF THE WOODS' are common figures in folklore throughout the world. In
medieval Britain they were known as 'woodwoses' or 'woodhouses', and can be seen
depicted in carvings in East Anglian churches. Though it is tempting to dismiss woodwoses as colourful figments of the rural
imagination, a recent stream of reports of
sightings from the North American continent of 'man-beasts' up to 8 feet (2.4 metres)
tall make these not so easy to ignore.

Bigfoot – or sasquatch, to give it the
Indian name that is used in the province of
British Columbia in Canada – makes the
headlines so frequently nowadays that similar sightings in more distant or less publicity-
conscious parts of the world tend to be
overlooked. Yet from time to time reports
emerge from the Himalayas, traditionally
thought of as the home of the yeti or abominable snowman, of strange footprints in the
snow or, less frequently, distant sightings of
what is taken to be the yeti itself. In 1974, a
Nepalese girl guarding a herd of yaks 14,000

Man-beasts around the world

feet (4250 metres) up in the mountains near Mount Everest was attacked by a yeti and in 1978 Lord and Lady Hunt, revisiting Nepal to commemorate the 1953 ascent of Everest, saw and photographed large tracks in the snow around their huts.

Much has been written about the yeti over the years, although the number of actual sightings has been fairly small. In contrast, very little has been written about sightings of 'wild men' or 'man-beasts' in China, but from what has been published it seems they are fairly active in some remote areas. In the mid-1970s strange encounters with unknown creatures were reported from Hopeh and Shansi provinces – forested, mountainous country in northern China.

Particularly dramatic was the report made by 33-year-old Pang Gensheng, a commune leader, in June 1977. Pang was chopping wood in the Taibai Mountains of central Shansi province when he saw a 'hairy man':

It came closer and closer. I got scared and kept retreating until my back was against a stone cliff and I couldn't go any further. The hairy man came up to 7 or 8 feet [2.1 or 2.4 metres], and then to about 5 feet [1.5 metres] from me. I raised my axe, ready to fight for my life. We stood like that, neither of us moving, for more than an hour. Then I groped for a stone and threw it at him. It hit him in the chest. He uttered several howls and rubbed the spot with his left hand. Then he turned left and leaned against a tree, then walked away slowly toward the bottom of the gully. He kept making a mumbling sound.

The 'man' was about 7 feet (2.1 metres) tall, with a sloping forehead and deep-set black eyes. His jaw jutted out, and he had broad front teeth. Dark brown hair hung long and loose over his shoulders, and his body and face were covered with short hair. His long arms reached below his knees, and he walked upright with his legs wide apart.

Researchers at the Institute of Palaeoanthropology and Vertebrate Palaeontology

Background picture: the Himalayas, home of the yeti, or abominable snowman

Below left: a footprint, allegedly of a yeti, found near the Menlung Base of the 1951 Himalayan expedition. It is regarded as the best piece of photographic evidence for the existence of the yeti

Below right: in February 1980, a Polish climber took this photograph on Mount Everest at 16,000 feet (4800 metres). The footprint measures 14 inches (36 centimetres) long and 7 inches (17 centimetres) wide

Mysterious man-beasts

of the 'wild men'. These mountains are a north-westerly extension of the Himalayas. In the summer of 1979 a Soviet expedition there found footprints 13½ inches (34.3 centimetres) long and 6½ inches (16.5 centimetres) wide at the toes, but no one actually saw who or what made them.

'Man-beasts' have also been seen in Siberia, in the inhospitable northern territory of the Soviet Union. In the early 1960s a hunter living near the River Ob saw two such creatures when they came out of the forest one evening, while he was walking with his dogs. The dogs ran off in terror, but were not harmed. Dogs are usually frightened by these unknown monsters; in America bigfeet seem to dislike dogs and have been known to injure or even kill them. The Siberian hunter noted that the wild men were covered with dark hair, had long arms and turned their feet outwards when walking. Their eyes glowed dark red – yet another characteristic that indicates a similarity with bigfeet.

In the 1920s, a chuchunaa (a name meaning 'outcast' given to the man-beast in the Yakutiya region of eastern Siberia) was seen by villagers out berry-picking.

It was also picking berries and stuffing them into its mouth with both hands. On catching sight of us, he stood up to his full height. He was very tall and lean, over 2 metres [over 6 feet], they say Barefoot and dressed in deerskin, he had very long arms and a mop of unkempt hair. His face was as big as a human's. His forehead was small and

of the Chinese Academy of Sciences have been investigating such reports, but so far have not been able to solve the riddle of the 'wild man'. Even so, it it significant that the detailed description given by Pang Gensheng is similar to those given by witnesses elsewhere in the world. And the creature's behaviour is quite typical.

Footprints in the snow
Research and investigation have also been undertaken in the Soviet Union, where Dr Jeanna Kofman has been on the trail of the so-called 'almas' in the Caucasus Mountains since 1955. She has received many eye-witness reports and has personally interviewed about 4000 people.

One of them was 39-year-old Mukhamed Tomakov, a farm manager, who in 1946 caught an almas in a mountain hut at Getmish. The creature was man-like, but covered with hair, and ran on all fours, standing on its hind legs whenever it stopped. (Sometimes, but not often, American bigfeet have been seen running on all fours.) Once the creature was safely inside the hut, Tomakov latched the door and went to get a rope. When he returned the door was open and the hut empty.

The Pamir Mountains on the southern border of the Soviet Union are another haunt

Above: the carved figure of a woodwose in the porch of Peasenhall Church, Suffolk. Woodwoses, or 'wild men of the woods', are said to have inhabited England in the Middle Ages, but they have apparently become extinct with the gradual spread of towns and villages

Right: a line of footprints said to have been made by a yeti. An alternative explanation, however, is that they were made by a mountain goat. The sun then melted the snow around the hoof marks, enlarging them

protruded over his eyes like the peak of a cap. His chin was large and broad, far bigger than a human's. Other than being a little taller, he was very much like a human. The next moment he ran away. He ran very fast, leaping high after every third step.

In America, too, bigfeet have been seen eating berries, and there have even been occasional reports of them actually wearing clothing.

'X' marks the spot

All continents still have some areas of wilderness, jungles or forested mountains that are rarely penetrated by outsiders. (Europe has the smallest area of uncivilised territory, which may explain why man-beast reports are almost non-existent there.) Vast tracts of unexplored land may conceal all manner of unknown creatures, not just wild men or man-beasts. In the East, man-beasts have been reported in Malaysia, where there is still plenty of jungle to conceal anything that wishes to stay hidden. Of course, the more remote the country, the less likely outsiders are to hear about unexpected encounters with these unknown life forms, unless expeditions are mounted with the intention of tracking them down.

This explains why we have only fragmentary data from South America and Africa. Yet what we do hear suggests there is plenty of activity. In 1978 Jacqueline Roumeguere Eberhardt of the Centre Nationale de la Recherche Scientifique in Paris published information on her research into the African man-beast, which she has somewhat unimaginatively named 'X'. At that time she had 31 accounts of sightings in 11 Kenyan forests, and she was able to identify four separate types of 'X'. One native was captured and carefully examined by an 'X' before being pushed away in the direction of his home.

Reports sometimes surface from far less promising areas. Our western image of Japan as a small, industrial nation leaves little room for remote uninhabited country able to support a population of man-beasts. Yet in the early 1970s there were several sightings of the Hibagon (as the beast became known) on Mount Hiba near Hiroshima. Farmer Albert Kubo saw this 5-foot (1.5-metre), big-eyed, smelly creature in 1974 when he was out in his rice fields spreading fertiliser. It was standing on a path, and Mr Kubo began to approach it before he realised what it was.

He said: 'I was petrified, but the stench was what really got me. He must have bathed in a septic tank and dried off with cow dung. I nearly passed out. Luckily enough, though, I managed to turn and run before it realised I was there. I ran 5 miles (8 kilometres) straight home without ever looking back over my shoulder.' The strong smell of many North American bigfeet is often described by witnesses in equally graphic terms.

The continent of Australia has many thousands of square miles of territory rarely visited by man and, as might be expected, it too has its man-beast. The Aborigines, who were apparently well aware of its existence,

Is this the yeti?

One of the most popular explanations of the yeti's origins is that it is descended from the giant ape *Gigantopithecus*, whose fossilised remains have been found in India and China. Examination of the fossils indicates that *Gigantopithecus* lived between 12 million and 500,000 years ago. Also during this period, the Himalayas were rising by as much as 8000 to 10,000 feet (2500 to 3000 metres). Because of this increase in height of the mountains, many species of animals, including the yeti's ancestor, may have become isolated.

Some experts argue that though the yeti's footprints have been discovered above the snowline (a bare terrain that is unable to support a large mammal) its present home is actually lower down in the forested valleys. Here, vegetation is dense, fog is common and there are few human inhabitants to disturb the yeti. But, as a result of seasonal changes, they must sometimes cross the high snow passes to reach nearby valleys – and leave those telltale footprints.

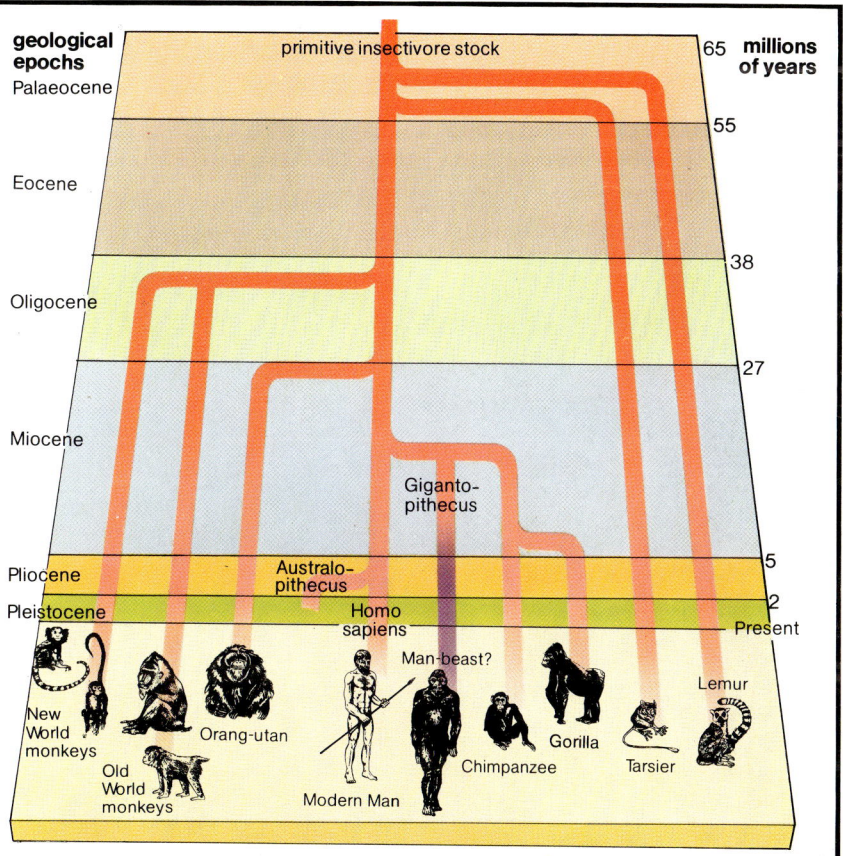

geological epochs — Palaeocene, Eocene, Oligocene, Miocene, Pliocene, Pleistocene. Present. millions of years: 65, 55, 38, 27, 5, 2. primitive insectivore stock. Gigantopithecus. Australopithecus. Homo sapiens. New World monkeys, Old World monkeys, Orang-utan, Modern Man, Man-beast?, Chimpanzee, Gorilla, Tarsier, Lemur.

gave it many different names, but today it is usually called the yowie. Sightings have been regularly reported, especially in New South Wales and Queensland, since the late 18th century. On 3 October 1894 a boy named Johnnie McWilliams saw one while he was riding from his home at Snowball to the Jinden Post Office in New South Wales.

'A big man covered with long hair' suddenly appeared from behind a tree and seems to have been as surprised at the encounter as was the young Johnnie, for he ran off across open country, knocking his foot against a log and crying out in pain. He kept looking back as he ran, until he went out of sight over a low hill. The 'man' was over 6 feet (1.8 metres) tall and heavily built.

Joseph and William Webb, preparing to camp out one night at the turn of the century in the ranges of Brindabella, New South Wales, had a rather more dramatic encounter with a yowie. They heard a 'deep guttural bellowing' and noises, as if something was crashing through the scrub. According to John Gale, founder and editor of *The Quean-beyan Age*, writing in his book *An Alpine excursion* (1903):

Next moment a thing appeared walking erect, though they saw only its head and shoulders. It was hirsute, so much of the creature as was visible, and its head was set so deep between its shoulders that it was scarcely perceptible. It was approaching towards their camp. Now it was in full view, and was of the stature of a man. moving with long strides and a heavy tramp. It was challenged: 'Who are you? Speak, or we'll fire'. Not an intelligible word came in response; only the guttural bellowing. Aim was taken; the crack of a rifle rang out along the gully; but the

thing, if hit, was not disabled; for at the sound of the shot it turned and fled.

That the men saw no evidence of the bullet having struck its target does not necessarily mean that they missed. There is some evidence from North America that ordinary guns are useless against the hairy giants, either because they are not powerful enough, or for some stranger reason.

Australian yowie researcher Rex Gilroy has collected more than 3000 sighting reports and, as in North America, there was a big increase in reports during the 1970s. A particularly close sighting, where the witness was able to get a good look at a yowie of 7 feet (2.1 metres), was reported by a National Parks worker in the Springbrook area of Queensland in March 1978. Hearing a grunting sound, he thought a pig was loose and went into the forest to look for it.

Then something made me look up and there, about 12 feet [3.7 metres] in front of me, was this big black hairy man-thing. It looked more like a gorilla than anything. It had huge hands and one of them was wrapped round a sapling.

It had a flat, black shiny face, with two big yellow eyes and a hole for a mouth. It just stared at me and I stared back. I was so numb I couldn't even raise the axe I had in my hand. We seemed to stand there staring at each other for about 10 minutes before it suddenly gave off a foul smell that made me vomit – then it just made off sideways and disappeared.

Both its appearance and behaviour suggest that the yowie is a close cousin to the North American bigfoot.

Bigfeet have been reported in North America since the 1930s. What are they? See page 38

Left: music teacher Richard Brown stands beside the fence near The Dalles, Oregon, where he saw a bigfoot in 1971. He followed the bigfoot's movements through the telescopic sights of his rifle

Below: Igor Bourtsev, a Russian 'snowman' hunter, holding a cast of a footprint found on 21 August 1979 in the Gissar Range of the Pamir-Alai Mountains, Tadzhikistan, in central Asia. The footprint, believed to have been made by an almas, measures 13.5 inches (34 centimetres) long and 6.5 inches (16 centimetres) wide at the toes. It is very nearly the same size as 'yeti' footprints found in the Himalayas

The exact nature of hypnosis has been debated for over 200 years. BRIAN INGLIS discusses its use in medicine, in crime detection and in exploring the possible evidence for reincarnation

MOST PEOPLE STILL THINK of hypnotists as slightly shady characters practising a highly dubious craft. We see in our mind's eye the evil Svengali, the character in George du Maurier's novel who lived off the unfortunate Trilby by putting the 'fluence on her so that she became an internationally acclaimed concert artist, though her ordinary voice was terrible. Today's stage hypnotist, however, is no longer the seedy villain of the story. He is a well-dressed and well-heeled smoothie with the patter of a conjuror, who exercises his talent before audiences in clubs.

The performance tends to follow a standard formula. Volunteers are called for, and one by one, the hypnotist addresses soothing words to them, like a mother putting her child to sleep. Those who respond remain on stage; the rest are sent back into the audience. Then, in groups or individually, those still on stage are told that they are very hot or very cold, very thirsty or very drunk – and they behave and feel as they are told to even if they make themselves look ridiculous.

The riddle of hypnosis

There is not, as yet, any clear explanation of the nature of hypnotism. Hypnosis is generally defined as a trance, that is, an altered state of consciousness. The extent of the alteration depends upon the individual. In any group, some of the volunteers will remember everything that has been done while they are on stage; others may recall nothing. But they will all have come under the hypnotist's influence.

What this means is that each of them has shed some of the controls, or thrown off some of the inhibitions, that training and habit normally impose on us. If somebody said to any of them, in ordinary conversation, 'You are a watchdog and you hear a burglar', it would raise only a laugh. On stage, the hypnotised subject gets down on hands and knees and barks. The hypnotist is he-who-must-be-obeyed; commands from other people are ignored unless he has given instructions that they should be obeyed, too.

Even more impressively, the accomplished hypnotist can give commands that will be obeyed after the subjects have come out of their trances and returned to their seats in the audience. If he gives them a 'post-hypnotic suggestion' that they should stand up and shout 'hip-hip-hooray' whenever the orchestra plays a certain tune, they will do so, without knowing why.

Hypnosis appears to switch off some part of our minds that ordinarily monitors our behaviour, instructing us what to do in any

The power of suggestion

given set of circumstances without thought on our part. We hand this control system over to the hypnotist, much as an airline pilot may hand over the controls of his aircraft to somebody on the ground, who guides it in by radar with the help of an automatic pilot.

Watching people behave in this way – and often, to the amusement of the audience, making fools of themselves – appears to demonstrate the hypnotist's powers. But this is an illusion. The powers really lie in the hypnotised subjects. And these powers are far greater and potentially far more valuable than is generally realised, in spite of numerous demonstrations of a more serious nature of just what can be achieved under hypnosis.

In one form or another, hypnotism has been used throughout history. It has been exploited by tribal witch doctors and by priests in the temples of ancient Greece. But we owe the form in which it is practised today to Franz Mesmer and his disciples. Two

An 18th-century hypnotist supposedly projecting magnetism from the palms of his hands to induce a 'healing crisis' in his patient. In the 18th and early 19th centuries hypnotist Anton Mesmer and his followers believed they had found a new healing force called 'animal magnetism', which became the rage in fashionable circles in the capital cities of Europe

Hypnosis

Below: unscrupulous stage hypnotists can give their profession a bad name. In this French hypnotist's show a girl from the audience, apparently under hypnosis, stripped off some of her clothes. But it was the same girl every night!

Bottom: a still from *Svengali*, the 1954 film version of George du Maurier's famous novel *Trilby*. Donald Wolfit played the evil hypnotist Svengali, Hildegarde Neff his victim, the cabaret singer Trilby

hundred years ago, they realised that subjects in the trance state could be made to obey every command. But more important, in the course of their experiments they made two discoveries of great potential significance.

For a start, they found that if they told a subject, 'You will feel no pain,' he could be struck, pricked and even burned without so much as a yelp. The Mesmerists proceeded to demonstrate that pain-free surgical operations could be performed under hypnosis – and this was before the invention of anaesthetic drugs.

The medical profession refused to accept the evidence. When distinguished surgeons were invited to watch the amputation of a leg under hypnosis, they insisted the man was only pretending to feel no pain! Hypnosis,

they argued, was occult; it could not work.

The second discovery was that some hypnotised subjects enjoyed talents they did not know they had in their ordinary lives. One might draw well under hypnosis; another sing melodiously (there was at least a grain of truth in du Maurier's story). A few appeared to become clairvoyant, describing places or events that they could not have seen. This, too, was dismissed as occultism. And to this day, hypnotism has never quite rid itself of its reputation of lying beyond the boundaries of orthodox science.

Yet we know now that the Mesmerists' claims were largely justified. Endless demonstrations have shown that a subject under hypnosis can put his finger into a candle flame and if told he will feel no pain, will feel no pain. Even more remarkable, if told he will have no blister, no blister appears.

Researchers have taken this further. If a hypnotised subject is told that he is going to be touched with a red-hot skewer, not only will he cry out in pain even if the skewer is cold, its touch will raise a blister.

A case for reincarnation?

Scepticism about the possibility that some subjects become clairvoyant under hypnosis has also been shaken by recent research into hypnotic regression. It has long been known that hypnotised subjects can be escorted back in time to earlier occasions in their lives. Asked to recall what they were doing on, say, New Year's Day 10 or 40 years ago, they will describe in detail episodes they have long since forgotten – and where it has been possible to check their stories, these have been found to be accurate. In the United States, the police have been exploiting this faculty by asking witnesses of crimes and accidents to allow themselves to be hypnotised to find out whether they can recall, say, the number of a stolen car which they did not consciously note at the time the event was taking place.

Hypnotic regression has been carried further. A hundred years ago researchers on the Continent found that some hypnotised subjects appeared to be able to recall events from past centuries. Recently this line of investigation has been taken up again, and the results described in detail in works like Jeffrey Iverson's *More lives than one*, an account of Arnall Bloxham's investigations, and Joe Keeton's *Encounters with the past*.

It remains to be established whether the hypnotised subjects are regressing to their own past lives, or tuning in to what might be described as a videotape from the collective unconscious, but it seems clear they are genuine; the material, even if not accurate in detail, is being picked up from sources other than books and conversations.

Hypnosis, then, is a trance state, or altered state of consciousness (some people prefer to describe it as a state of altered *awareness* of consciousness) in which certain faculties and

Right: the French hypnotist Oudet extracts a tooth after having put his patient into a trance, 14 November 1836. Although doctors at first regarded the idea of using hypnosis as an anaesthetic with suspicion, they were soon using it in a wide range of operations

Below: Dr Malcolm Rawson, chief neurologist at Hull Royal Infirmary, questions 13-year-old Gail Rogers after putting her in a hypnotic trance. Police used hypnosis to try to cast light on the mysterious disappearance of Genette Tate, also aged 13, who vanished while delivering evening papers on Friday, 18 August 1978 in her home town of Aylesbeare in Devon. The oil painting (inset) was produced by an artist from descriptions given by Gail and her mother, Mrs Matilda Rogers, under hypnosis, and for a time police were hopeful it might give them a lead. By the end of 1981, however, the case remained unsolved

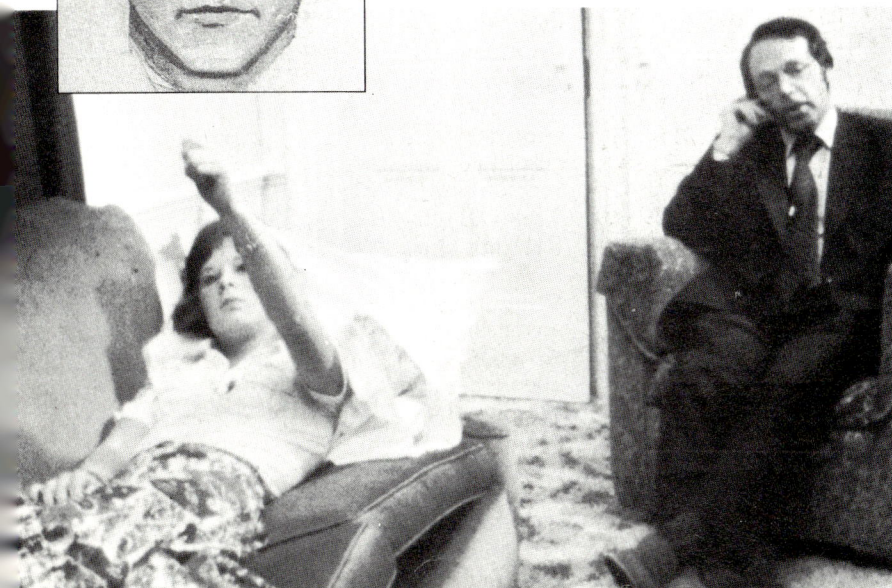

abilities can be liberated. Clearly the potential benefits, for anybody prepared to master the art of auto-hypnosis, can be considerable. Why, then, is more use not made of it?

Fear is partly responsible; the lingering fear that hypnosis is in the occult category and not scientifically respectable, or the more reasonable fear that to undergo it is to put oneself into the hands of a Svengali.

Yet the fact that a stage hypnotist can so easily manipulate volunteers is misleading. The volunteers know it is a game. They choose to play it, presumably out of curiosity in most cases; they would not volunteer if they thought they might be made to do something dangerous or criminal – or even immoral, by their standards.

A celebrated experiment demonstrated this a century ago. A girl subject taking part in an experiment in Paris was told to kill one of the students; she appeared to try to do so and had to be restrained. Yet when asked to take off her clothes, she blushed, came out of her trance and ran from the room.

In the experiment she must have sensed, in some way, that she would be prevented from doing anything dangerous or criminal, so she could put on an act. But to have undressed would have compromised her own moral code and was therefore unacceptable.

The implications of hypnosis for medicine are striking, yet until very recently they have been largely ignored. It is only in the past 10 years that the results of research into hypnosis have been confirmed and amplified with the help of investigations involving biofeedback. These have shown how individuals can control many bodily functions – heartbeat, blood pressure, gastric secretions – by auto-suggestion: self-hypnosis.

And hypnosis, or auto-suggestion, can do much more. Individuals like the American Jack Schwartz have demonstrated how they can control bleeding, staunching the blood flow as if by turning off a tap. Much the simplest way to remove warts and other skin

blemishes is by suggestion under hypnosis. It can also be a help in curing allergies and in stopping smoking (though good hypnotherapists emphasise that they can only help those who want to help themselves).

The distinguished Australian psychiatrist Ainslie Meares and Americans Carl and Stephanie Simonton have shown how hypnosis and auto-hypnosis can be used to help terminal cancer patients, not merely by enabling them to control pain, but also by giving them a welcome distraction from their worries. In some cases this has prolonged survival; in a few, x-rays have revealed actual regression of tumours. No false hopes are raised of miracle cures, as has so often happened with other forms of cancer treatment. Patients are, told that it is how they react to their own voyages of discovery in altered states of consciousness that counts.

Hypnotherapy has two major advantages. It can be taught, so that patients can learn to control, for instance, their own headaches – sometimes even prevent them. And it costs nothing, except the practitioner's time.

Outside the medical field, too, the possibilities of hypnosis are just beginning to be appreciated, particularly by sportsmen. Post-hypnotic suggestion can send a golfer out onto the course in a relaxed frame of mind – which in golf is half the battle.

The nature of hypnosis remains unexplained, but it is clear from the research that has been done that altered states of consciousness can provide fascinating insights into the human mind as well as enabling us to heal our own minds and bodies.

Hypnosis has provided startling new evidence that reincarnation does occur. See page 54

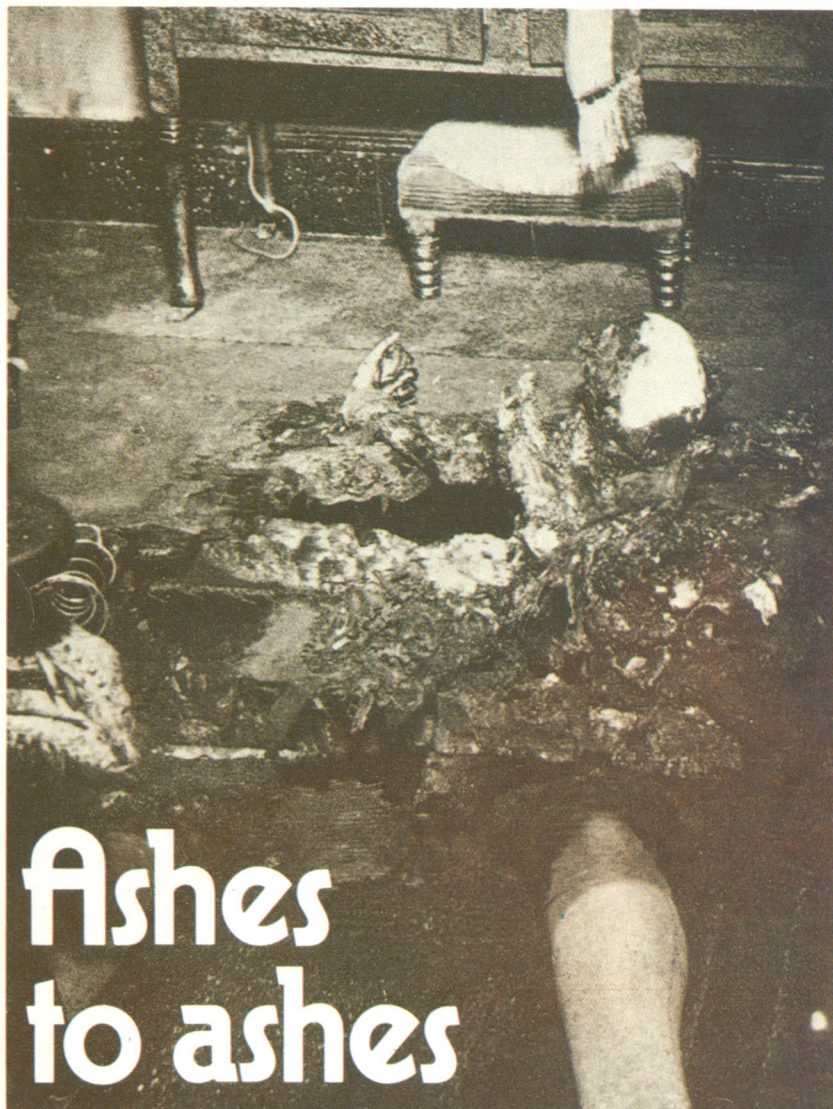

Ashes to ashes

Of all the strange and inexplicable fates that may befall a person, perhaps the most bizarre is to burst into flames without warning and without apparent cause. BOB RICKARD describes cases that still defy science

PEOPLE HAVE LONG BELIEVED that in certain circumstances the human body can burst into flames of its own accord. Flames, furthermore, of such ferocity that within minutes the victim is reduced to a heap of carbonised ashes. This idea – some call it a superstition – has been around for centuries, smouldering in the belief in divine retribution. 'By the blast of God they perish,' says the author of *Job*, 'and by the breath of his nostrils are they consumed.'

This Gothic horror was hugely popular in the 18th and 19th centuries, and its literary use is still extensively discussed in the pages of *The Dickensian*, stimulated by Charles Dickens' own fascination with the subject. Dickens had examined the case for spontaneous human combustion (SHC) 'as a Judge might have done', and knew most of the early authorities and collections of cases. He probably based his description of Krook's death

The aftermath of spontaneous human combustion. The fire has reduced most of the body to ashes, leaving only parts of the lower legs, the left hand and portions of the skull, and was intense enough to burn a hole in the floor. Enormously high temperatures must have been involved, yet for some mysterious reason the fire has been contained, causing little further damage to the surroundings

in *Bleak House* (1852–3), upon the cases of Countess Bandi and Grace Pett.

The death of the 62-year-old Countess Cornelia Bandi, near Verona, is perhaps one of the first of the more reliable reports of SHC. According to a statement by Bianchini, a prebendary of Verona, dated 4 April 1731, the Countess had been put to bed after supper, and fell asleep after several hours' conversation with her maid. In the morning the maid returned to wake her and found a grisly scene. As the *Gentlemen's Magazine* reported: 'The floor of the chamber was thick-smear'd with a gluish moisture, not easily got off . . . and from the lower part of the window trickl'd down a greasy, loathsome, yellowish liquor with an unusual stink.'

Specks of soot hung in the air and covered all the surfaces in the room, and the smell had penetrated adjoining rooms. The bed was undamaged, the sheets turned back, indicating the Countess had got out of bed.

Four feet [1.3 metres] from the bed was a heap of ashes, two legs untouch'd, stockings on, between which lay the head, the brains, half of the back-part of the skull and the whole chin burn'd to ashes, among which were found three fingers blacken'd. All the rest was ashes which had this quality, that they left in the hand a greasy and stinking moisture.

A hole burnt in the floor

Bianchini could have been describing some of our modern cases. The diligent researches of Larry E. Arnold unearthed the fate of Dr J. Irving Bentley, a 93-year-old retired physician of Coudersport, Pennsylvania. Gas company worker Don Gosnell discovered the remains after smelling a 'light-blue smoke of unusual odor'. The fire had been so intense that it almost totally consumed the old man. John Dec the deputy coroner said: 'All I found was a knee joint atop a post in the basement, the lower leg from the knee down, and the now-scattered ashes 6 feet [2 metres] below.' And yet the fire had, mysteriously, been contained; firemen testified to the existence of a few embers around the hole, and a slight scorching on the bathtub about a foot (30 centimetres) away was the only other sign of this fiercely fatal fire. The burns on the bath were still visible when Arnold investigated nine years later.

It was suggested that Bentley was a careless smoker – small burns riddled his everyday clothes and the bedroom floor – and that he had wakened to find himself on fire, struggled to the bathroom in search of water, and there collapsed and died. Arnold, in his report on the case in the journal *Pursuit*, 1976, points out that there are several inconsistencies in this account, though it was accepted by the local newspaper and the coroner.

Bentley's pipe had been 'carefully placed' on its stand by his chair; not the action of a man on fire. A broken hip six years before had left him with no feeling in his left leg, and he walked with difficulty – his 'walker' can be seen fallen across the hole. He was enough of a doctor to realise that his only chance of survival, had his clothes been on fire, would be to take them off there and then, rather than risk the precarious trip to the bathroom.

It is more likely that whatever happened to Bentley occurred when he visited the bathroom for some other reason, and that he was beginning to burn before he took off his robe, setting fire to it in the process – it was found smouldering in the bathtub. The autopsy was a mere formality, yet despite having so little to go on – just half a leg; the ashes

A villain meets his end

In chapter 32 of *Bleak House*, Charles Dickens' characters, William Guppy and Tony Weevle, discover that the evil Krook has been mysteriously burned to a few charred lumps and ashes, filling the room with 'hateful soot' and objects coated with an offensive 'thick yellow liquor'. 'Call the death by any name . . . attribute it to whom you will, or say it might have been prevented how you will, it is the same death eternally – inborn, inbred, engendered in the corrupt humours of the vicious body itself, and that only – Spontaneous Combustion, and none other of all the deaths that can be died.'

were never analysed – the coroner decided that Dr Bentley had died of *asphyxiation*, probably because that is the usual cause of death during fires.

Primarily due to the efforts of Charles Fort, the pioneer collector of accounts of strange phenomena, and the small number of people and journals who continue his work, we have accumulated a respectable number of records, from newspapers and medical journals, of SHC right up to the present. Very few of the accounts mention SHC, because officially there is no such phenomenon, and coroners and their advisers have the unenviable task of dealing with evidence that seems to contradict accepted physical laws and medical opinion. Inevitably, suppositions are made about knocked over heaters, flying sparks, careless smoking, and in the case of child victims, playing with matches. Faced with the alternative – a nightmare out of the Dark Ages – it is not surprising that they are accepted.

There are occasional exceptions, which are far more useful to those who truly wish to solve the enigma, like the report in *Lloyds Weekly News* of 5 February 1905. A woman asleep by a fireplace woke to find herself in flames and later died. The honest coroner said he could not understand: the woman had gone to sleep facing the fire, so any cinder that shot out from the grate would ignite the front of her clothes. Yet it was her back that bore the severe burns.

Fear of the truth

At worst, a story may be rejected out of fear or disbelief, as in the case of the elderly spinster, Wilhelmina Dewar, who combusted near midnight on 22 March 1908, in the Northumberland town of Whitley Bay. Wilhelmina was found by her sister Margaret who, in a shocked state, managed to summon her neighbours. In the house they found the severely charred body of Wilhelmina in an upstairs bed. The bedclothes were unscorched and there was no sign of fire anywhere else in the house.

When Margaret told this story at the inquest, the coroner thought it preposterous and asked her to think again. Repeatedly she said she was telling the truth and could not change her story – even after a policeman testified that Margaret was so drunk she couldn't have known what she was saying. As Fort points out, the policeman 'was not called upon to state how he distinguished between signs of excitement and terror, and intoxication.' The coroner adjourned the inquest to give her more time to think. When it was reconvened a few days later it was obvious that a great deal of pressure had been placed upon poor Margaret.

Both sisters were retired school teachers and, up until then, lived respectably. Now the coroner was calling her a liar, the papers called her a drunk, and friends and neighbours turned away, leaving her to face a hostile court. Not surprisingly, she said she had been inaccurate. This time she told a story of finding her sister burned, but alive, in a lower part of the house. Then she helped her upstairs to bed, where she died.

This sounded superficially more plausible, was accepted, and the proceedings promptly closed. The court was not interested in how Wilhelmina was transformed from someone who could be helped upstairs into the cindered corpse with charred abdomen and legs; or how, if she continued to smoulder after being helped into bed, there was no mark of fire in the house. 'But the coroner was satisfied,' wrote Fort sarcastically. 'The proper testimony had been recorded.'

Yet it was medico-legal interest that kept alive the notion of SHC, with pathologists endorsing the phenomenon, than rejecting it in favour of 'preternatural combustibility'. In addition, there was the perennial possibility that a murderer may simulate SHC to hide his crime. One of the earliest test cases occurred in Rheims in 1725 when an innkeeper, Jean Millet, was accused of having an affair with a pretty servant girl and killing his wife. The wife, who was often drunk, was found one morning about a foot (30 centimetres) away from the hearth.

'A part of the head only, with a portion of the lower extremities, and a few of the vertebrae, had escaped combustion. A foot and a half (45 centimetres) of the flooring under the body had been consumed, but a kneading-trough and a powdering tub very near the body sustained no injury.' A young assistant doctor, named Le Cat, was staying at the inn and managed to convince the court that this was no ordinary fire death but a 'visitation of God' upon the drunken woman, and an obvious result of soaking one's innards with spirits. Millet was vindicated, and Le Cat went on to qualify with distinction, and publish a memoir on SHC.

Spontaneous human combustion received its severest criticism from the great pioneer chemist, Baron Justus von Liebig, who wrote a spirited refutation of both spontaneous and preternatural combustion, on the grounds that no one had seen it happen. As a scientist he saw the historical evidence as an unsupported record of the *belief* in SHC, rather than actual proof of spontaneous burning deaths. Further, he lamented the lack of expert witnesses, and dismissed the accounts generally because they 'proceed from ignorant persons, unpractised in observation, and bear in themselves the stamp of untrustworthiness.'

Despite Liebig's assertion, however, there is plenty of evidence from both medical and police sources. Many of these bear witness to the ferocity of the phenomenon, as in the case investigated by Merille, a surgeon in Caen, recorded in Trotter's *Essay on drunkenness* (1804). On 3 June 1782, Merille was asked by 'the king's officers' in the city to report on the death of Mademoiselle Thaurs, a lady of over 60 who had been observed, that day, to have drunk three bottles of wine and one of brandy. Merille wrote:

The body lay with the crown of the head resting against one of the handirons . . . 18 inches [45 centimetres] from the fire, the remainder of the body was placed obliquely before the chimney, the whole being nothing but a mass of ashes. Even the most solid bones had lost their form and consistence. The right foot was found entire and scorched at its upper junction; the left was more burnt. The day was cold but there was nothing in the grate except two or three bits of wood about an inch in diameter, burnt in the middle.

Dr Wilton Krogman, who investigated a famous case of SHC, and experimented with

Left: the great chemist Baron Justus von Liebig. He rejected tales of spontaneous human combustion because of the lack of expert witnesses – and because his attempts to make flesh burn with the same intensity as SHC were, without exception, a dismal failure

Below: an anonymous victim of SHC lies with its apparently unburnt head resting in a grate. An electric fire is also visible – but how did the body burn so thoroughly without setting fire to the rest of the room?

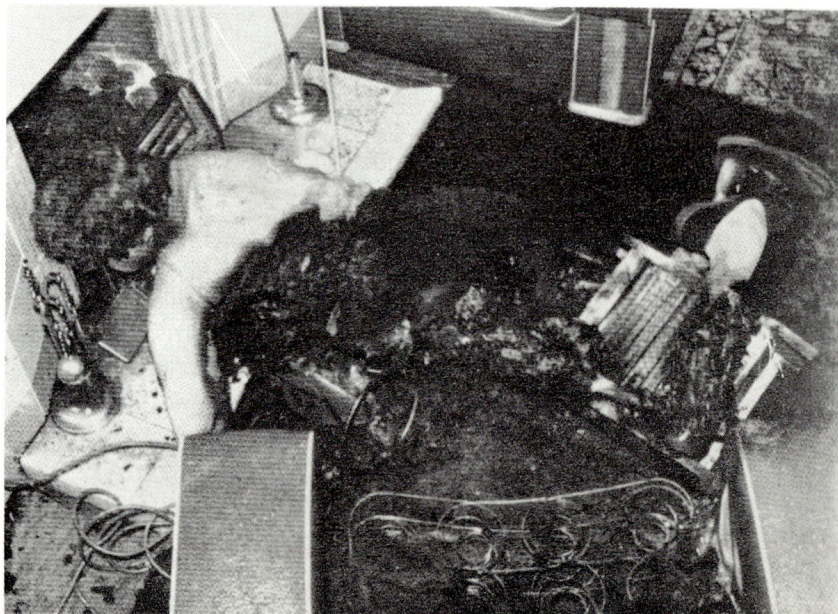

The burning of Dr Bentley

Dr J. Irving Bentley, a retired physician, lived on the ground floor of an apartment building in Coudersport, northern Pennsylvania. On the cold morning of 5 December 1966, Don Gosnell entered the building's basement to read the meter for the North Pen Gas Company. In the basement a 'light-blue smoke of unusual odor' hung in the air. Scattering an unfamiliar heap in the corner with his boot, Gosnell found it was ashes. There had been no answer to his greeting on the way in, so he decided to look in on the old man. There was more strange smoke in the bedroom but no sign of Bentley. Gosnell peered into the bathroom and was confronted with a sight he will never forget. A large hole had burned through the floor to the basement, exposing the joists and pipework below. On the edge of the hole he saw '. . . a brown leg from the knee down, like that of a mannequin. I didn't look further!' Gosnell fled from the building.

sophisticated crematorium equipment, said: 'Only at 3000°F (1500°C) plus have I seen bone fuse or melt so that it ran and became volatile.' Such a heat would certainly char everything within a considerable radius and set the house ablaze, yet the meticulous Merille writes:

> None of the furniture in the apartment was damaged. The chair on which she was sitting was found at the distance of a foot from her, and absolutely un-touched . . . the consumption of the body had taken place in less than 7 hours, though according to appear-ance, nothing around the body was burnt but the clothes.

Reluctant admissions

Modern researchers into SHC readily quash the idea that the phenomenon is as rare as some commentators suggest. Similarly, there is a growing number of cases testified to by doctors and pathologists, and this number would probably increase if the fear of ridicule could be completely removed. A Dr B. H. Hartwell reported to the Massachusetts Medico-Legal Society an unusual case of SHC that he witnessed while driving through Ayer, Massachusetts, on 12 May 1890.

He was stopped and called into a wood where he saw a horrible sight. In a clearing a woman was crouching 'in flames at the shoulders, both sides of the abdomen, and both legs.' Neither he nor the other witnesses could find an obvious cause for the fire.

This doctor's experience was not unique. Support for the suspicion that many a doctor would be able to tell of an encounter with mysterious and fatal fires comes in a coincid-ental and roundabout way. Maxwell Cade and Delphine Davis, authors of the im-aginative study of ball lightning *Taming of the thunderbolts* (1969), confessed they them-selves would not have put much faith in the above story, or in the existence of SHC, 'if a doctor friend had not told us of a lecture which he attended at the Massachusetts Medico-Legal Society, where several such cases were discussed. When we expressed cautious doubts, the doctor assured us that he had been called to a similar case himself as recently as the autumn of 1959.'

When Dr D. J. Gee of the University of Leeds delivered his well-known paper on 'A case of spontaneous combustion' he was surprised by the candid discussion that fol-lowed. He is quoted as saying:

> Dr George Manning described his ex-perience of several similar cases, and indicated that the phenomenon was certainly not as rare as might be sup-posed from the literature. This view was supported by Dr David Price, who said that he met with this phenomenon approximately once in every four years.

For a closer look at the many peculiar and frightening aspects of SHC, see page 46

At about 7.45 p.m. on 11 May 1950 at his farm close by the Salmon River Highway, about 10 miles south-west of McMinnville, Oregon. Paul Trent and his wife claimed they saw a UFO – and took a photograph of it which has still not been proved a fake.

Mrs Trent was in the yard on the south side of the house feeding the rabbits when she saw, to the north-east, moving westwards, a disc-shaped object. She called her husband, who was inside the house. When he realised the unusual nature of the object in the sky, Mr Trent ran to his car for his camera, but his wife remembered that he had left it in the house and hurried to fetch it. The camera already had a partly used film in it.

The object was tilted up a little as it approached, and appeared bright and silvery; it made no noise, and the Trents saw no smoke or vapour. Mr Trent took a picture (*above*) and wound on ready for the next frame, moving to the right to keep the object in the view-finder, and taking a second shot some 30 seconds after the first. Mrs Trent said the object seemed to be gliding, with no rotating or undulating motion. It moved off westwards and 'dimly vanished'.

The couple said there was a 'breeze' as the object tilted before flying overhead. Mr Trent estimated its diameter as 20 or 30 feet (6 or 9 metres).

A few days later, when he had used up the remaining frames, Mr Trent had the film developed locally. He mentioned the incident to only a few friends. He did not seek publicity, telling his friends he didn't want to be 'in trouble with the government'. However, a reporter from the local *McMinnville Telephone Reg-*

ister heard of the sighting from two of Mr Trent's friends; he followed it up and found the precious negatives on the floor of the Trents' house, under a writing desk where the Trent children had been playing with them! The *Telephone Register's* story appeared on 8 June 1950. On 9 and 10 June newspapers in Portland, Oregon, and in Los Angeles ran the story, and *Life* magazine carried the photographs a week later.

None of this publicity had been sought by the Trents. When, 17 years after the sighting, they were visited by an investigator from the US Air Force-sponsored Colorado University Commission of Enquiry (whose findings were

later published as the Condon Report) he found them completely unchanged by their experience, well liked locally and known as reliable.

The McMinnville UFO (above left) is remarkable for its similarity to an object (above right) seen and photographed from an aeroplane by a French Air Marshal near Rouen, France, in March 1954.

After submitting the photographs to rigorous scientific examination the Condon investigation was forced to admit they might be genuine. The official report concluded: 'This is one of the few UFO reports in which all factors investigated, geometric, psychological and physical appear to be consistent.'

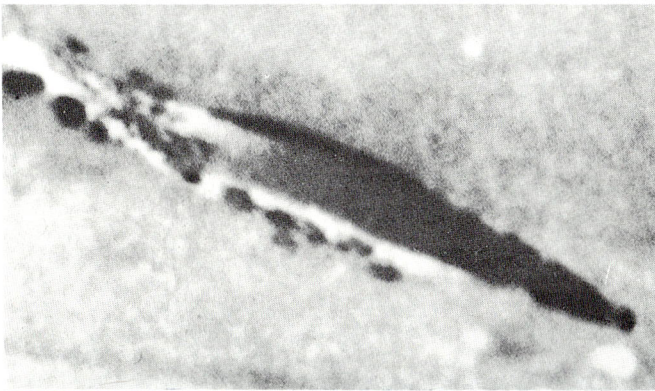

One warm, clear afternoon in early April 1966, Mr Brown (he wishes his real name to remain secret) was in his garden in Balwyn, near Melbourne, Australia, when it suddenly 'lit up' and he saw in the sky a bright object, shaped like a mushroom (left), about 20 to 35 feet (6 to 10 metres) in diameter. It was about 150 feet (50 metres) from the ground and seemed to float down towards him, spinning through a 180° angle on its vertical axis, 'during which time I photographed it'. It then shot off northwards at high speed. A carpenter working in the house witnessed the object and saw Brown photograph it.

Mr Brown is a qualified engineer. director of a large family business, and is a respected citizen of Balwyn. It is difficult to believe he would perpetrate a hoax. And yet an American UFO organisation, Ground Saucer Watch Inc., of Phoenix, Arizona, has recently cast doubt on the authenticity of the photograph. Using computer techniques to analyse the photograph, GSW has claimed it is a fake. And yet GSW has often been wrong in the past. Who is right? It is a question that is impossible to answer.

A promotional photograph of a B-57 aeroplane in flight (below) found its way into a set of UFO photographs offered for sale by NICAP (National Investigations Committee on Aerial Phenomena). An unknown object appeared in the top right-hand corner of the photograph. According to UFO investigator Robert Schmidt, the object 'appeared to be streamlined, and to have dark ''ports'' on its lower periphery.'

Schmidt wrote to the manufacturers, the Martin Aircraft Company, asking for a bigger enlargement (inset left) from the NICAP file. When questioned about the picture, the company replied that the unexplained image had been caused by a tear, a rub or an abrasion. Analysis, however, subsequently showed that in the original negative the emulsion grain extended over the area of the unknown object; a tear or rub would have destroyed the grain.

The Martin Company also said they had filmed another 'fly-by' to see if the same effect could be obtained again – a strange thing to do if, as they claimed, the original image had been caused by a flaw in the film.

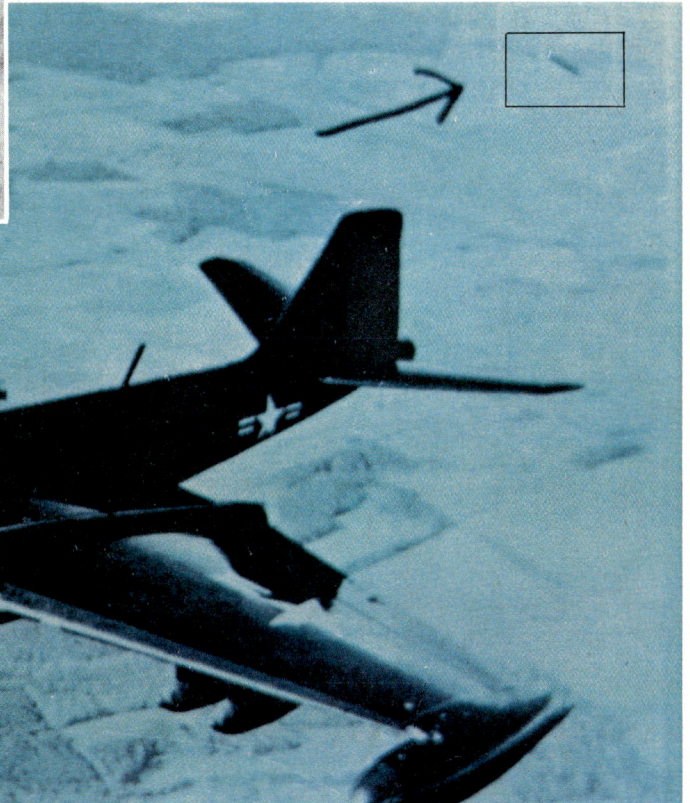

Black holes:
Where time stops, space collapses

Black holes can turn everything we know about reality on its head: infinitely dense, they warp space and time, and they may even connect directly with other, alternate universes. Yet, as NIGEL HENBEST shows, these enigmatic objects seem to evolve naturally from heavy stars

A BLACK HOLE is quite literally a hole in the fabric of space, torn from our Universe by a star collapsing in on itself. It is a region into which matter has fallen and from which nothing, not even light itself, can escape. Within the black hole, there is no up or down; no left or right. Time and space have changed roles with one another.

Just as we on Earth cannot help but travel forward in time, so any space traveller unfortunate enough to fall into a black hole would be sucked into the centre by an infinite density and crushed out of existence. Around the black hole itself is left a gaping hole, a few miles across, where space *does not exist*. Here, the pull of gravity is stronger than anywhere else in the Universe. Nothing can ever escape from it.

Both the theory of black holes and the evidence for their existence are products of 20th century science. But, surprisingly, the first prediction of black holes was made in 1798 by the French astronomer Pierre Laplace. In his *Exposition du système du monde*, Laplace proposed the startling and contradictory theory that the most luminous stars might in fact be invisible.

Laplace derived this conclusion from Newton's law of gravitation. If a star had the same density as the Earth, Laplace argued, it would be so massive that its surface gravity would prevent light from escaping. Since such heavy stars should produce a lot of light, Laplace concluded that the most brilliant stars were invisible.

In his idea of strong gravity preventing light from escaping, Laplace anticipated current astronomical thinking. But in other ways, Laplace was quite wrong. The modern view is that stars as heavy as those described by Laplace cannot exist in reality. Astronomers now think that black holes are formed not by the massive explosion predicted by Laplace, but by a cataclysmic *implosion* – matter being dragged inwards and compressing to an incredible density.

But the main source of contemporary research and knowledge of black holes was provided not by Laplace but by Albert Einstein. In his *General theory of relativity*, published in 1916, Einstein replaced Newton's 'force' of gravity with an entirely new concept of time and space 'warps' (see p. 42). Subsequent measurement and experimentation seem to have confirmed Einstein's theory, with profound results for black hole theory. With Einstein's view of the Universe, astronomers are now confident in being able to calculate their way around – and into – a black hole.

Using Einstein's equations, the German astronomer Karl Schwarzschild produced a general description of black holes only months after publication of the general

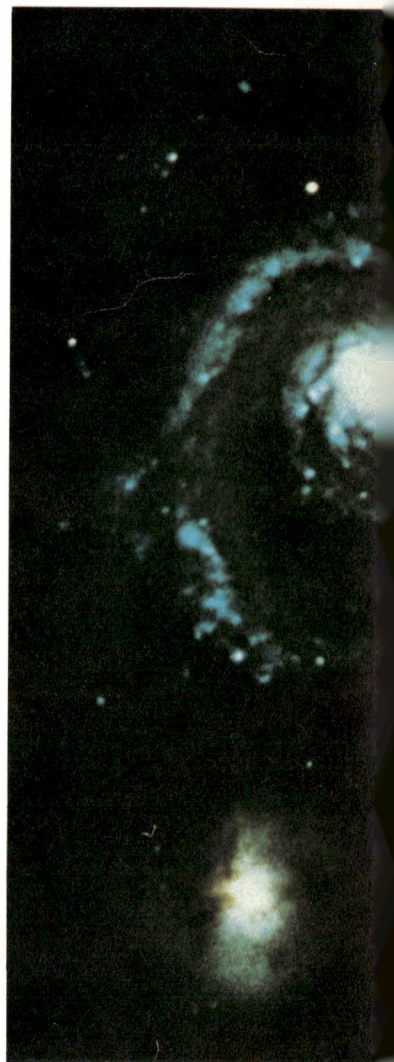

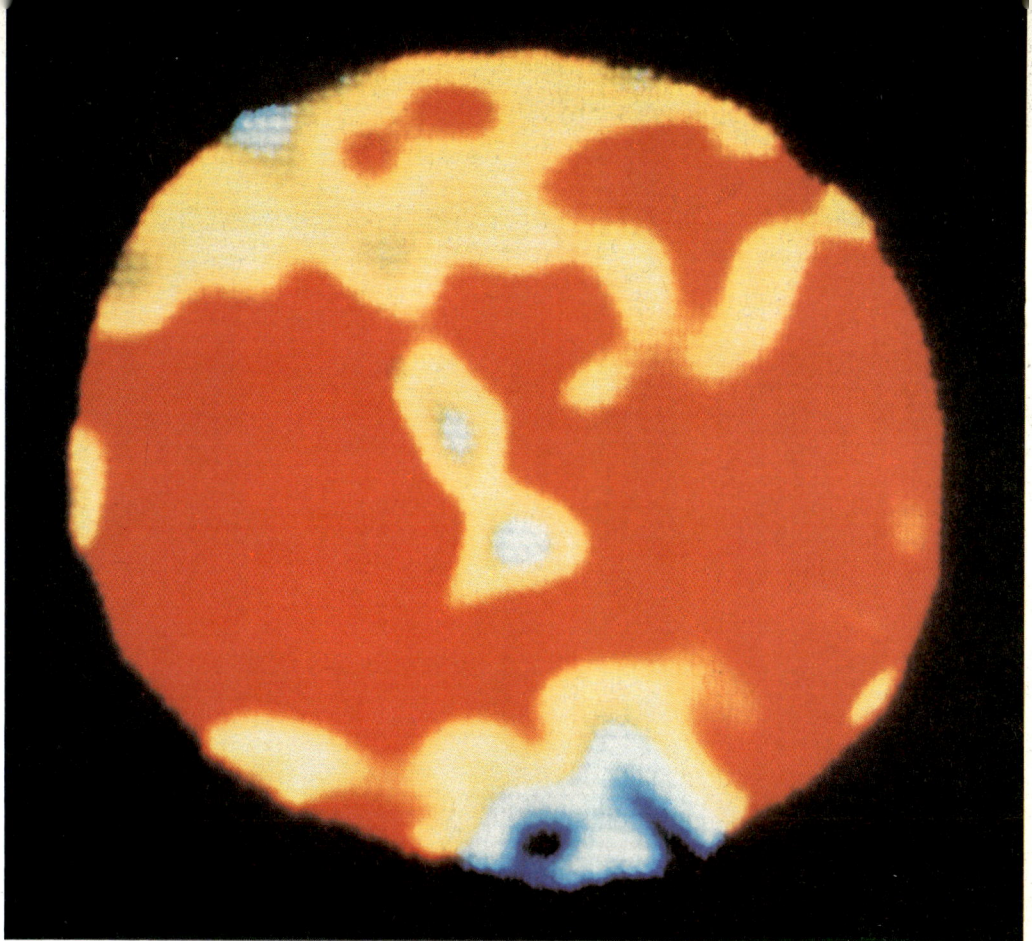

theory. At the time, however, no one could conceive of such strong gravitation as predicted by Schwarzschild. His calculations lay in obscurity, collecting dust. But by 1939 American physicists J. Robert Oppenheimer ('father of the atom bomb') and H. Snyder calculated that black holes could form at the heart of a massive implosion of a star.

But black holes were still not taken seriously by the astronomical establishment. Even if they did exist, how could we ever know? How could you possibly detect an entirely black, extremely small object millions of miles away? It seemed that no new advances in black hole theory were possible. Then, in the 1960s and 1970s, thanks to the advances made in radio-astronomy, strange objects were seen on the fringe of the Universe that put astronomy in a turmoil and led to the resurrection of black hole theory.

Using radio and x-ray techniques, astronomers spotted objects that emitted huge amounts of radiation, but no light. And although black holes cannot emit radiation themselves, they may capture streamers of gas which wrap themselves around a black hole in a rotating disc before being sucked into the hole. Caught in the intense gravitation near the hole, the gas becomes hot and turbulent and its energy may shine out as radiation. Astronomers now think that some celestial x-ray sources consist of a black hole pulling gas off a companion star. Quasars – quasi-stellar objects were thought to be huge black holes capturing gas in the centre of a whole galaxy of stars.

Schwarzschild had assumed that if black holes do exist they would not rotate. But all real stars do rotate, and as a dying star collapses to a black hole, it should spin round even faster. What was the explanation?

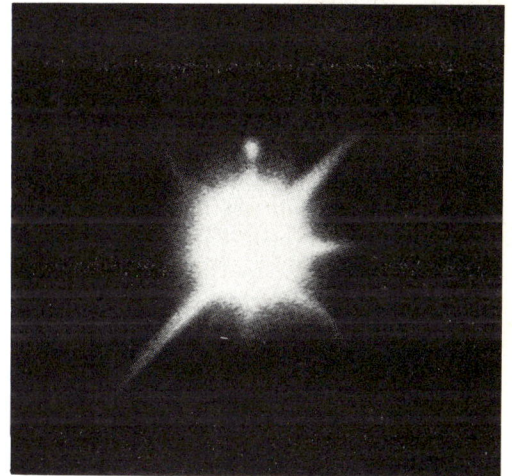

One of the most important contributions to black hole theory in recent years has been the work of New Zealand mathematician Roy Kerr. Calculations based on Einstein's theory convinced Kerr of the existence of 'rotating black holes'. Although the collapsed star's matter ends up as a central point, the space around it is still distorted, curved, by its original rotation. Kerr found that there is a region surrounding the hole where matter is dragged around by virtue of the hole's rotation.

Kerr's work on rotating black holes was further elaborated by Oxford mathematician Roger Penrose. Although some mathematicians have thought that the collapsed point-like star can sometimes be visible, Penrose

suggested that such a 'naked singularity' is always decently 'clothed' by a surrounding black hole that keeps its light from reaching the Universe beyond.

Other important work on black hole theory was done by Stephen Hawking, of Cambridge – described as the man who has contributed more to our understanding of gravity than anyone since Einstein himself. Hawking revealed his most amazing result in 1974: black holes are very slowly evaporating away.

In practice, Hawking's evaporation mechanism is far too slow to affect black holes formed from collapsed stars. But it is very important for smaller holes. If black holes, the size and density of small hills, had formed when the Universe began some 15,000 million years ago, they should evaporate so fast that they are now 'exploding' in a burst of energy. Astronomers have looked for such explosions, but failed to detect them. This, however, is not a refutation of Hawking's theory; it just means that there were few such holes created in the early Universe.

But with evidence for star-mass black holes, astronomers are on firmer ground. Astronomers now think the heaviest stars in the Universe must end their lives by swallowing themselves up in black holes.

Birth of a star
To understand how this happens we must begin with the birth of a star. Stars are formed in huge clouds of diffuse gas which come together under their own gravitational inpull. Near the centre, the turbulent gas becomes so dense that it breaks up into

individual fragments – each of which becomes a new-born star. The result is a cluster of stars of different masses – ranging from one ten-thousandth the Sun's mass to 100 times heavier than our star.

At first, the new-born stars light up the surrounding gas cloud (nebula), as we see in the Orion Nebula today. Eventually the gas cloud is blown away, and the cluster breaks up into individual stars. Our Sun, a typical star, was born this way 4,600 million years ago.

During a star's lifetime its core is a raging nuclear furnace, where hydrogen is continuously turning to helium – as in a hydrogen

Above: new-born stars of Orion Nebula lighting up the surrounding gas cloud. Eventually, the nebula will break up to form individual stars

Below: an x-ray photograph showing some of the most distant objects in the Universe. The bright object, lower right, is quasar 2C278, about the size of Earth but with the brilliance of 100,000 million Suns

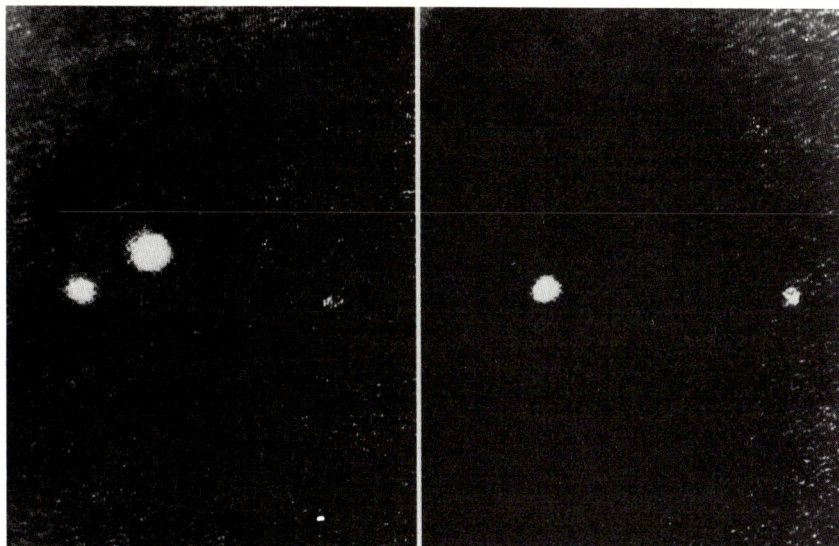

Above: the Crab pulsar.
Pulsars are stars that spin
rapidly in space emitting
radio waves that are received
on Earth as a flash or pulse
every few seconds. In the
picture above, the pulse is
'on', while the one next to it
shows the pulse 'off'

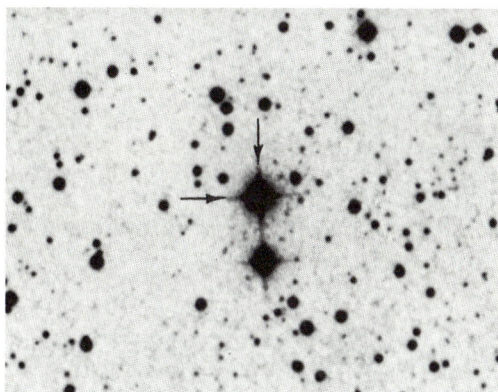

Right: the recently
discovered x-ray star Cygnus
X-1. Some 6000 light years
from Earth, Cygnus X-1 is
thought to provide the best
evidence for the existence of
black holes. The arrowed star
shows HDE 226868, a
companion star three times
the density of our Sun

inwards on itself. The subatomic particles (electrons and protons) within it amalgamate to make up neutrons. Because neutrons are much smaller than atoms, the resulting *neutron star* is tiny, smaller even than a white dwarf. It is only 15 miles (25 kilometres) across – and so dense that a drop of matter from it would weigh over a million tonnes.

Many neutron stars spin rapidly, and send out beams of radio waves. When these sweep across the Earth, a radio telescope detects the star appearing to 'flash' or 'pulse' – just as a lighthouse seems to flash as the beam of light from its rotating lantern sweeps across our eyes. Radio astronomers at Cambridge discovered these flashing neutron stars in 1967, and labelled them *pulsars*.

Invisible corpse in orbit

Studying x-rays from space, astronomers have also found neutron stars in orbit around normal stars. Here, the compact neutron star pulls gas off its companion. As gas spirals down through the neutron star's gravitational field it heats up by friction, until it is hot enough to beam out x-rays, not light.

Satellites have revealed many of these unequal double acts, and astronomers studying the ordinary star's light in each case have found that it is indeed in mutual orbit about a star that can't be seen. Theory suggests that neither a white dwarf nor a neutron star can be heavier than three Suns; yet some stars associated with x-ray sources seem to have invisible companions heavier than this limit.

The best-known is Cyg X–1, an x-ray star in the constellation Cygnus. Uhuru, the x-ray detecting satellite, discovered that the radiation comes from the spiralling disc of gas which surrounds the unseen companion of a giant star (catalogued as HDE 226868). But the motion of the giant star, revealed by its light, shows that its companion is at least six times heavier than the Sun. Too heavy to be a neutron star (or a white dwarf), the invisible star in the Cyg X–1 system must be a black hole. Millions of years ago it must have been an ordinary but very heavy star, which lived its life in a rush, exploded as a supernova, and left its invisible corpse still in orbit about its companion HDE 226868. Streams of gas from the latter fall towards the black hole, and fleetingly emit x-rays before disappearing into the hole.

Half a dozen other x-ray sources have similar characteristics to Cyg X–1, and probably also harbour black holes. Indirect though the evidence is, most astronomers accept that these sources do indicate that black holes are not just a theorist's dream. Matter in our Universe can indeed collapse past the point of no return, and tear out of the structure of space a black hole – a hole that can perhaps lead out of our Universe altogether and into another.

On page 41 we take you to the edge of a black hole and beyond – into other universes

bomb – and the nuclear energy released keeps the star shining. Eventually, though, the hydrogen at the centre will be replaced by spent helium 'ash'. Now the star must change. Its core shrinks, while its outer layers swell up enormously – to around a hundred times the star's previous size. When our Sun's central reactor becomes choked with helium, it will expand to become a red giant, engulfing Mercury and Venus in the process.

A star exists as a red giant for only a short period. Eventually it ejects its distended outer gas as a beautiful 'planetary' nebula (so-called because it resembles a planet's disc in a small telescope), while its core settles down as a small, very dense star, called a white dwarf. White dwarfs are very small, about the size of the Earth, one hundredth the Sun's present size, made of a 'gas' some million times denser than water.

Heavier stars live for a shorter time, for they consume their central hydrogen much more quickly. They have more chequered careers as red giants, too. The core of a heavy star can convert helium into other elements – carbon, silicon and iron in particular. But they too must die: blowing themselves apart in a vast supernova explosion, during which they outshine 1000 million Suns.

While the outer layers explode outwards, the central core of the supernova collapses

Messages in the mind

Modern research has succeeded in actually recording the 'tuning in' of one mind to another. But, explains ROY STEMMAN, scientists still cannot tell us how telepathy works

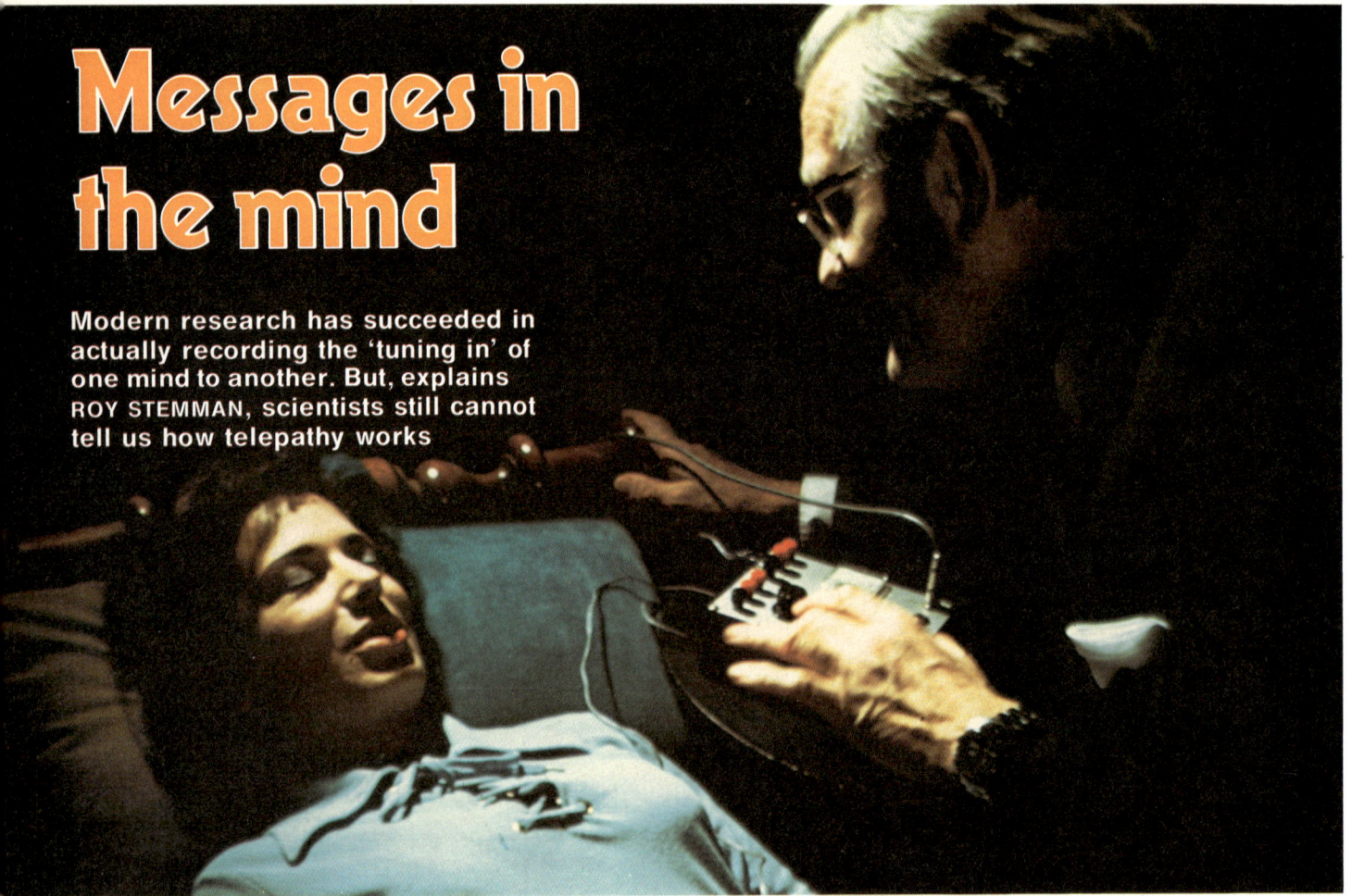

Above: Douglas Dean, one of America's leading psychical researchers, using a plethysmograph to monitor blood volume. The machine shows that telepathic activity can actually increase blood volume

Below: Sir William Barrett (1845–1926), Professor of Physics at the Royal College of Science, Dublin, who was one of the first psychical investigators

EARLY ONE MORNING in 1980, a very frightened old lady walked feebly into a Barcelona police station. Senora Isabel Casas, an 81-year-old widow, had been so scared by a terrible dream that, despite her age and infirmity, she had managed to walk to the local police station to raise the alarm. Almost incoherent with fear, she told the officer on duty that she had seen the face of her friend and neighbour, Rafael Perez, 'twisted in terror' – and heard a voice say, 'They are going to kill us.'

The Spanish police were inclined to dismiss Senora Casas's experience as a mere nightmare. But they became curious when they learned that she had not seen Perez, the only other resident in the block of flats where she lived, for 10 days. Normally the 56-year-old chef called to see her every day, but he had written her a note saying he was going away for several weeks. It was odd, the police thought, that this note had not been delivered until three days after she had last seen her neighbour. And why had Perez not called to see her personally?

They decided to investigate and eventually found Perez tied up in a shed on the roof of the block of flats. He told them two men had broken into his apartment, made him sign 28 cheques so that they could draw his £15,000 life savings a little at a time, then forced him to write the letter to Mrs Casas so

that her suspicions would not be aroused. Then they tied him up and said they would be back, once they had all the money, to kill him and his neighbour.

Astonishingly, the old woman seems to have picked up the thoughts of her friend as he waited in terror for his captors to return. His life was saved by her vivid telepathic dream – and the police ambushed and arrested the men when they returned to the scene of their crime.

This ability of one person to 'look into' the mind of another was one of the first subjects to be studied by the early psychical researchers a century ago.

The case of Canon Warburton

Typical of the spontaneous cases of telepathy investigated by early researchers was the experience of an English clergyman in 1883. Canon Warburton sat in an armchair in his brother's flat and began to doze. Suddenly, he woke up with a start exclaiming, 'By Jove! He's down!' The canon had just had a vivid dream in which he had seen his brother come out of a drawing-room on to a brightly illuminated landing, catch his foot on the edge of the top stair and fall headlong down the stairs, just managing to save himself from serious injury by using his hands and elbows. The house in the dream was not one he recognised. All the canon knew, having just arrived in London from Oxford, was that his brother had left him a note explaining that he had gone to a dance in the West End and would be back at about 1 a.m.

Recovering from the experience, Canon Warburton dozed off again for half an hour until his brother came in and woke him up. 'I have just had as narrow an escape of breaking my neck as I ever had in my life!' he exclaimed. 'Coming out of the ballroom, I caught my foot, and tumbled full length down the stairs.'

The canon's uncanny dream experience is one of many hundreds of equally impressive cases of spontaneous telepathy collected by the Society for Psychical Research in Britain and America.

The word 'telepathy' was coined in 1882 by a leading Cambridge scholar and investigator, F. W. H. Myers, and the first major study of such experiences – the *Census of hallucinations*, published in 1890 – examined replies to 20,000 questionnaires. But science needed to examine telepathy under more controlled conditions.

One of the pioneers of scientific research into telepathy was Sir William Barrett, professor of physics at the Royal College of Science, Dublin, who conducted experiments with hypnotised subjects that satisfied him that telepathy was real.

When Sir William submitted his paper, *Some phenomena associated with abnormal conditions of the mind*, to the British Association for the Advancement of Science, it was

refused by the biological committee. He eventually presented it to the anthropological sub-section, where it was accepted only on the casting vote of its chairman, Dr Alfred Russell Wallace, who was also a keen investigator of psychical phenomena.

By the early part of this century many groups of researchers were involved in imaginative telepathy tests. In the 1920s Rene Warcollier conducted group telepathy experiments between France and the United States, many of which produced very impressive results. But not all early research is acceptable by today's strict scientific standards. The famous physicist Professor Oliver Lodge (later Sir Oliver Lodge) carried out tests with two girls who claimed to be able to read each other's minds. He found their demonstrations convincing and published them in 1909 in his book *The survival of man*. But since the girls were allowed to hold hands while 'sending' their telepathic images of playing cards, the possibility that they were using a code cannot be eliminated. This suspicion is reinforced by Lodge's statistics, which show that when the girls were not touching, results fell nearly to chance levels.

'Sinclair goes spooky'
In the 1930s the work of the well-known writer Upton Sinclair caught the public imagination. Sinclair's wife had considerable psychic abilities and was able to 'receive' by telepathy pictures that were drawn by her husband or other senders. Sometimes these experiments were carried out in adjoining rooms, at other times over long distances. Sinclair published his results in his book *Mental radio*, revealing that in 290 experiments Mrs Sinclair scored 23 per cent successes, 53 per cent partial successes and 24 per cent failures.

The similarity between the original drawings and Mrs Sinclair's 'copies' was often striking, ruling out coincidence, but making a statistical analysis of the results difficult. In fact, partial successes were often as impressive as direct hits because they gave an interesting insight into how Mrs Sinclair perceived the images. On one occasion, Upton Sinclair drew a volcano with billowing black smoke. His wife drew a very good likeness, but was unable to identify it and guessed that the smoke was a beetle. Had this been a telepathy test which required a verbal response, her description of a beetle would have been judged a miss. In fact, her drawing showed that she had picked up the image very accurately.

Sinclair, a committed socialist, was well aware that most intelligent people still regarded the phenomenon of telepathy with scepticism. Some of his socialist friends felt that his interest in ESP conflicted with their rationalist outlook on the world, and one of them attacked him in a newspaper article headed 'Sinclair goes spooky'.

Above: Sir Oliver Lodge (1851–1940), who carried out psychical experiments with two girls who claimed to be able to read each other's minds. But later investigations have cast doubt on Lodge's results

All in the mind's eye

Pictures drawn by American novelist Upton Sinclair and their images 'received' telepathically by his wife Craig reveal a startling degree of similarity. In the first pair (left) Sinclair's original was of a volcano erupting. His wife interpreted it as a beetle – which, as Sinclair put it, 'hardly sounds like a triumphant success.' But in fact the billowing smoke looks very like a beetle's body in Mrs Sinclair's drawing, while the sides of the mountain can easily be interpreted as its antennae.

The second and third pairs of pictures need no explanation. Mrs Sinclair had difficulty, however, with her husband's drawing of a cow. She failed to identify it, but noted that she saw 'something sending out long lines from it.'

In the last pair of pictures Mrs Sinclair again failed to identify the target picture – but the similarity between the two drawings is striking. Her comment reads, 'May be elephant's snout – but anyway it is some kind of a running animal. Long thing like a rope flung out in front of him.'

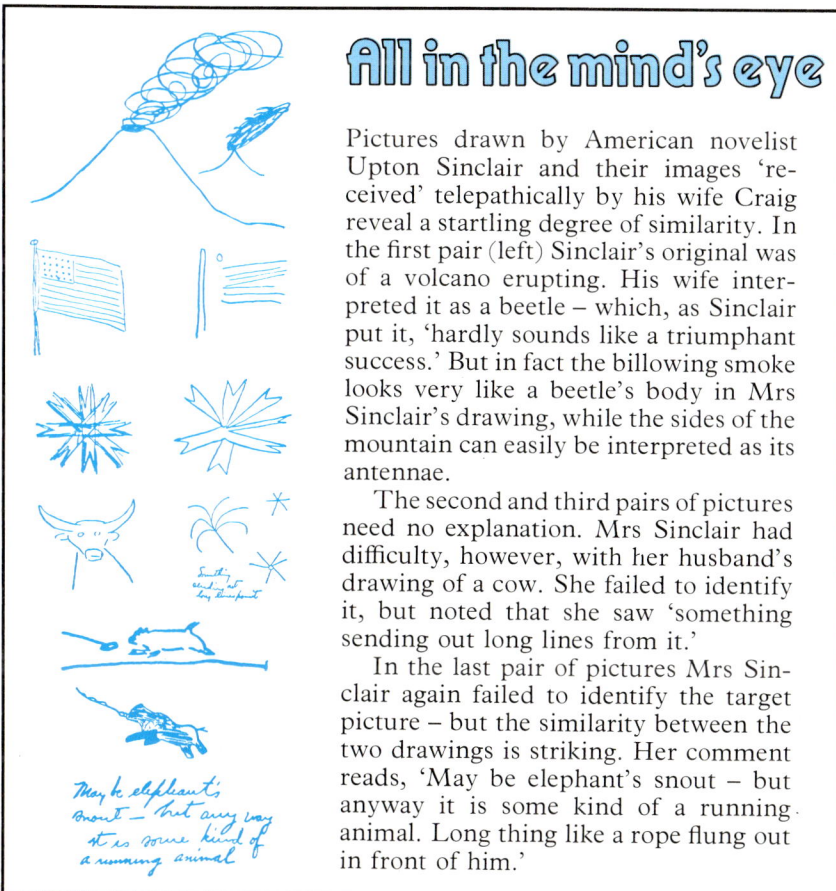

May be elephant's snout – but any way it is some kind of a running animal

35

Extra-sensory perception

It was to give the subject respectability in the eyes of science that Dr J. B. Rhine began to research telepathy in the laboratory. Rhine used new methods and easily identifiable targets – Zener cards – to ensure that there was no doubt whether a subject was scoring a hit or a miss in his tests. The results were impressive and satisfied Rhine and many other scientists that mind-to-mind communication was real.

But there were still sceptics, one of whom was the psychologist Bernard Riess. When Dr Rhine was invited to lecture about his ESP work at Barnard College, Riess questioned him so fiercely and in such a manner that Rhine protested he was, in effect, accusing him of being a liar. Instead of defending his own experiments, however, Rhine suggested to Riess that he should carry out his own tests, using all the controls he believed necessary. Riess's students urged him to accept the challenge and they found a young lady with psychic abilities who agreed to act as subject. For several months, Riess conducted his own card-guessing experiments with the girl. Seventy-four runs of 25 cards were made (1850 trials) and they averaged a phenomenal 18 hits out of 25.

Riess, once a denigrator of ESP research, was called upon to defend his experiment in 1938 when the American Psychological Association organised an ESP symposium. He told the meeting:

> There can be no criticism of the method used. I had the deck of cards on my desk, shuffled them, and at the stated time turned them over one by one, making a record of each card. I kept the records locked up in my desk and sometimes it was a week before I totalled up the scores and found the number of high scores she was making. . . . The only error that may have crept in is a possibility of deception, and the only person who could have done the deceiving was myself since the subject at no time knew how well she was doing nor had any idea of cards which were being turned by myself. . . .

ESPionage!

Rhine's work continued to be a subject of public debate for many years, but with more and more researchers carrying out their own research programmes into various ESP subjects, telepathy was soon overshadowed by subjects such as clairvoyance and precognition, which brought startling experimental results. Then, in the late 1950s, telepathy was suddenly back in the news with the publication in the French press of reports that successful telepathy tests had been carried out between a subject in the submerged American submarine USS *Nautilus* and an agent on shore. The military implications of such methods of communication, if they proved to be reliable were obvious; and

ESP in dreams

Recent research suggests that telepathy may occur much more often than is generally thought.

In a series of dream telepathy experiments carried out at the Dream Laboratory in Brooklyn, New York, an 'agent' studied a picture postcard and transmitted the image telepathically while the subject was asleep in another room. An electro – encephalograph monitored brain patterns: when a change in the patterns indicated the subject was dreaming, he or she was woken up and asked to describe the dream.

There was a high degree of similarity between the transmitted images and the dreams, although the target pictures were never received whole. The images were interwoven with the dream the subject was having at the time.

they aroused great interest.

Despite the United States Navy's denial of the *Nautilus* story, the Soviets took it seriously – with the result that the work of Russian psychical investigators, which had been classed as top secret for 30 years, was made public. Among them was physiologist Dr Leonid Vasiliev. He claimed that Soviet parapsychologists had received encouragement for their research from high up in the party organisation – which suggests that Stalin himself may have been interested in the use of telepathy for military purposes.

Dr Vasiliev had been using hypnotised subjects to investigate 'mental radio', and when a book about his work was published in 1962 he revealed that he and other researchers had been able to make hypnotised

patients carry out actions by telepathic order, and even hypnotise people by telepathy. In one extraordinary case, a woman whose body was paralysed down the left side was the subject of the experiments. Her condition was psychosomatic, and under hypnotism she was able to move her left arm and leg with ease. Vasiliev discovered, however, that he had only to give *mental* commands and she would move her left hand, arm, or foot as requested – without the use of hypnotism.

He was able to demonstrate this mental communication before a group of observers. As an extra precaution the patient was blindfolded and not a word was spoken. Each instruction was written down and witnessed by the group before either Vasiliev or his co-worker, hypnotist Dr Finne, concentrated on it. The woman obeyed with remarkable accuracy, and she was even able to say whether it was Vasiliev or Finne who was giving the instruction.

More recently, the Russians have carried out even more startling demonstrations of telepathy using a biophysicist, Yuri Kamensky, and a Moscow actor and journalist, Karl

Nikolaiev. Kamensky was in Novosibirsk in Siberia, Nikolaiev in Moscow, and a committee of scientists supervised the session. The results provided overwhelming evidence for mental communication between the two men.

In one test, Nikolaiev correctly described six objects that had been given to Kamensky; he was also able to identify 12 out of 20 ESP cards. What is particularly impressive about this Russian series is that the scientists succeeded in producing independent instrumental confirmation that something paranormal was going on.

They wired Nikolaiev to an electro-encephalograph (EEG) machine, which monitors brain waves. They found that as soon as Kamensky began to transmit images,

Nikolaiev's brain waves altered. Using this knowledge they devised a technique for sending messages in Morse code. Instead of asking Kamensky to think of an object, they asked him to imagine he was fighting Nikolaiev. As the scientists in Moscow watched the recording of Nikolaiev's brain waves on the EEG, they found that there was a distinct change in the pattern whenever Kamensky imagined he was fighting him. Kamensky was able to transmit Morse 'dots' and 'dashes' by imagining 'fighting bouts' of various lengths: a 45-second bout produced a burst of activity that was interpreted as a dash, while a 15-second bout was read as a dot. In this way, the scientists in Moscow were able to identify the Russian word *mig* – meaning 'instant' – which Kamensky had transmitted in Morse code from 2000 miles (3200 kilometres) away in Siberia.

Interestingly, a similar technique using different methods has been successfully demonstrated in the West. It followed the accidental discovery by a Czechoslovakian researcher, Dr Stepan Figar, that intense thought about a person produced an increase in that individual's blood volume – a change that could be accurately measured by a device called a plethysmograph.

Mental radio

Douglas Dean, a British-born electrochemist and professor of computing who is also a leading psychical researcher, saw the potential of this discovery for telepathy tests. His research revealed that, when a telepathic sender concentrates on the name of someone with whom a subject wired to a plethysmograph has an emotional tie, a change in the subject's blood volume is often recorded. Together with two engineers of the Newark College of Engineering in New Jersey, Dean designed a system using a plethysmograph for sending messages in Morse code.

If the sender concentrates on the name of a person who is emotionally significant to the subject, the plethysmograph produces a measurable response which is interpreted as a Morse dot. If no response is registered during a specified period of time, this is noted as a Morse dash. Using this technique, Dean has successfully communicated over short and long distances. In one remarkable instance he sent a Morse message over a distance of 1200 miles (2000 kilometres), between New York and Florida.

Despite these discoveries and the outstanding individual results that some experiments have produced, not all researchers are so successful when they attempt to duplicate telepathy tests. Mental radio remains an elusive phenomenon, although it is one that has occurred often enough – spontaneously and in the laboratory – to satisfy most investigators of its reality.

Top: the nuclear submarine USS *Nautilus*. In the late 1950s it was rumoured that the US Navy had been carrying out telepathy experiments with an agent on shore and a sender aboard the submerged craft

Above: Karl Nikolaiev (left) and Dr Yuri Kamensky (second from right). They devised a method of sending Morse messages by telepathy

Left: Dr Leonid Vasiliev, the Soviet psychical researcher

Clairvoyance – mental television – can be used in crime detection. See page 66

On the bigfoot trail

Hundreds of sightings all over the North American continent suggest that the fabled bigfoot really does exist. But how can this primitive creature survive in the world's most developed society? JANET and COLIN BORD consider the most reliable reports

RELIABLE REPORTS OF 'man-beasts' on the North American continent have been traced as far back as the 1830s. We have to rely on old newspaper accounts for our data before 1900, but determined researchers have found some intriguing descriptions of beasts very similar to those reported today. For example, in 1851 a local newspaper carried the story of two hunters in Greene County, Arkansas, who saw a herd of cattle being chased by 'an animal bearing the unmistakable likeness of humanity'.

He was of gigantic stature, the body being covered with hair and the head with long locks that fairly enveloped the neck and shoulders. The 'wild man', after looking at them deliberately for a short time, turned and ran away with great speed, leaping 12 to 14 feet [3.6 to 4.3 metres] at a time. His footprints measured 13 inches [33 centimetres] each.

The newspaper reporter added that the beast was thought to be 'a survivor of the earthquake disaster which desolated that region in 1811'. In nearly all these early reports the man-beasts are referred to as 'wild men', the assumption being that they must be humans who have taken to the woods and in so doing somehow developed a thick coat of body hair. Modern evolutionary theory, however, suggests that this is unlikely.

The location of the 1851 sighting in Arkansas shows that bigfoot reports are not confined to the north-western states (northern California, Oregon and Washington) and British Columbia, where so many originate. Although these areas, with their vast tracts of forested mountains, have produced more reports than other regions, bigfeet or their footprints have been seen in nearly all the American states and Canadian provinces. Florida, far away from what is thought of as traditional bigfoot territory, has been particularly rich in sightings of the similar 'skunk ape' in recent years.

Many reports simply describe a man-beast, seen briefly in wooded country. But there are enough detailed reports for trends and characteristics to be apparent. Bigfeet seem to be timid, not wishing to get too close to humans. However, they also have a streak of curiosity and sometimes come close to people camping in the woods at night, look through their belongings, and occasionally also rock their camper or car. This behaviour, and early reports of the destruction of mineral prospectors' camps, may suggest a wish to frighten intruders away.

Bigfeet have also been seen wandering near rural houses and settlements, possibly attracted by the easy availability of food in such places. But despite their frightening appearance and the provocative behaviour of their discoverers, (whose reaction is frequently to shoot first and ask questions afterwards), bigfeet are not aggressive towards humans. Reports of injuries caused by them are rare.

As the 20th century progressed and more people became aware of bigfeet, so more reports came in concerning old as well as

Above and right: Five stills from the only cine film ever taken of a bigfoot at Bluff Creek, California, in 1967. Rigorous analysis has not proved the film to be a fake – but sceptics still insist that the creature is a large actor dressed in animal skins. Casts (below) were taken of footprints found in the area after the sighting

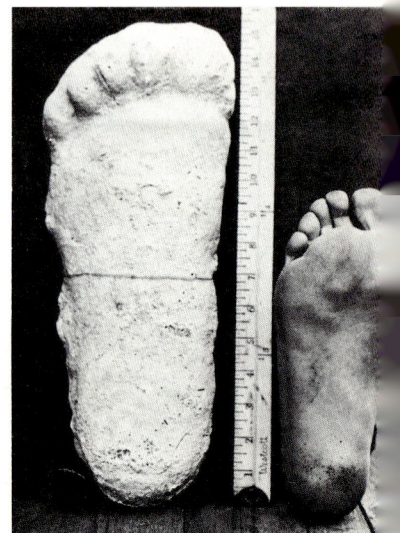

recent sightings, until in the 1960s and 1970s there was a vast number of reports on file. Although this was obviously due in part to the greater publicity, did it also mean that bigfeet were being seen more frequently? Since their habitat must gradually be shrinking as civilisation advances, it would be reasonable to expect their numbers to be declining. Perhaps it is this very pressure on living space that forces them to visit settlements for food and this might explain the increased number of reported sightings.

The *Bigfoot casebook* records nearly 1000 sightings in the past 150 years and this collection of cases is by no means complete. If, as has been estimated, only about one tenth of all sightings are ever reported, then there may have been as many as 10,000 sightings during that period. There are also many other reports of large, human-like footprints being found, usually in mud, snow or sand where they show up well, and it is usually assumed that a bigfoot left these tracks, even when the creature has not been

a very large man-like creature about 6½ or 7 feet [2 or 2.1 metres] tall came into view.

It was walking on its hind legs, was covered with dark hair, had a bearded face and large chest and so far as I could see was not wearing clothes of any kind. Startled, I let out a yell of alarm and the creature instantly turned and ran off into the woods, still on its hind legs. I told some of my co-workers about it and some laughed but others said they, too, had seen it. No one had an explanation for it and no name was given to it, but all agreed that it was a large ape-like something and that it also resembled a very large man.

Kidnapped by a man-beast

Another bigfoot report, dating from 1924, describes what, if it is true, is the most dramatic bigfoot encounter on record. Albert Ostman claims to have been kidnapped by a bigfoot and held captive for several days

Top: prospector Albert Ostman claimed to have been held captive by a bigfoot family in British Columbia in 1924

seen. Sometimes researchers investigating reports also find hair and faeces that are suspected to be a bigfoot's, but analyses done on these substances are usually irritatingly inconclusive.

A selection of a few of the many sightings reported this century will give a clear picture of bigfoot and his behaviour. In 1969 Albert M. Fletcher wrote about his encounter 50 years before, when he was a lumber-camp worker in Washington.

In the fall of 1917 when I was 17 years old I was working for a lumber camp on the Cowlitz River in the state of Washington. One moonlit evening I was walking down a logging road en route to a dance when I had the uneasy feeling that something was following close behind me. I kept looking over my shoulder but could not see anything. When I came to a bend in the road I ducked behind a tree and waited to see what it was. Almost immediately

before he managed to escape. The kidnap took place near Toba Inlet in British Columbia, when Ostman was prospecting and camping in the mountains. An 8-foot (2.4-metres) bigfoot picked him up in his sleeping bag one night and carried him across country for what seemed to the hot and cramped captive like three hours.

It was still dark when they arrived at their destination, but when it got light Ostman saw there were four bigfeet, male and female adults and male and female children. During his captivity Ostman was able to study the family's way of life, and to ponder his best method of escape. All attempts were blocked by the 'old man', as Ostman called him, whose mere size was an imposing deterrent. Ostman had his rifle with him but was loth to cause the creatures any injury, since they had not harmed him. He finally escaped by feeding the 'old man' a huge quantity of snuff and thereby incapacitating him. While the bigfoot rushed to find some water, Ostman grabbed his belongings and ran for his life.

Encounters in which the witness is able to get a long, close look at the creature are the most interesting; a perceptive and unflurried witness can add greatly to our knowledge of the creature. One of the best reports of this kind was made by William Roe, who saw a bigfoot on Mica Mountain in British Columbia in October 1955.

Roe was hidden in a bush, so the bigfoot, a female about 6 feet (1.8 metres) tall and 3 feet (1 metre) wide and weighing around 300 pounds (135 kilograms), came towards him unaware she was being watched. When the bigfoot was 20 feet (6 metres) away, she squatted by the bush Roe was hiding in.

He later wrote a careful description of the bigfoot's head, face and hair, of the shape of her body and the way she walked. He wondered briefly if he had unknowingly stepped into a film set and was looking at a made-up actor, but soon discarded that idea. His report continues:

> Finally, the wild thing must have got my scent, for it looked directly at me through an opening in the bush. A look of amazement crossed its face. It looked so comical at that moment I had to grin. Still in a crouched position, it backed up three or four short steps, then straightened up to its full height and started to walk rapidly back the way it had come. For a moment it watched me over its shoulder as it went, not exactly afraid, but as though it wanted no contact with anything strange.

Roe considered shooting what would be a unique specimen, and even raised his rifle. But he could not fire. 'Although I have called the creature "it", I felt now that it was a human being and I knew I would never forgive myself if I killed it.'

Human or animal? The witnesses are not sure, and neither are the researchers. 'If only we had a corpse to examine,' they cry. But those who feel that the priority is to kill a bigfoot and thus prove its existence once and for all are opposed by those who feel equally strongly that the creature should be left in peace. What gives man the right to commit murder simply to satisfy his curiosity?

A few reports suggest that someone with enough patience and nerve might even be able to make friends with a bigfoot. In the autumn of 1966 a couple living near Lower Bank in New Jersey found footprints 17 inches (43 centimetres) long outside their house, and saw a face peering in at a window over 7 feet (2.1 metres) high. They regularly left vegetable scraps for the bigfoot, which it ate, but one night they left nothing and their visitor showed its annoyance by throwing a dustbin against the wall. A shot fired into the air failed to deter it, so the man fired *at* the bigfoot, which ran away and did not return.

Thirty feet (9-metres) of wobbly 16-millimetre colour film shook the bigfoot-hunting world in 1967, and the questions posed by the film still have not been answered to everyone's satisfaction. Behind the camera was bigfoot-hunter Roger Patterson, who in October that year was riding through the remote forests of the Bluff Creek area of northern California with Bob Gimlin, on the lookout for signs of bigfeet. Their horses reared in fright when they suddenly came across a female bigfoot squatting beside a creek. Patterson leapt down, grabbed his camera and began to run after the retreating figure, filming as he went. Before the bigfoot was lost to sight among the trees, it turned to look back at the men. The famous strip of film has been analysed many times since 1967, but although no one has been able to prove it a hoax, scientists remain suspicious.

This may be due to natural caution, or the curious argument that 'Bigfoot can't exist, therefore it doesn't'. Meanwhile this creature continues to appear regularly in North America, to alarm but not hurt the witnesses who are invariably taken by surprise, and to puzzle all who ponder its presence.

Are man-beasts from the natural world or could their origins be much stranger? See page 74

Bigfoot hunter Rene Dahinden stands beside a statue of a bigfoot, sculpted by Jim McClarin, at Willow Creek, California. The figure, modelled on descriptions of bigfeet seen in the area, is 8 feet (2.4 metres) tall, 41 inches (1.04 metres) wide at the shoulder and has feet measuring 18 by 10 inches (46 by 25 centimetres)

Doorway to beyond: Inside a black hole

Some astronomers have suggested that we can travel through a black hole and reappear instantaneously in another universe. NIGEL HENBEST explores the scientific basis for believing such a journey possible

NOTHING, NOT EVEN LIGHT, can ever escape from a black hole. But some astrophysicists believe that an astronaut falling into one might suddenly, almost instantaneously, reappear in a strange and alien universe quite unlike the one he had left only moments before: a universe existing not only in another dimension of time, but one where the fundamental laws of nature are reversed.

Of course, no one knows for certain what would happen if an astronaut were to fall into a black hole. But modern astronomy, based on Einstein's theory of relativity, has pieced together an account of what *could* happen.

Take the case of an astronaut approaching a simple, static, black hole of the type described by Karl Schwarzschild in 1916 (see

Above: an artist's impression of a rotating black hole. The brightness surrounding the hole is light from distant stars that has gone into temporary orbit, before being flung into space

Right: diagram 1 shows the structure of a static black hole. The event horizon marks the boundary beyond which nothing, not even light, can ever escape. Anything falling to the point of singularity would be crushed to oblivion

diagram 1). Not everything that strays into the outer fringes of a black hole is inevitably sucked in. A spaceship, for example, could journey to the outer limits, despatch an astronaut, then safely escape by firing its rocket motors or by going into orbit: letting centrifugal force balance the spaceship's gravitational pull.

As the astronaut begins to fall towards the brightly lit outer fringe of the black hole – called the event horizon – strange things begin to happen. Relativity theory says that time runs more slowly in regions of strong gravitation. And the gravitation exerted by a black hole is more powerful than anywhere else in the Universe. As we watch the astronaut fall closer to the event horizon, time for him runs slower and slower. His watch slows down to such an extent that, to us observing him, he never seems to reach it. If we calculate, for example, that he's just one second from falling in, then that last second on his slow-running watch will be stretched to an infinite amount of time. However long we wait, he'll never quite make it. But to him, his watch keeps perfectly steady time. Although to us his fall to the event horizon takes an infinite time, to him it passes in only a matter of seconds. And once beyond the event horizon we cannot see or hear from him again.

Crushed to oblivion

Inside a Schwarzschild black hole, our astronaut would be dragged to the single point of infinite density at the centre, called the 'singularity'. Within a fraction of a second – to him – he too, becomes part of that infinitely compressed point, crushed to oblivion. Few astronomers now think, however, that static black holes of the type described by Schwarzschild actually exist. Every star in the Universe rotates – indeed our whole Universe may itself rotate – and black holes are probably no exception. Indeed, black holes may well rotate more rapidly than most stars. And for an astronaut approaching a rotating black hole, his fate is not as grim as the certain oblivion he would meet in a static hole.

To help us visualise what would happen inside and around a rotating black hole, Roger Penrose has devised a set of space-time diagrams. To plot a course through a Penrose diagram the basic rule is that we can only

1

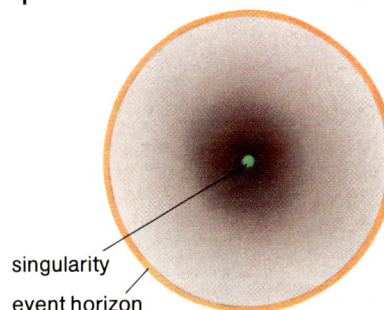

singularity

event horizon

Left: German astronomer Karl Schwarzschild was the first to apply Einstein's theory of relativity to the study of black holes

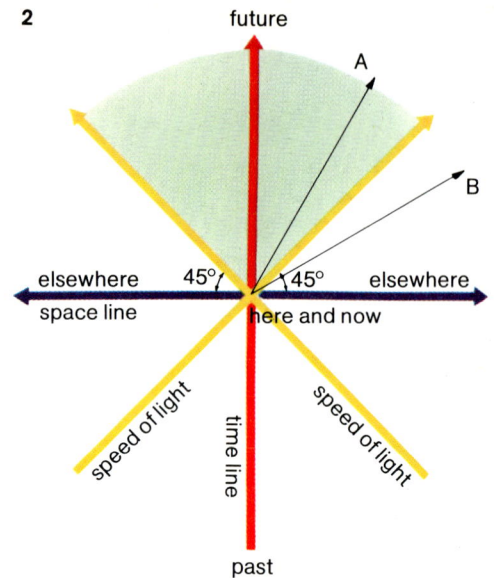

Right: diagram 2, the standard space-time chart. Journey A is possible because it is less than the speed of light. Journey B, which exceeds the speed of light, is impossible. The shaded area defines the area of possible space travel

Space, time, and relativity theory

Imagine you are flying in an aeroplane at 500 mph (800 km/h). Another jet is flying straight towards you, also at 500 mph (800 km/h). How quickly are you approaching each other? In other words, what is your *relative* velocity? Common sense says it is 1000 mph (1600 km/h); to get the answer, you add the velocities.

Now imagine you are aboard a spaceship travelling at three quarters the speed of light towards a distant star. How fast is the light from the star reaching you? Again, common sense says that the relative velocity is one and three-quarters the speed of light; but if you measured it, you would find that the speed at which the light was reaching you was still only 186,000 miles per second (300,000 km/s).

This seemingly paradoxical state of affairs is both predicted and explained by the theory of special relativity, proposed by Albert Einstein in 1905. It states that the speed of light is constant, no matter what the speed of the source or the speed at which you travel towards it. It explains this by saying that *moving clocks run slow* – and not only clocks: *time itself* runs more slowly the faster you travel. If you could travel fast enough in your spaceship you would find, on your return to Earth, that many years had elapsed during the few months that the clock in your spaceship says you were away. You could actually be younger than your own children.

In formulating his theory of special relativity, Einstein made use of a new concept of space and time in which he saw the world as having four dimensions – the familiar three dimensions of space,

Below: common sense says that two jets travelling each at a speed of 500 mph (800 km/h) will be coming together at a relative velocity of 1000 mph (1600 km/h). But relativity theory states that the speed of light cannot be exceeded. The speed of light approaching a stationary spaceship is 186,000 miles per sec (300,000 km/s); but even if the spaceship is travelling towards the source of light at a speed as high as (say) 139,500 miles per sec (225,000 km/s) the relative velocity of approach will still be only 186,000 miles per sec

plus one of time. He called this new concept *spacetime*. It was to be of crucial importance in his revolutionary new theory of gravitation.

In 1915 Einstein announced his theory of general relativity. This explains gravity not, as we are taught at school, as a force of attraction between two objects, but as a property of spacetime itself.

Imagine a horizontal frame, over which is stretched a rubber mattress. On the mattress are a number of balls of various sizes and weights. Each ball will sink into the mattress to a different depth, according to how big and how heavy it is. Now imagine rolling a smaller ball along the mattress; it will be 'attracted' to the others as it rolls down the slope towards them.

This is the principle of general relativity: matter causes spacetime to 'warp', and spacetime in turn tells matter how to

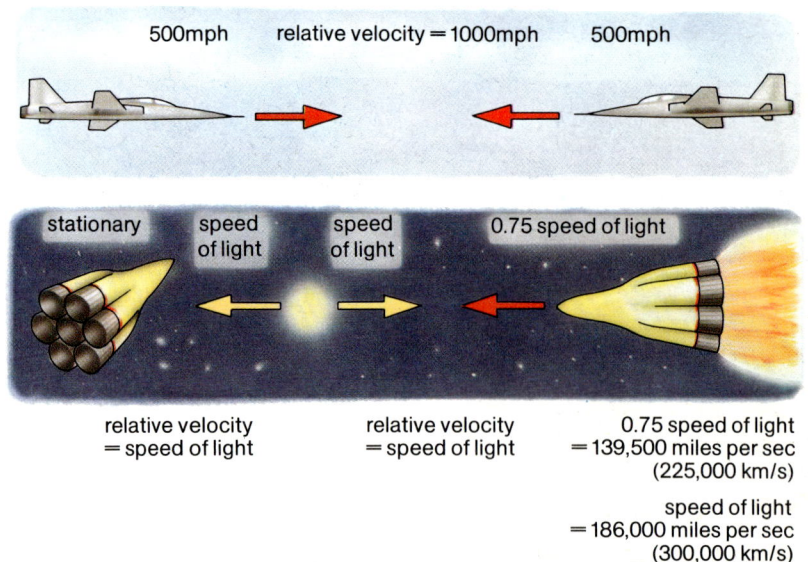

500mph relative velocity = 1000mph 500mph

stationary | speed of light | speed of light | 0.75 speed of light

relative velocity = speed of light

relative velocity = speed of light

0.75 speed of light = 139,500 miles per sec (225,000 km/s)

speed of light = 186,000 miles per sec (300,000 km/s)

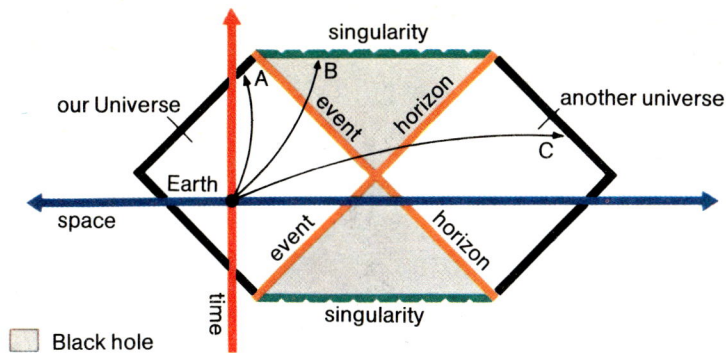

Black hole

Above: diagram 3, showing the impossibility of travelling through a static black hole and entering other universes. Journey A shows the route of possible spaceflight in our Universe; by entering the black hole journey B inevitably hits the singularity and is destroyed; journey C is impossible since to cross the event horizon and enter another universe would require travelling faster than the speed of light. Before such a journey can be made, the hole must rotate

travel through space in a generally upward direction, that is, forward in time. In diagram 2, light rays travelling at a speed of 670 million mph (1000 million km/h) mark the speed limit of possible space travel beyond which we can never, according to Einstein, travel. Our entire Universe, out into infinity of space, from its birth to eventual extinction along the time scale, is reduced to a diamond shape in diagram 3. The hour-glass shape (at 45 degrees to the vertical) represents the event horizon and the singularity is at the top. As our astronaut begins to fall towards the event horizon of a rotating black hole, he does not just fall straight inwards. Because of the rapid rotation of the black hole, he would be dragged sideways, no matter how powerful his rockets.

Astronomers working on black hole theory are agreed upon the sequence of events so far. But from this point, the picture becomes slightly more complex. Some astronomers claim that not only do black holes rotate, they are also electrically charged. And this fact makes a difference to our astronaut as he is about to enter the hole.

Within an electrically-charged black hole (see diagram 4), there is a second 'inner' event horizon, lying inside the 'outer' horizon which seals the hole from the rest of the Universe. Here space and time change roles again. So although an astronaut falling through the outer event horizon must pursue a one way path inwards, this now takes him only as far as the inner event horizon. And once inside the inner horizon, our astronaut can manoeuvre how he likes, although he cannot know where he will end up. According to simple calculations, he may re-emerge in another universe, or at the same instant, elsewhere in this Universe.

Into another universe

We can trace the course of the journeys an astronaut could possibly take on Penrose diagram 5. Here the singularity is shown as two vertical lines bordering a 'tunnel'. An astronaut travelling near vertically in the diagram can enter the tunnel through the outer event horizon, travel through the inner event horizon and into a totally different universe at the top of the diagram.

A rotating, non-electrically charged black hole (see diagram 6) also has an inner event horizon through which we could, theoretically, reach another universe. But here the singularity is not a single point, but a ring. If an astronaut could aim through this ring, he might find himself not only in a universe that was different from our own, but one where gravity, for example, instead of being a force that attracts two objects, is a force that repels. He might find himself, that is, in a 'negative universe'. Leaving aside this 'negative universe', some writers have proposed that future space travellers will journey through such tunnels within rotating black holes and hop from universe to universe.

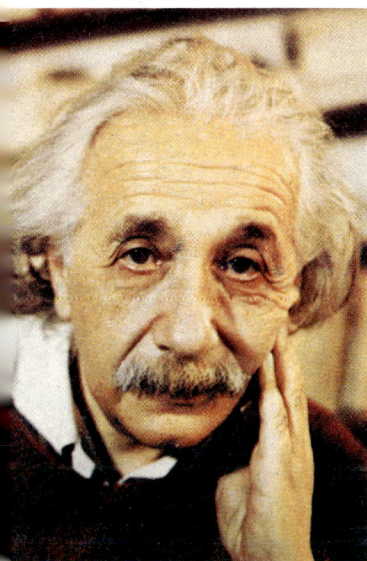

Above: Albert Einstein (1879–1955), inventor of the 'spacetime' concept

behave. In general, spacetime is fairly flat, but near large masses it becomes curved. This curvature influences not only the movement of the smaller masses, but also time itself. General relativity predicts that gravity slows down time.

By 1960, five years after the death of Albert Einstein, scientists had developed clocks accurate enough to prove that the prediction was correct. If you take two identical accurate clocks, synchronise them and place one on the ground floor and one on the top floor of a high building, you will find the one on the ground floor ticks the more slowly – because its region of spacetime is more strongly curved by gravity.

Now imagine placing a very small, but immensely heavy, object on the rubber mattress so that it stretches the mattress to an infinite extent without tearing it. This is the riddle of the black hole.

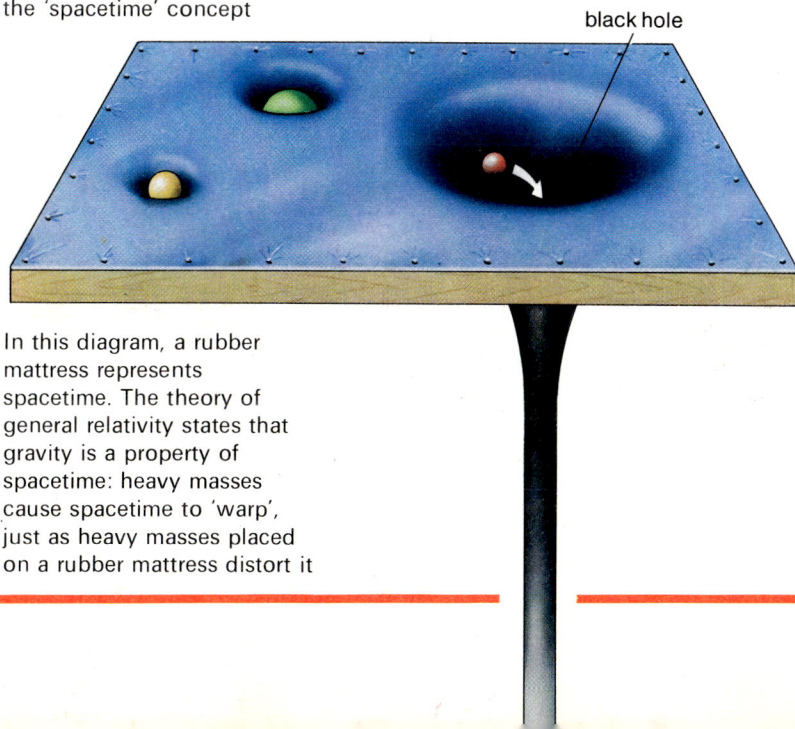

In this diagram, a rubber mattress represents spacetime. The theory of general relativity states that gravity is a property of spacetime: heavy masses cause spacetime to 'warp', just as heavy masses placed on a rubber mattress distort it

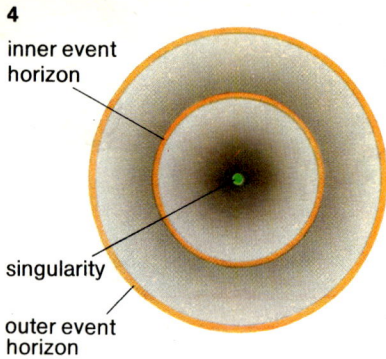

4

inner event horizon

singularity

outer event horizon

But there are problems with this proposal. An adventurous astronaut would encounter his first problem before he even entered the black hole. Suppose the astronaut is falling feet first. His feet, being nearer to the hole, would feel a stronger gravitational pull than his head. The difference in gravitational pull along his body would stretch him out as he falls inwards. Physicists Charles Misner, Kip Thorne and John Wheeler have carried this gruesome calculation through, and according to their results the astronaut would be stretched to breaking point still hundreds of miles from the black hole.

Strangely enough, this problem is worse for smaller black holes where the force of gravitation changes more sharply with distance. For the smaller holes, the effect is so marked that gravitation is gradually shredding the structure of space itself and creating particles of matter outside the event horizon. These particles stream off into space gradually robbing the hole of its strength, and indirectly, its matter. These have been described by Stephen Hawking as 'evaporating' and 'exploding' black holes.

At the heart of the galaxy

An astronaut could, however, safely enter a very heavy black hole, where the gravitation changes more gradually with distance from the hole. Such holes may form at the centres of galaxies, where matter was tightly packed at the time of their birth. Some astronomers believe that our own Galaxy, the Milky Way, harbours a black hole five million times the Sun's weight at its centre. There's an even better indication of a black hole a thousand times more massive still, in the heart of the galaxy M87. Although it's invisible, this black hole's immense gravitational pull distorts the paths of nearby stars in the galaxy. And most astronomers now believe that the distant, very bright quasars are simply hot discs of gas surrounding massive black holes at the centre of far-off galaxies.

So massive black holes probably do exist and, in theory at least, could be used as gateways to other universes. In this Universe, the traveller would emerge through a white hole – the exact opposite of a black hole. Just as anything inside a black hole falls inwards, so anything inside a white hole must

Left: diagram 4, an electrically-charged black hole. The outer event horizon seals the black hole from the rest of the Universe. An astronaut falling inside the inner event horizon, however, could manoeuvre wherever he wanted and could, in theory, emerge into another universe

Below: an astronaut approaching a rotating black hole in diagram 5 has a number of options. He can follow route A and remain in our Universe; he can take route B and hit the singularity and meet instant death. The course of C involves faster-than-light travel, which Einstein rules out. On route D he could pass through both the outer and inner event horizons, avoid the singularity, and reappear in another universe

travel outwards, and must emerge through the event horizon. If white holes exist, they are 'cosmic gushers', spewing matter and light out in a seemingly inexhaustible fountain.

White holes are present in the Penrose diagrams already discussed. In diagram 2, for example, the lower half of the 'hour-glass' is a white hole, while the top half is a black hole. Remembering that all objects must travel more or less vertically in the diagram, it's obvious that everything within this lower triangle must eventually shoot out of the event horizon. And for the more complicated case of the rotating black hole (see diagram 3), the upper of the two diamonds making up the tunnel is, in fact, a white hole opening into the upper universe.

If white holes do exist, they would certainly be fascinating to peer into. The view into a rotating black hole would reveal not just its central singularity, but also two other universes (see diagram 2). One of these universes is the 'negative universe' seen through the centre of the ring-shaped singularity; surrounding this is the singularity itself, and the rest of the white hole would contain a distorted view of another universe,

5

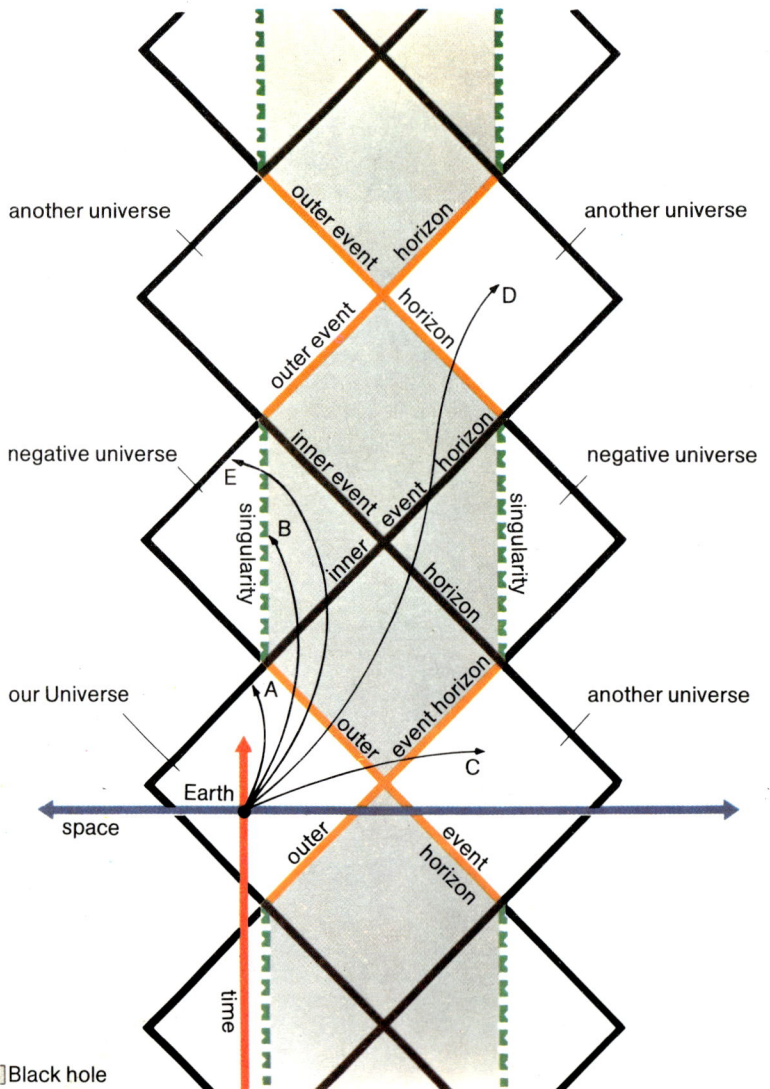

another universe

outer event horizon

another universe

negative universe

inner event horizon

negative universe

singularity

our Universe

another universe

outer event horizon

Earth

space

time

☐ Black hole

7

our Universe

time

Earth

space

A

negative universe

singularity

B

D

singularity

negative universe

E

previous universe

C

☐ Black hole

⇨ Light rays

which is seen reflected within the white hole.

But there are severe theoretical difficulties with white holes. For a start, despite their 'gushing' nature they have strong gravitational fields around them. And white holes can't form in space as black holes can: if they exist they must have been around since the beginning of our Universe, 15,000 million years ago. Most astronomers now accept that our Universe began with a 'Big Bang'. Any white holes that did form would have trapped so much radiation around themselves that the sheer mass of radiation would have created a black hole *around* the white hole. The white hole would have been swallowed up in the black hole it created around itself.

The tearing effects of the changing gravitational force within a white hole also mean that the central singularity of a white hole is unstable. And effects of both these kinds are likely to happen at the inner event horizon. So although there's still a lot of detailed calculation to be done, scientists are now distinctly dubious about universe-hopping through black/white hole tunnels.

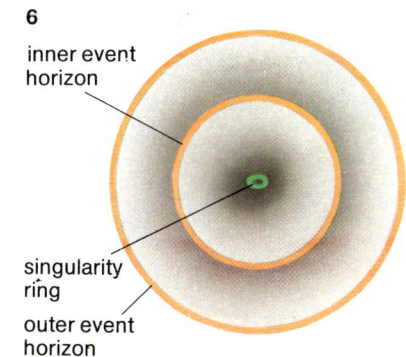

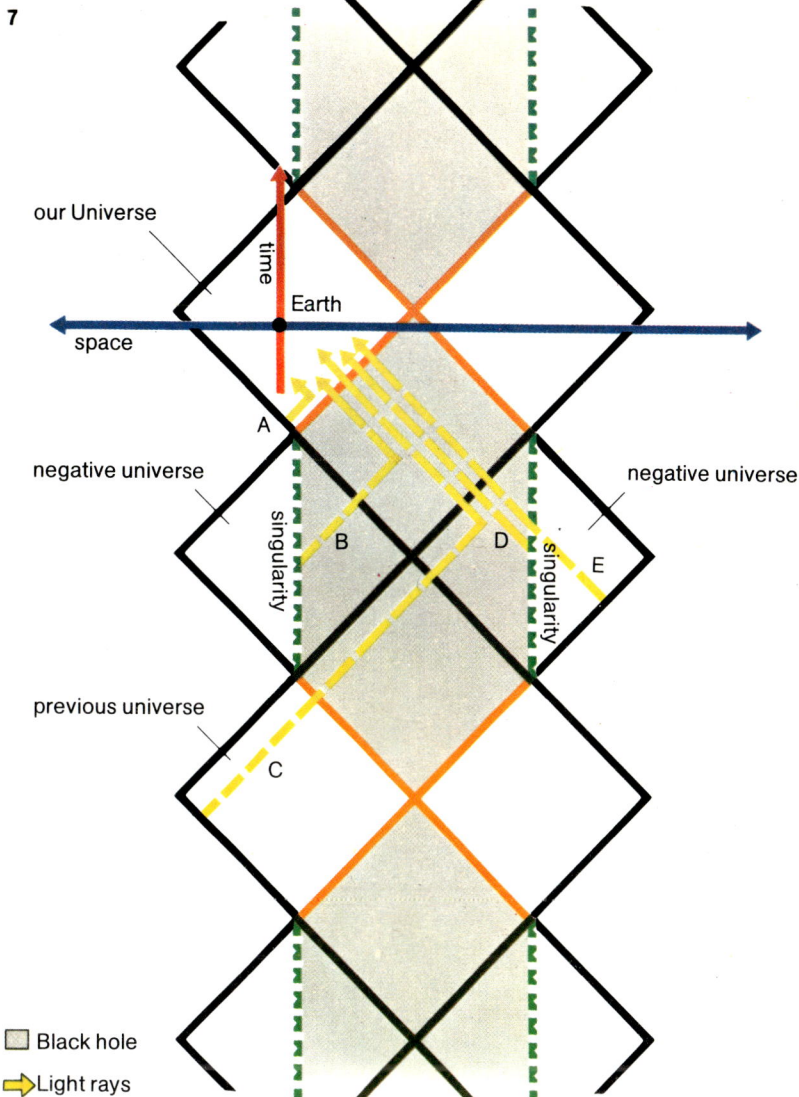

6

inner event horizon

singularity ring

outer event horizon

Above left: an x-ray photograph of the distant galaxy M87

Left: diagram 6, a rotating black hole as seen from above. To enter another universe, an astronaut would have to pass through the singularity ring

Above: diagram 7. An observer standing on Earth could, theoretically, receive light rays through a white hole from sources reflected back into positive space from a rotating black hole. From A he would see events happening millions of years ago in this Universe. From B and D he would see into a black hole and from E he would catch a glimpse of a negative universe where the fundamental laws of nature were reversed. Light from C would show events from other, previous, universes

Even so, if the space-time diagrams shown here are correct, interesting questions arise as to the nature of the 'other universes'. They may be totally disconnected from our own; or they may be different regions or different times of our Universe. If so, a black hole *could* be a time machine – and a journey through one could end up in the age of the dinosaurs or far in the future.

But while this aspect of black hole research seems to have come to a full stop, at least in terms of conventional science, observational astronomers are gathering more and more evidence that black holes do exist in our Universe, both in double star pairs like Cyg X-1 and in the centres of galaxies like M87 and the quasars. No doubt black holes have many more surprises – both observational and theoretical – in store for us. And given Man's pioneering urge it can only be a matter of time before manned spaceships are in orbit about a black hole. And someone may just be brave enough to find out what's inside.

On page 81 Adrian Berry shows how, by creating artificial black holes, we can make instantaneous journeys across space

A strange unnatural fire

The idea that human beings can burst into flames of their own accord is odd enough. But, as BOB RICKARD shows, everything about spontaneous human combustion is bizarre

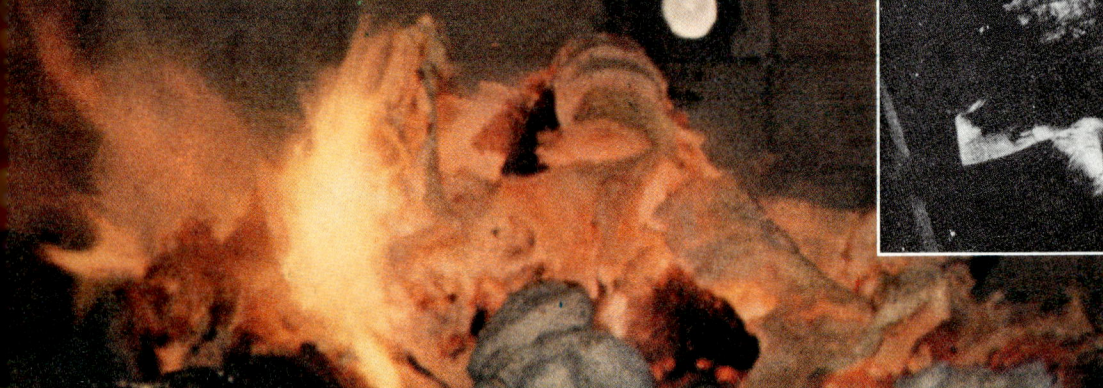

Spontaneous human combustion strikes with astonishing speed, yet the heat generated is sufficient to char even the bones of the victim. In contrast, a body can take hours to burn away in the sustained fire of a crematorium – and even then only the flesh is thoroughly destroyed

PERHAPS THE MOST common characteristic of SHC is the sheer speed with which it strikes. Many victims were seen alive only a few moments before the fire struck from nowhere. An Italian surgeon called Battaglio reported the death of a priest, named Bertholi, in the town of Filetto, in 1789. Lodging with his brother-in-law, he had been left alone in his room reading a prayerbook. A few minutes later he screamed. People came running to find him on the floor surrounded by a pale flame, which receded as they approached.

Bertholi wore a sackcloth under his clothes, next to his skin, and it was immediately apparent that the outer clothes had burned away leaving the sackcloth intact. Under the sackcloth the skin on the man's trunk was not burned, but detached from the flesh and hung in shreds.

Some writers deduce that the fire develops with particular rapidity, from the fact that the victims are often discovered still sitting calmly, as though nothing had happened.

A dramatic example is given in Ron Willis's article on SHC in *INFO Journal* 8 (1972). In 1960, five charred bodies were found in a burned-out car near Pikeville, Kentucky. The coroner commented: 'They were sitting there as though they'd just gotten into the car. With all that heat it seems there'd be some sort of struggle to escape. But there hadn't been.'

Another almost universal characteristic of SHC is the extreme intensity of heat that is involved. Under normal circumstances the human body is very hard to set alight, especially if still alive, and people who die in fires usually sustain only partial or superficial damage to the body. Reduction to a pile of calcined ashes, experts all agree, demands a fierce heat which needs to be externally fuelled and maintained for hours, and even so crematoria still have to grind up the bones that remain afterward.

The death of Mrs Reeser (see box) was investigated by Dr Wilton M. Krogman, a renowned forensic anthropologist from the University of Pennsylvania School of Medicine, who has researched and experimented the causes and effects of deaths by and during fires. He said he has watched bodies in a crematorium burn for over 8 hours at 2000°F (1110°C) without any sign of the bones becoming ashes or powder; and that it takes a heat of about 3000°F (1650°C) to make bone melt and become volatile. Willis mentions the case of Leon Eveille, aged 40, found burnt to a crisp in his locked car at Arcis-sur-Aube, France, on 17 June 1971. The heat had melted the windows. It was estimated that a burning car normally reaches about 1300°F (700°C), but to melt glass the temperature must have been over 1800°F (1000°C).

Time and again in cases of SHC, we encounter a further strange effect: the confinement of the heat. Charred bodies are found lying in unscorched beds, sitting on slightly singed chairs, or with their clothing intact.

In 1905 the *British Medical Journal* reported the death of 'an elderly woman of intemperate habits'. Authorities broke into a house from which smoke was issuing to find a small pyramidal heap of broken calcinated human bones, on the top of

Dr Wilton Krogman, an expert on the effects of fire on the human body. He was astonished by the state of Mrs Reeser's corpse, and constructed an elaborate theory to account for it

which was a skull, on the floor in front of a chair. All the bones were completely bleached and brittle; every particle of soft tissue had been consumed, and yet a tablecloth within three feet of the remains was not even scorched. . . . Curiously, the ceiling was scorched, as if the woman had become a pillar of fire.

Fort, in his *Complete books* (1941) gives two startling cases. The first, from the *Daily News* of 17 December 1904, describes how Mrs Thomas Cochrane, of Falkirk, was found in a bedroom burned to death 'beyond recognition'. There had been no outcry, and little else burned, with no fire in the grate. Her charred corpse was found 'sitting in a chair, surrounded by pillows and cushions'. The second is from the *Madras Mail* of 13 May 1907 concerning a woman in the village of Manner, near Dinapore. Flames had consumed her body, but not her clothes. Two constables had found the corpse in a room in which nothing else showed signs of fire, and had carried the smouldering body to the District Magistrate.

In 1841 the *British Medical Journal* reported an address by Dr F. S. Reynolds to the Manchester Pathological Society on the subject of SHC. Although rejecting the idea of 'spontaneous' combustion, he admitted there were baffling cases, and gave an instance from his experience of a woman of 40 who fell near a hearth. She was found next morning still burning. What astonished him was the damage to the legs: inside unharmed stockings her femora were carbonised and knee-joints opened.

Some chroniclers of SHC have drawn attention to the lack of outcry and struggle by victims. 'In their grim submission,' Fort wrote, 'it is almost as if they had been lulled by the wings of a vampire.' There is more to it than being overcome by drink and fumes – some psychic or psychological component of the phenomenon prefaces or accompanies the burning, and this may explain the lack of escape, and the inability of surviving victims to tell what happened to them.

For example, the *Hull Daily Mail* of 6 January 1905 describes how an elderly

The destruction of Mary Reeser

Workmen are seen here clearing away the remains of the chair in which Mrs Mary Reeser, a widow of 67, of St Petersburg, Florida, departed this life on a pillar of fire, during the night of 1 July 1951. Damage to the surroundings was minimal. The overstuffed chair was burned down to its springs, there was a patch of soot on the ceiling above and a small circle of carpet was charred around the chair, but a pile of papers nearby was unscorched. Dr Wilton Krogman, a forensic scientist who specialised in fire deaths, was visiting in the area and joined the investigation. He said:

I cannot conceive of such complete cremation without more burning of the apartment itself. In fact the apartment and everything in it should have been consumed. Never have I seen a human skull shrunk by intense heat. The opposite has always been true; the skulls have been either abnormally swollen or have virtually exploded into hundreds of pieces . . . I regard it as the most amazing thing I have ever seen. As I review it, the short hairs on my neck bristle with vague fear. Were I living in the Middle Ages, I'd mutter something about black magic.

Police considered every likely theory, and a few unasked-for ideas from cranky members of the public: suicide by petrol, ignition of methane gas in her body, murder by flame-thrower, 'atomic pill' (whatever that meant), magnesium, phosphorus and napalm substances . . . and even a 'ball of fire' which one anonymous letter-writer claimed to see. In the end the coroner accepted the FBI theory, that she had fallen asleep while smoking and set her clothes alight.

Dr Krogman himself proffered the idea that Mrs Reeser had been burned elsewhere by someone with access to crematorium-type equipment or materials, then was carried back to the apartment, where the mystery assailant had added the finishing touches, like heat-buckled plastic objects, and a doorknob that was still hot in the morning. A year later, the police confessed the case was still open.

woman, Elizabeth Clark, was found in the morning with fatal burns, while her bed, in the Trinity Almshouse, Hull, was unmarked by fire. There had been no outcry or sounds of struggle through the thin partitions. She was 'unable to give an articulate account' of her accident, and later died. Of course that could mean that the authorities – not for the first time – simply didn't believe her account.

In *Lo!* (1930), Fort describes the complex fires that plagued Binbrook Farm, near Grimsby, in the winter of 1904–5. One incident involved a young servant girl who was burning without her knowledge, and might have been another SHC statistic had not her employer roused her from her daydreaming (or trance). According to a local newspaper, the farmer said:

Our servant girl, whom we had taken from the workhouse . . . was sweeping the kitchen. There was a very small fire in the grate; there was a guard there so that no one can come within 2 feet [0.6 metres] or more of the fire, and she was at the other end of the room, and had not been near. I suddenly came into the kitchen and there she was, sweeping away while the back of her dress was on fire. She looked around as I shouted, and seeing the flames, rushed through the door. She tripped and I smothered the fire out with wet sacks.

The girl had obviously been on fire for some time and was 'terribly burned'.

As we have seen in the Pikeville car case, several people have combusted together, but such cases are extremely rare. Baron Liebig thought that the occurrence of multiple SHC cases disproved the 'disease' theory (see box), since in his experience a disease has never run the same course in two or more people, detail for detail, culminating in their simultaneous death. Certainly none of the 'diseases' that are suggested by the theory's apologists has done so.

Willis describes the case of the Rooneys who lived in a farmhouse near Seneca, Illinois:

On Christmas Eve 1885, Patrick Rooney and his wife and their hired man, John Larson, were drinking whiskey in the kitchen. Larson went to bed and woke up Christmas morning feeling sick. Downstairs in the kitchen he found everything covered with an oily film, and on the floor, Patrick Rooney dead. Larson rode to get help from Rooney's son John, who lived nearby. Back at the farm the two men noticed that there was a charred hole next to the kitchen table. Looking into the hole they found, on the earth under the kitchen floor, a calcined skull, a few charred bones and a pile of ashes. Mrs Rooney had been obliterated by a fantastically hot fire that had not spread beyond her immediate area.

The coroner soon found that Patrick had been suffocated by the smoke of the burning body of his wife.

Charles Fort, who spent a lifetime collecting reports of SHC and other inexplicable occurrences. Fort wondered if SHC might be connected with demonology: 'I think our data relate not to "spontaneous combustion of human bodies" but to things or beings, that with a flaming process consume men and women, but like werewolves or alleged werewolves, mostly pick women.'

Fuelling the human fireball

Among the early pathologists the theory arose that in certain circumstances the body may produce gases that combust on exposure to quantities of oxygen. The distinguished scientist Baron Karl von Reichenbach wrote of the 'miasma of putrefaction' of human bodies, for instance. But Liebig could find no evidence of such a gas, 'in health, in disease, nay not even in the putrefaction of dead bodies.'

Dixon Mann and W. A. Brend, in their *Forensic medicine and toxicology* (1914) give the case of a fat man who died two hours after admission to Guy's Hospital, London, in 1885. The following day his corpse was found bloated, the skin distended all over and filled with gas, although there was no sign of decomposition. 'When punctures were made in the skin, the gas escaped and burnt with a flame like that of carburetted hydrogen; as many as a dozen flames were burning at the same time.' Had the man died at home near a fire, another case of 'spontaneous combustion' would have been reported to confuse researchers further.

However, gases within the body tissues of the sort suggested would be fatally toxic, and the victim would have been gravely ill or dead. And generally there are no such symptoms: victims have often been seen alive shortly before their flaming. Nor does this theory account for the observed fact of clothes that are left unburnt on a charred corpse.

As an alternative to the disease theory, we might consider organic or mechanical malfunctions of normal processes within the body. Ivan Sanderson and, before him, Vincent Gaddis, speculated about the build-up of phosphagens in muscle tissue, particularly the vitamin B10, vital to normal energy supplies. A technical paper in *Applied Trophology* (December 1957) included this relevant paragraph:

Phosphagen is a compound like nitro-glycerine, of endothermic formation. It is no doubt so highly developed in certain sedentary persons as to make their bodies actually combustible, subject to ignition, burning like wet gunpowder under some circumstances.

This may explain the readiness of some bodies to blaze, but we still have to identify the source of ignition.

An unmistakable case of simultaneous SHC is summarised by Fort, of an elderly couple named Kiley, who lived near Southampton. On the morning of 26 February 1905, neighbours heard a curious 'scratching' and went next door to investigate. They entered the house and found it in flames inside. Kiley was found burned to death on the floor. Mrs Kiley, burned to death, was sitting in a chair in the same room, 'badly charred but recognisable'. Both bodies were fully dressed,

judging by the fragments of clothes, indicating they had been burned before their time for going to bed . . . the mystery was that two persons, neither of whom had cried for help, presumably not asleep in any ordinary sense, should have been burned to death in a fire that did not manifest as a general fire until hours later.

There are on record two cases of SHC which coincided with suicide attempts, the implication of which is obscure unless one presupposes some form of the 'psychic suicide' theory in which victims combust because they have given up on life.

On 13 December 1959, 27-year-old Billy Peterson, of Pontiac, Michigan, said goodbye to his mother and drove to his garage where he hooked a pipe from the car's exhaust into the car itself. Only 40 minutes after Billy had left his mother, a passing motorist saw the smoke and investigated. Inside the car Billy was dead from carbon monoxide poisoning, but it was the condition of his body that puzzled pathologists. His back, arms and legs were covered in third-degree burns, and some parts of him were charred to a crisp. Despite all this, his clothes and underclothes were quite unharmed.

On 18 September 1952, Glen Denney, 46, a foundry worker in Louisiana, cut the arteries in his left arm and both wrists and ankles, but he had died from inhaling smoke. When found, he was a 'mass of flames' with nothing else in the room ablaze. The coroner guessed that he had poured kerosene over himself and lit a match, though no container was found, and just how he could hold, let alone light, a match with arterial blood pumping over his hands at about 4 per cent of body volume per second was not explained. The investigator, Otto Burma, wrote: 'There is no doubt in my mind that Denney did in fact attempt suicide. But while in the process of carrying out this act his body caught fire due to some unknown cause.'

Many other aspects of SHC would reward investigation. There are, for instance, demonstrable connections with poltergeist phenomena, which frequently involve mysterious spontaneous fires. Then there are people who are fire-prone, in whose presence fires repeatedly break out. Examining these and other facts that surround SHC may lead us nearer to understanding the phenomenon – and perhaps to identifying its causes.

Many causes have been suggested for SHC.
A review of the theories starts on page 84

The end of an old soldier

On 19 February 1888, Dr J. Mackenzie Booth, a lecturer at Aberdeen University, was called to the loft of a stable in Constitution Street, where he found the charred corpse of a 65-year-old pensioner. There was considerable damage to the body: most of the fleshy parts had burned away exposing the calcined ends of bones. The floor around the man had burnt through so that the corpse rested on a charred beam. The heat had also burned the roofing slats above him, causing some slates to fall onto his chest and damage his brittle form further. He was last seen going into the loft with a bottle and lamp the previous evening.

It was thought that he had knocked the lamp over and then been overcome by drink and smoke. (Booth's report describes the 'old soldier' as being 'of inebriate habits'.) But the lamp had been seen to go out shortly after he went into the loft, and no fire was seen during the night. Furthermore, it is clear from this engraving (from the *British Medical Journal* of 21 April 1888, and based directly on a photograph of the scene) that the bales of hay surrounding the man did not catch fire. The carbonised face retained recognisable features, from which, and from 'the comfortably recumbent attitude of the body' Booth noted that 'it was evident that there had been no death struggle.'

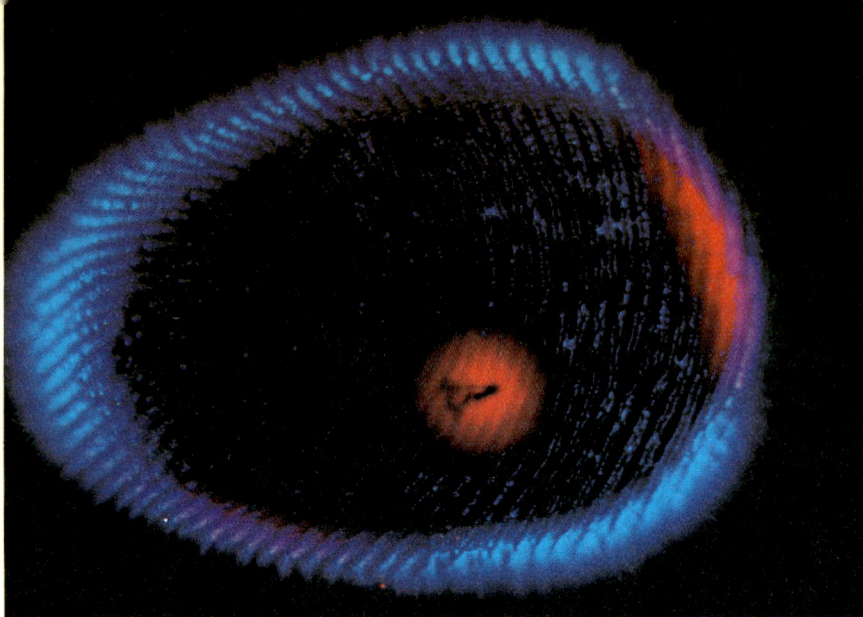

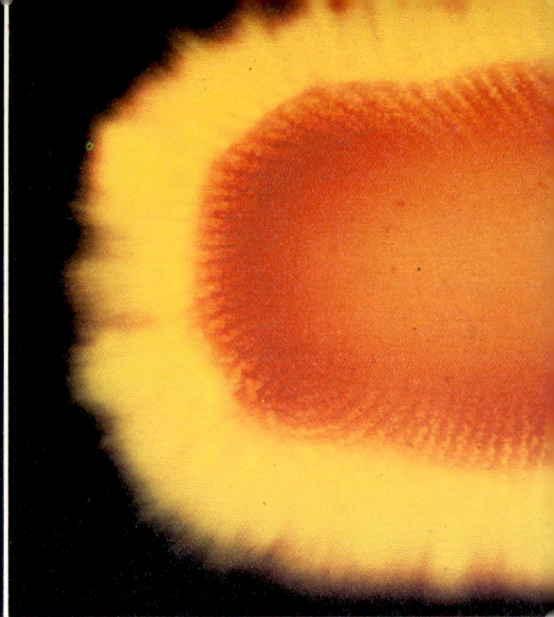

Images of the unseen

Do we have a spiritual body that exists separately from our physical body? For centuries mystics and clairvoyants have claimed that there is a halo of brightly-coloured light surrounding the human body. Then, in 1970, news was received that Russian scientists had photographed this 'aura'. BRIAN SNELLGROVE reports on their revelations

IN 1939 A RUSSIAN engineer, Semyon Kirlian, was repairing an electro-therapy machine in a research laboratory in the Ukrainian town of Krasnodar. Accidentally he allowed his hand to move too close to a 'live' electrode. The shock he received was accompanied by a brilliant flash of light given off by a large spark of electricity. His curiosity aroused, Kirlian wondered what would happen if he placed a sheet of light sensitive material in the path of the spark. Placing his own hand behind a piece of light-sensitised paper, Kirlian found on developing the film strange streamer-like emanations surrounding the image of his fingertips. On closer inspection, Kirlian found that each emanation was seen to have a different radiation pattern.

Fascinated by his 'discovery', Kirlian set up a laboratory in his tiny two-roomed flat and spent all his spare time investigating this phenomenon. Kirlian's research into high-voltage photography over the next 40 years led to intense scientific speculation and debate, and the claim, by some, that the strange emanations captured on film by Kirlian were proof of the existence of the so-called 'astral body'.

For centuries mystics and clairvoyants had claimed that they were able to see a brilliant halo of light surrounding the physical body of all living organisms. This 'halo', they believed, was the spiritual 'double' of our physical selves, but independent of it and surviving the death of the body.

Was the image that Kirlian was able to photograph that of the 'astral body'? Some

have believed so. But at present it is not at all clear what causes the brilliant glow surrounding the hands, feet, plant leaves and other objects that have been photographed using the Kirlian technique.

Nor indeed were the effects that Kirlian thought he had discovered entirely new or unknown. In the 1890s, Nikola Tesla, a Serbian scientist working in the USA, had

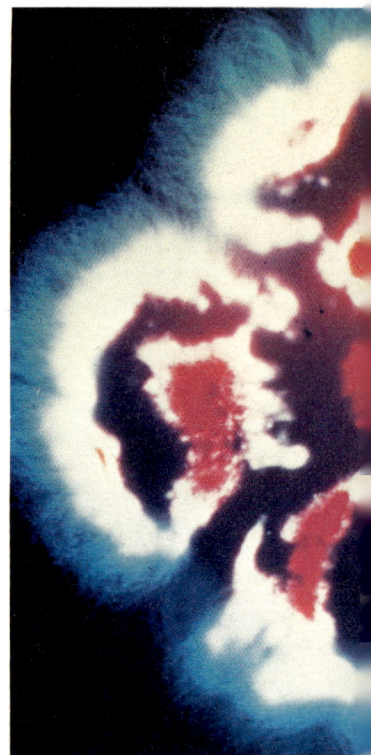

Top left: a fingertip photographed by the Kirlian method, which shows the surrounding radiation pattern. The vivid colour is not in fact significant. The colour of the aura tends to vary according to the type of film used

Left: Semyon and Valentina Kirlian, the husband and wife team who spent over 40 years developing a technique to capture on film the strange streamer-like emanations that, in varying degrees of strength, surround almost all objects

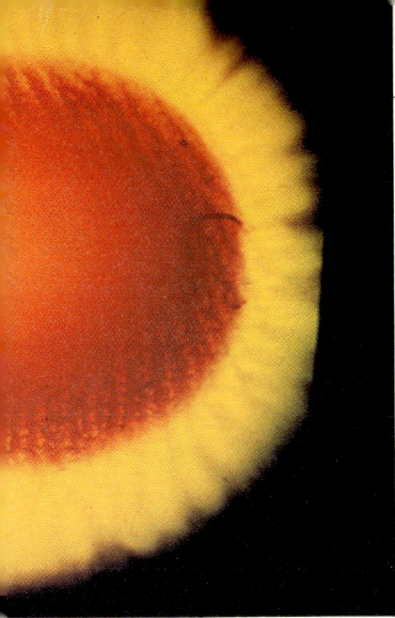

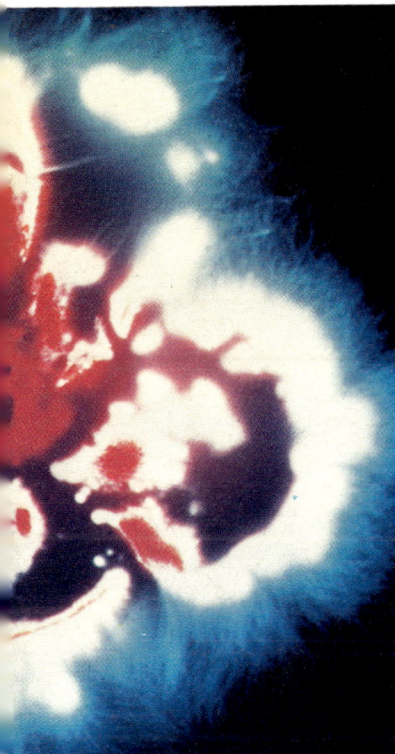

An amazing inventor

Born in Smiljan, Yugoslavia, 9 July 1856, Nikola Tesla became a driving force in the invention of electrical devices and equipment, as well as being something of a prophet.

Unable to interest European engineers in a new alternating current motor he had conceived, Tesla went to the United States in 1884 and joined Thomas Edison in the designing of dynamos. But the two men soon fell out. Tesla left his employ and set up his own laboratory dedicated to showing the feasibility of Alternating Current.

In 1891 Tesla unveiled his famous coil, which is still widely used today in electronic equipment, including television and radio. Tesla's coil is an electrical device for producing an intermittent source of high voltage. It consists of an induction coil with a central cylindrical core of soft iron onto which are wound two insulated coils: an inner (primary) coil of a few turns of copper wire, and a surrounding, secondary coil with a large number of turns of thin copper wire. An interrupter is used for making and breaking the current in the primary coil automatically. This current magnetises the iron core and produces a large magnetic field through the induction coil. For experimentation with the high voltage output of power from his coil, Tesla produced a gas-filled, phosphore coated tubular light – forerunner of today's fluorescent light.

A measure of Tesla's inventiveness can be seen by his tele-automatic boat of 1898 which was guided by remote control. Then in 1900 he made what many have claimed as his finest discovery – terrestrial stationary waves. He proved with this discovery that the earth could be used as a conductor and would be as responsive as a tuning fork to electrical vibrations of a certain pitch. He also lighted 200 electric lamps without wires from a distance of 25 miles and created man-made lightning, producing flashes of some 135 feet. Tesla was convinced at one time that he was receiving signals from another planet at his Colorado laboratory. But his claims were met with derision from the scientific press.

His ideas later became even more speculative. He asserted that he was able to split the world in half like an apple and that he had invented a 'death ray' that could destroy aircraft 250 miles away. His ideas concerning communication with other planets met with incredulity. Yet in 1917 he accurately forecast the coming of radar.

Top: a brilliantly illuminated Kirlian picture of a fingertip. A strong 'aura' is said to show ESP powers, sometimes latent, in the subject of the photograph

Above: as this picture of an oleander leaf shows, plants also respond to the Kirlian method. This fact has been taken by some to prove that all life is essentially spiritual

used high-voltage photography, with much the same results as those achieved by Kirlian. In the early 1930s an English researcher, George de la Warr, discovered the existence of weak 'electromagnetic force fields' surrounding areas of the human body and at a distance from it. These fields extended in a lattice-like formation and contained voltage peaks as high as 70 millivolts. The vividness of these fields was also seen to fluctuate according to the physical and emotional state of the subject.

But undoubtedly the major advances in the field of high voltage photography were indeed made by Kirlian himself. Some of his most interesting contributions were made quite by chance. On one occasion, Kirlian was preparing his equipment for a demonstration he was giving to a distinguished visitor. To his dismay, on the day the visitor was to arrive the machine failed to produce the normal clear results. Kirlian took his machine apart, checked for faults and made further tests, but with the same negative results. In frustration he asked his wife, Valentina, to be the subject. To their mutual surprise, a perfect image was produced. A few hours later, Kirlian discovered what he believed to be the cause of his failure to produce a clear image. He developed a particularly virulent form of influenza, and to Kirlian it seemed reasonable to suppose that his illness had caused the weak image. The photograph, Kirlian claimed, had in some way given warning of the influenza.

A further possible use of the Kirlian method was revealed when the chairman of a major scientific research institution arrived. He brought with him two apparently identical leaves for the Kirlians to photograph, the

Controlling the Kirlian aura

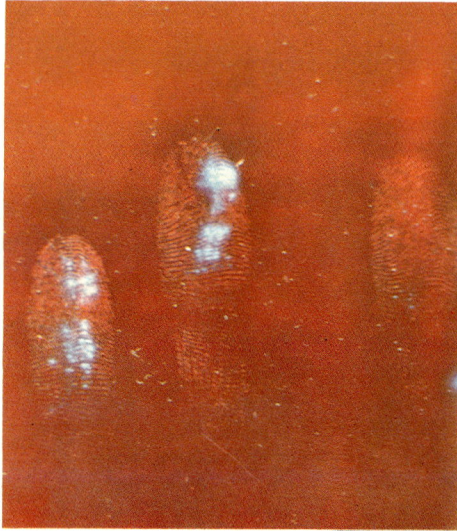

From the age of 11 Matthew Manning, below left, has been aware of possessing a wide range of psychic powers. Powers that he could, with practice, turn on at will. In 1974 a group of 21 scientists met to investigate these powers. Was Matthew being used by supernatural forces outside himself, or could his 'gift' be explained in terms of science? The evidence remains inconclusive. But Kirlian photographs taken of Matthew's fingertips produced startling results. The picture on the left shows Matthew's 'normal' corona, but the picture below, taken when he had 'switched the power on', shows a remarkably intense aura.

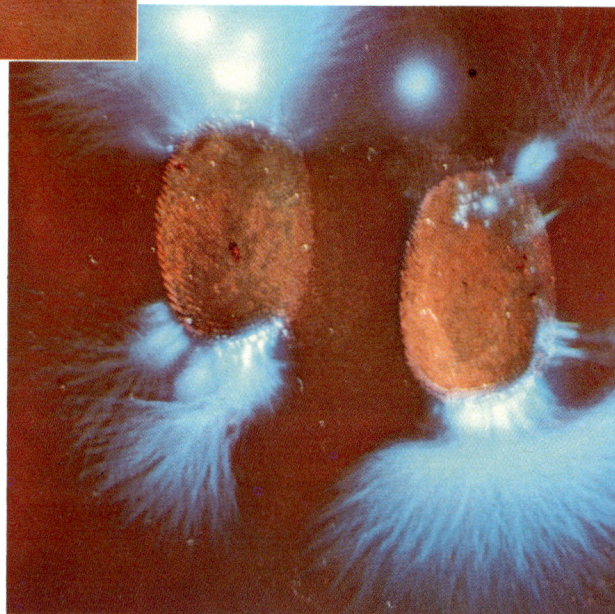

A Kirlian photograph of a rose petal (top right) shows a characteristic aura. But when a portion of the petal is cut away (below right) the Kirlian photograph still shows, quite clearly, the section that has been removed. This is known as the 'phantom leaf effect' and Russian investigators say that it proves that 'bioplasma' surrounds all living things

Below: a 50p coin with the characteristic outer 'glow'. If, as some claim, this glow is really the 'aura', then it would imply that even inanimate matter has some form of spiritual existence

Bottom: the same coin photographed after two psychic healers had placed their hands 4 inches (10 centimetres) above the coin for five minutes. The outer glow is noticeably brighter

two samples had been taken from the same species of plant, torn off at the same time. From one leaf the husband and wife team obtained the characteristic flare patterns surrounding the leaf. But from the other leaf, no clear patterns were obtained. The Kirlians adjusted their machine in every possible way, but with the same inconsistent results. Next morning they related their failure to produce the same results to their visitor. To their surprise he was delighted. The leaf with the weak pattern, he told them, had been taken from a plant that had contracted a serious disease. The other leaf, with the clear pattern, had been taken from a perfectly healthy plant. The experiment seemed to confirm Kirlian's hypothesis: his machine was able to give warning of disease. The high voltage photograph had detected illness and disease in advance of any physical symptoms appearing on the surface.

Further experiments seemed to produce equally startling results. If a section of a leaf was cut off and photographed an image of the outline appeared on the photograph. This phenomenon, known as the 'phantom leaf', seemed to confirm the claims of clairvoyants that they could see clearly the 'phantom limb' on people with an amputated limb, but who continued to feel pain from the severed limb.

Though the Kirlians themselves did not describe the results of their investigations as evidence for the existence of an 'astral body', many were only too eager to do so. What other explanation was there, they asked, for the startling pictures Kirlian was able to take? But in one sense even the clairvoyants were disappointed with the results of Kirlian photography. Even the richly colourful images achieved by Kirlian lacked the subtlety of the 'aura' seen by clairvoyants.

While working at St Thomas's Hospital in London at the turn of the century, Dr Walter Kilner found that if he observed his patients through a glass screen coated with a blue dye,

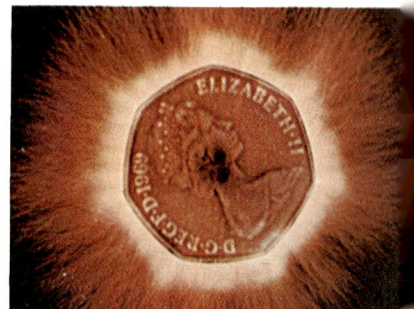

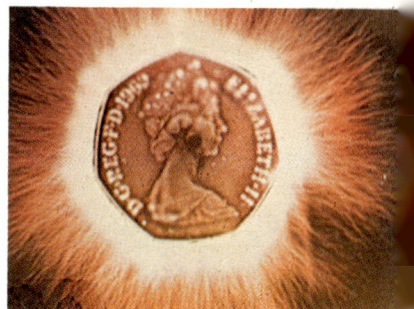

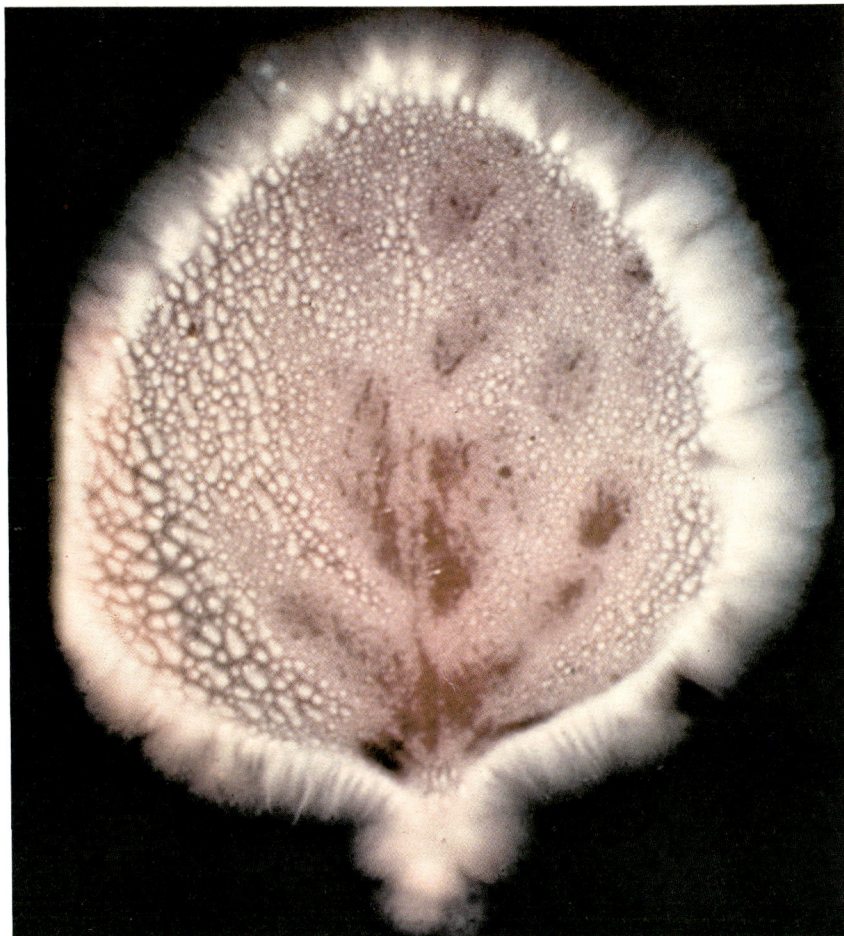

but also a counterpart body of energy'.

Much evidence already exists, claim the enthusiasts, to support Inyushin's theory. And there is also evidence that the nature and extent of these fields of energy, surrounding every living organism, corresponds to the image on the Kirlian print. Not so, reply the critics. Kirlian photography cannot be considered of scientific interest, since it is not repeatable under stringent laboratory conditions; a necessary requirement of all scientific phenomenon. Also, they argue, those experiments that have been conducted produce different results every time, not as the result of underlying physical or psychological causes, as Kirlian claimed, but due, simply, to such factors as sweat secretion and the primitive nature of the equipment used in Kirlian photography.

The debate continues. No one knows for certain what the images the Kirlians photographed are. Some, while rejecting the spiritual aspects of Kirlian, accept that, whatever the emanations mean, they can be used to achieve insight into the physical and psychological condition of the subject. Others, including practising scientists, claim far more. But all are agreed that the Kirlians have opened up a hitherto invisible world, once known only by the exceptional few, for everyone to see.

On page 94 we show how the Kirlian technique works and some of its outstanding successes

he could see a 'faint cloud' surrounding them that seemed to vary according to the physical and mental state of the patient. The dye had, Kilner later came to believe, acted as a stimulant to his own innate ability to perceive the 'glow' without any artificial aid. But the ability of those like Kilner to see this 'aura' clearly is of little help to scientists. Because it is such a personal quality, it is difficult to measure, control, analyse and subject to scientific scrutiny in the laboratory.

Research in the West into the possible cause of Kirlian photography is still in its infancy. Certainly, no definite conclusions have been reached. Research in Russia has been of much longer duration and has contributed many interesting theories as to the possible cause of the Kirlian effect. Working at the University of Alma Atta, Dr Victor Inyushin has spent several years investigating Kirlian photography. As a result of his investigations, Inyushin has come to the conclusion that the 'aura' effect shown in Kirlian photography is evidence of what he calls 'biological plasma' and not the result of any electrical state of the organism. Dr Inyushin describes 'biological plasma' in terms that closely resemble those used by clairvoyants to describe the 'astral body'. 'All living things' writes Dr Inyushin '– plants, animals and humans – not only have a physical body made of atoms and molecules,

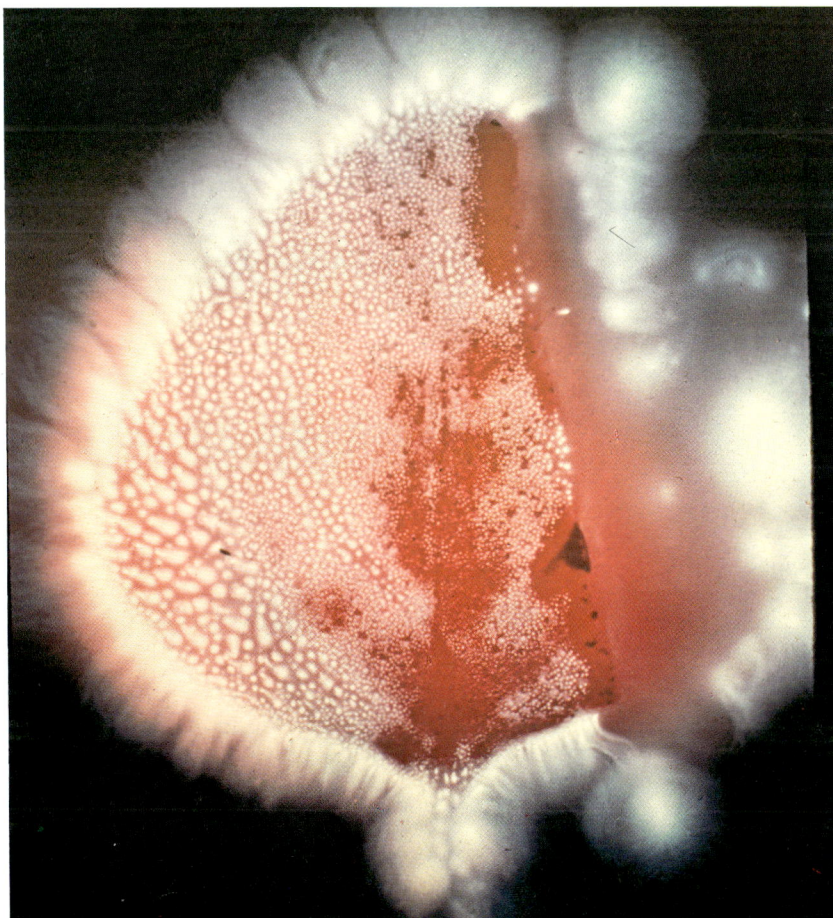

Other voices, other lives

It has long been known that under hypnosis some people regress to what appears to be a previous life. They not only assume another personality, but, as DAVID CHRISTIE-MURRAY shows, they can describe details from the past that are completely unknown to them outside of the trance state

HYPNOTIC REGRESSION into alleged previous lives is one of the most exciting and fascinating of psychic phenomena – and one of the most frustrating. During the past 20 years it has been brought to the attention of the general public every so often by programmes on radio and television, articles in the press and books written either by hypnotists themselves or by collaborators working with them.

Morey Bernstein's *The search for Bridey Murphy*, published in 1965, is still remembered if the small talk veers towards the occult; Arnall Bloxham's tapes, featured on radio and television programmes, and given a longer life by Jeffrey Iverson's *More lives than one?*, are widely known. Recently, Peter Moss has collaborated with Joe Keeton, prodigious in his expenditure of hypnotic man-hours, in the book *Encounters with the past*, which describes recordings of extracts from sessions with chosen subjects.

It is not generally realised that hypnotic regression into previous lives is not a recent discovery and has, in fact, been studied for nearly a century. The work of pioneers in this field, much of it lost because it was done long before the advent of the tape-recorder, is nevertheless valuable to students of reincarnation, whether they believe in it or not.

Travelling back in time

Part of the fascination of hypnotic regression lies in the very frustration that it engenders. Its revelations are both positive and negative, some bolstering the faith of reincarnationists and puzzling sceptics, others bewildering believers and encouraging doubt. Regression is positive in that the dramatisations of former existences are vividly portrayed far beyond the acting abilities of subjects in their waking condition, so that observers repeatedly say: 'If this be acting, neither an Olivier or a Bernhardt could better it.'

Positive, too, is the consistency with which many subjects, regressed repeatedly to the same historical period, take up the previous life, so that the same personality, outlook and intonation of speech appear without effort or hesitation. The same incidents and facts are remembered even when trick questions are introduced to try to trap the speakers. This happens even when years separate the sessions.

Regression is positive in two further ways. The first is that obscure historical facts, apparently completely unknown beforehand to either hypnotist or subject and confirmed only after considerable research, are revealed in reply to general questions. An example of this is shown by one of Joe Keeton's subjects, Ann Dowling, an ordinary housewife who, during over 60 hours of regression, became Sarah Williams, an orphan living a life of utter squalor in a Liverpool slum in the first half of the 19th century.

When asked what was happening in Liverpool in 1850, Ann Dowling mentioned the visit of a foreign singer whose name had 'summat to do wi' a bird'. Research showed

Hypnotherapist Joe Keeton (top) has conducted more than 8000 regressions. One of his subjects, Ann Dowling (above), went back over 100 years and became Sarah Williams, who lived in Liverpool in the 1850s (top right). Among the facts recalled by Mrs Dowling was the visit of Swedish singer Jenny Lind (below)

that Jenny Lind, the 'Swedish Nightingale', on her way from Sweden to America, sang for two nights in Liverpool's Philharmonic Hall in August 1850.

The second positive aspect of hypnotic regression is found in the tiny details of past usage that slip naturally into the subject's conversation while reliving the past life. These details *might* have been picked up by the subject in his present lifetime and held in his subconscious memory, but they are unlikely to have been formally taught or known to people of ordinary education.

David Lowe, a member of the Society for Psychical Research, lectures about a woman whom he has regressed into a number of lives, some of them in different generations of the same family (an unusual feature), illustrating his talks with copious tape-recordings of her conversations in previous existences.

During a 17th-century regression, David Lowe asked the woman how a certain word containing a 'w' was spelt. Her spontaneous answer was 'double v' – the common pronunciation of the letter at that time. This

The belief in reincarnation

The belief in reincarnation – that man's soul is reborn over and over again in another body or form – stretches far back into the past. The doctrine appears in primitive religions such as those of the Indian tribes of Assam, Nagas and Lushais, who believed that after death the soul took the form of an insect. The Bakongs of Borneo believed that their dead were reincarnated into the bearcats that frequented their raised coffins. The Kikuyu women of Kenya often worship at a place 'inhabited' by their ancestral souls in the belief that to become pregnant they must be entered by an ancestral soul.

According to Buddhist and Hindu thought man or the soul is reborn in accordance with merits acquired during his previous lifetime. But some sects of Hinduism hold that a man does not necessarily assume a human form in the next life. If he has been involved with vice or crime it is possible he may return as a cactus, toad, lizard, or even as poison ivy! The Buddhists believe that man is made up of elements: body, sensation, perception, impulse, emotion and consciousness, which fall apart at death. The individual, as such, ceases to exist and a new individual life begins according to the quality of the previous life, until at last achieving perfection and nirvana – eternal bliss.

Although reincarnation is not mentioned in Western texts until the late Greek and Latin writers, the idea dates back to at least the 6th century BC. It appears in the Orphic writings, which

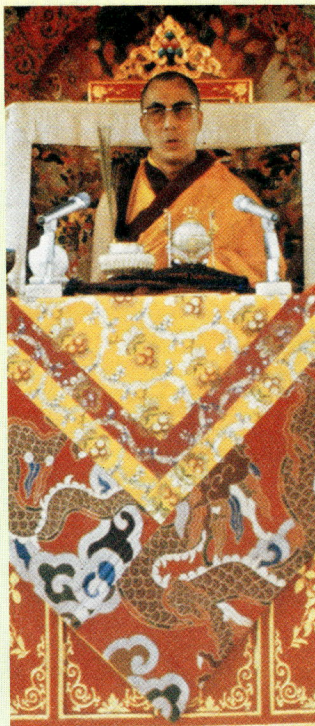

Tibetans believe that their spiritual leader, the Dalai Lama, is the reincarnation of a previous Dalai Lama whose soul enters the body of a child born at the precise moment of his death

appear to have played a great part in the thought of Pythagorus. He believed that the soul had 'fallen' into a bodily existence and would have to reincarnate itself through other forms to be set free. He himself claimed to have had previous existences including one as a soldier in a Trojan war.

Plato was greatly influenced by the Orphico-Pythagorean views and mentions reincarnation in his concluding part of the *Republic*. The soul, according to Plato, is immortal, the number of souls fixed, and reincarnation regularly occurs. Although discarded by Aristotle and other Stoic views, Plato's derivation was taken up by later schools of thought such as the Neoplatonists. Within the Christian church the belief was held by certain Gnostic sects during the first century AD and by the Manichaeans in the fourth and fifth centuries. But the idea was repudiated by eminent theologians at the time, and in AD 553, the Emperor Justinian condemned reincarnation, at the Second Council of Constantinople, as heresy.

Today the Westerner does have some difficulty in identifying with the Eastern idea of reincarnation. Most Western religious denominations share the view that the individual retains individuality after death, and finds the idea of returning as an animal or plant distinctly foreign. In 1917 the Roman Catholic Church denounced the idea as heresy.

Most adherents of reincarnation are now claiming the evidence from regressive hypnosis as proof for their case.

trivial detail was more telling to some listeners than all the researched dates and genealogies that substantiated the woman's story, remarkable as these were. When asked if she were engaged (to be married), the subject failed to understand the modern expression, but later talked happily of her recent betrothal.

Fact or fiction

The negative side of hypnotic regression is nevertheless considerable. There are many anachronisms, occasional historical howlers, instances of extraordinary ignorance and, with some subjects, inconsistencies (although much rarer than, and more balanced by, the consistencies).

One 19th-century character mentioned her 'boyfriend' in the modern sense of someone with a sexual love-interest in her. Another, regressed to the early 1830s and asked who ruled England, replied 'Queen Victoria', although four years of William IV's reign had still to run and Victoria's accession could not have been known for certain.

A common difficulty in substantiating historical facts is the scarcity of records of ordinary folk before the 19th century. Even when subjects mention landowners and comparatively important people, there is often no record of their existence in local archives. It is therefore sometimes extremely difficult to separate fact from fiction, especially as there may be a great deal of 'role-playing', the incubation in the subconscious mind of an imaginary personality around a nucleus of fact read in a history book or a novel.

Origins of modern hypnosis

Hypnosis is still so misunderstood and thought of as occult in the minds of many that it is as well to describe its place in modern thought.

Modern hypnosis began with Franz Mesmer, an Austrian physician who became a fashionable figure of Parisian society in the 18th century. He mistakenly believed that human beings emitted a force that could be transferred to objects such as iron rods. He 'magnetised' the rods by stroking them, then placed them in tubs filled with water in which his patients immersed their legs. Many and various were the ills allegedly cured by this method.

The extravagance of Mesmeric theory and its claims, together with the undertones of occultism that went with them, aroused intense opposition; and throughout the 19th century, serious investigators into hypnosis, and the few medical men bold enough to experiment with its use, met the kind of hostility once reserved for witches.

The Society for Psychical Research, which was founded in Britain in 1882, set up a committee to investigate hypnosis that continued to exist until a few years ago. Its findings, however, were not easily communicated to the general public and the phenomena it showed to be genuine were remarkable enough to maintain hypnotism's occult reputation, in spite of the Society's careful, objective and scholarly approach. But the therapeutic value of hypnosis was slowly established, especially in the treatment of psychological disorders.

After much investigation, it was discovered that subjects under hypnosis could be told either to *remember* what had happened on, say, their fifth birthday, or to *be* five years old again and to relive the day.

In the latter case, subjects would be led back to that day, write as they wrote at that age, relive the opening of their presents and each incident of the birthday party. They would have no knowledge of anything that happened after their fifth birthday until led forward by the hypnotist. It was as if all the layers of experience from five years old onwards had completely disappeared. The first man to attempt this age regression is said

The founder of modern hypnosis, Franz Anton Mesmer, believed that people emitted a force that could be transferred to iron rods. Parisians of all classes flocked to his salon in the 18th century where they sat round a large wooden tub called a *baquet*. This was filled with water, iron filings and bottles of 'magnetised' water. Projecting from the tub were iron rods, which patients held against their afflicted parts

to have been a Spaniard, Fernando Colavida, in 1887.

Further discoveries led to the investigation of pre-birth experiences in the womb and within a few years Dr Mortis Stark was studying the possibility of actually regressing subjects to a life before the present. At about the same time, in 1911, a Frenchman, Colonel Albert de Rochas, published an account of regressions that he had collected over several years.

A therapeutic role

The method employed in hypnotic regression is simple. After hypnotising the subject, the operator takes him back step by step to the beginning of his present life, then into the womb, and then instructs him to go back and back until he comes to some experience that he can describe. This is sometimes an 'existence' in the intermission between death ending a former life and birth beginning the present, sometimes experience of the former life itself, the period and circumstances of which the hypnotist can elicit by careful questioning.

The process is not merely used for interest's sake or to prove reincarnation – it can be therapeutic. Neuroses and other psychological disorders may be caused by traumas, the existence of which has been caused by shocks or other experiences in childhood or youth apparently too horrible for the conscious mind to face. To cure the neurosis, the trauma must be discovered and faced by the patient, and hypnosis is one technique able to dig it out.

By an extension of the process, neuroses and phobias may be caused by traumas experienced in alleged former lives that are revealed under hypnosis. Thus, one woman's terrible fear of water was caused by her having been bound with chains as a galley-slave in a previous existence, thrown into a river and eaten alive by crocodiles. A man terrified of descending in lifts had been a Chinese general who had accidentally fallen to his death from a great height. A young American girl about to dive from a high board was suddenly paralysed with fear after a moving bystander had been reflected in the water. Hypnosis revealed the hideous end of a former life in which she had been a girl in Florida who, just as she was jumping into the water, had seen the shadow of the alligator that was to devour her moving below the surface.

Whether or not these are memories of genuine previous experiences, they are convincing to many who have them. Much of the investigation into this particular aspect of hypnosis challenges the sceptics to find an explanation other than that of reincarnation. There *are* alternative explanations, which will be presented in future articles.

One of the most famous hypnotic regressions is that of Bridey Murphy. See page 78

Ten more lives to remember

Madame J, a soldier's wife and mother of one child, was delicate in health and as a girl had 'hated history'. She was regressed by Colonel de Rochas to 10 previous lives, some extremely detailed.

In the first she died at eight months. She then lived as a girl named Irisée in the country of the Imondo near Trieste. She next became a man, Esius, aged 40, who was planning to kill Emperor Probus in revenge for taking his daughter, Florina.

The fourth life was that of Carlomée, a Frankish warrior chieftain captured by Attila at Châlons-sur-Marne in AD 449. Abbess Martha followed, born in AD 923, who tyrannised young girls in a Vincennes convent as late as 1010. The Abbess was succeeded by Mariette Martin, aged 18 in 1300, daughter of a man who worked for the king – 'le beau Philippe'.

Madame J. then became Michel Berry, who was killed at the age of 22 in 1515 at the Battle of Marignano. This life was extremely detailed, Michel's career developing from his learning the art of fencing at 10, through his life as a page at the courts at Versailles and the Sorbonne and sundry love affairs to his presence aged 20 at the Battle of Guinegatte in Normandy.

Top: Colonel Albert de Rochas caused a sensation in 1911 with an account of hypnotic regression

Centre: the Emperor Probus, who was hated by Esius, the third personality in Madame J's previous lives

Above: the Battle of Marignano, in which Michel Berry died

After an eighth life as a wife and mother aged 30 in 1702, Madame J again became a man, Jules Robert. Jules was aged 38 in 1776 and a 'bad' worker in marble. Nevertheless one of his sculptures reached the Vatican.

Jules Robert reincarnated as Marguerite Duchesne, born in 1835, daughter of a grocer in the rue de la Caserne, Briançon. She went to school in the rue de la Gargouille. Research showed that the school existed, but there had never been a grocer Duchesne in the rue de la Caserne. Otherwise Madame J's description of places was accurate.

Tantalising evidence: The New Zealand UFO film

LATE IN THE EVENING of 30 December 1978 an Argosy freight plane set off from Wellington, New Zealand. Its skipper was Captain Bill Startup, who had 23 years' flying experience behind him, and the co-pilot was Bob Guard. On board was an Australian TV crew from Channel 0-10 Network: reporter Quentin Fogarty, cameraman David Crockett and his wife, sound recordist Ngaire Crockett. Their purpose was to try to film UFOs, for there had been reports of 'unknowns' during the preceding weeks in the region of Cook Strait,

One of the most impressive UFO sightings of all time took place in 1978 when a New Zealand television crew made two flights searching for UFOs – and actually succeeded in filming them. CHARLES BOWEN describes this extraordinary event

which separates New Zealand's North and South Islands. They were spectacularly successful in the quest. So successful that, after the story had appeared in hundreds of newspapers and clips from the films had been shown repeatedly on television around the world – the BBC, for instance, gave it pride of place on the main evening news – critics and droves of debunkers lined up to try to explain what the television crew had seen, in terms ranging from the sublimely astronomical to the ridiculously absurd.

'Bright lights over the ocean'

Radar-visual: Blenheim, New Zealand, 30 December 1978

This spinning, luminous sphere was filmed by a New Zealand television crew on the night of 30 December 1978. The crew made two flights, looking for UFOs, on the same night – and, incredibly, saw them both times

The Argosy had crossed Cook Strait and was flying over the Pacific Ocean off the north-east coast of South Island when the excitement began. The television crew was down by the loading bay filming 'intros' with Quentin Fogarty when Captain Startup called over the intercom for them to hurry to the flight deck; the pilots had seen some strange objects in the sky. According to Dave Crockett, they had already checked with Wellington air traffic control for radar confirmation of their visual sighting.

Quentin Fogarty stated that when he reached the flight deck he saw a row of five bright lights. Large and brilliant, although a long way off, they were seen to pulsate, growing from pinpoint size to the size of a large balloon full of glowing light. The sequence was repeated, the objects appearing above the street lights of the town of

Kaikoura, but between the aircraft and the ground.

Dave Crockett, who was wearing headphones, received a call from Wellington control warning the pilots that an unknown target was following the Argosy. Captain Startup put his plane into a 360-degree turn to look for the unidentified object but the passengers and crew saw nothing. Control however, was insistent: 'Sierra Alpha Eagle . . . you have a target in formation with you . . . target has increased in size.' This time lights were seen outside the plane, but because of interference from the navigation lights of the plane, Crockett was unable to film. So First Officer Bob Guard switched off the navigation lights – and everyone saw a big, bright light. The plane was now back on automatic pilot, so Bob Guard gave up his seat for Crockett, who obtained a clear shot

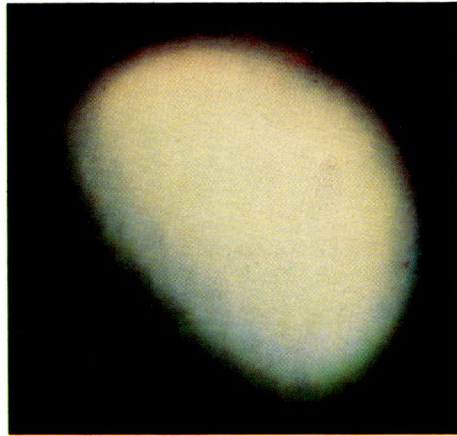

moonlight via cabbage leaves'. A more reasonable explanation was that the films showed a planet – but which one? One newspaper claimed it was Venus (left), another said it was Jupiter (right). But even the quickest glance at the planets themselves show these explanations to be unlikely. The *Daily Telegraph*, surprisingly, printed a strong condemnation of the Venus theory: 'The scientist who suggested that all [the television crew] were seeing was Venus on a particularly bright night can . . . be safely consigned to Bedlam.'

Rogue planets?

For a time it was thought that the New Zealand films might provide solid scientific evidence for UFOs.

Faced with this possibility, scientists were quick to react by putting forward a whole range of alternative explanations of what the object in the films might be. Some of their theories were wildly implausible – one even claimed the television crew had seen 'reflections from

Right and far right: two stills from the New Zealand television crew's film. The presence of the strange objects was confirmed by Wellington air traffic control, who saw their traces on their radarscopes

Below: Captain Bill Startup, pilot of the aircraft from which the UFO film was taken

of the object with his hand-held camera. Dave Crockett has since explained that this changing of seats with the camera running was responsible for the violent shake seen at that point in the movie film.

After this, Bill Startup put the plane into another 360-degree turn. They then lost sight of the UFO, although Wellington control said its echo was still on the radar scope.

It should be noted that, although there was no room for a camera tripod to be mounted on the flight deck, the unidentified object stayed steady enough for David Crockett to be able to keep it dead centre in his camera viewfinder for more than 30 seconds.

As the plane approached Christchurch, the fuel gauge went into a spin, but the captain said that this occasionally happened and was not necessarily caused by interference by the UFO. At this point they were

tuning in on the UFO off Banks Peninsula and were out of touch with Wellington control. Christchurch control had the object on its radar scope but later, when Captain Startup and American investigating scientist Dr Bruce Maccabee asked to see the radar tapes, the Christchurch supervisor replied that they had been 'wiped' clean as part of routine procedure.

The Argosy landed at Christchurch and journalist Dennis Grant joined the team in place of Dave Crockett's wife Ngaire. They left on the return flight to Blenheim at about 2.15 a.m. on 31 December 1978.

Early in this flight the observers saw two more strange objects. Through the camera lens Crockett saw what he described as a sphere with lateral lines around it. This object focused itself as Crockett watched through his camera – without adjusting the lens. He said the sphere was spinning. Significantly, one of the objects swayed on the Argosy's weather radar continuously for some 4 minutes. Later, as the aircraft approached Blenheim, they all saw two pulsating lights, one of which suddenly fell in a blurred streak for about 1000 feet (300 metres) before pulling up short in a series of jerky movements.

True or false?

Were the objects 'flying saucers'? Many alternative explanations were put forward: the film depicted a 'top secret American military remote-control drone vehicle', plasma or ball lightning, a hoax, meteorites, 'helicopters operating illegally at night', mutton birds, lights on Japanese squid boats, 'reflections from moonlight via cabbage leaves' (at Kaikoura), while Patrick Moore hedged his bets with a guess of 'a reflection, a balloon or an unscheduled aircraft.'

One newspaper claimed the film showed the planet Venus, out of focus because it was filmed with a hand-held camera. Another offered Jupiter as a candidate; an amateur astronomer had enhanced the light values of the film by putting through a line-scan analyser and had identified four small points of light that could be taken to correspond to the positions of the four largest moons of Jupiter. Venus and Jupiter appeared in

completely. They definitely moved, varying between 50 and 100 knots (92.5 km/h and 185 km/h). I certainly couldn't identify them as anything. It's pretty inconclusive. They were purely the sort of radar echoes that constantly pop up. It is not unusual to get strange echoes appearing on what we call primary radar. They usually amount to nothing at all.

Nevertheless, the Royal New Zealand Air Force was concerned enough about the incident to put a Skyhawk jet fighter on full alert to intercept any other UFOs that might appear in the area. By the end of January, however, the fuss had died down and the New Zealand Defence Ministry stated that the radar images were 'spurious returns' and the unidentified objects 'atmospheric phenomena'.

What is the truth of the New Zealand affair? The film appears to be genuine; computer enhancement has not proved it to be a fake. It seems almost too good to be true that a television crew that had set out with the deliberate intention of filming 'flying saucers' should come up with such spectacular results; and yet it has to be assumed that the objects they saw were real enough to those who beheld them – and were not mere hallucinations. The case remains on file, a fascinating question mark.

Below: this unique frame from the New Zealand film seems to show the UFO performing an extraordinary feat of aerobatics – looping the loop in 1/24 of a second. An alternative explanation for this typical UFO behaviour: the hand-held camera was jogged

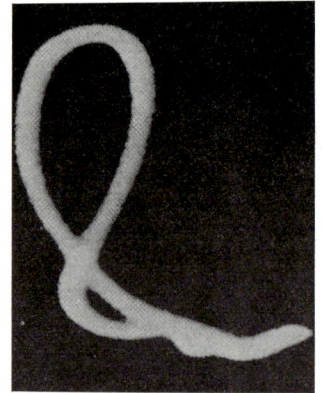

With the navigation lights of the aircraft switched off, the television crew was able to obtain this film of one of the objects. It pulsated from a pinpoint to the size of 'a large balloon'

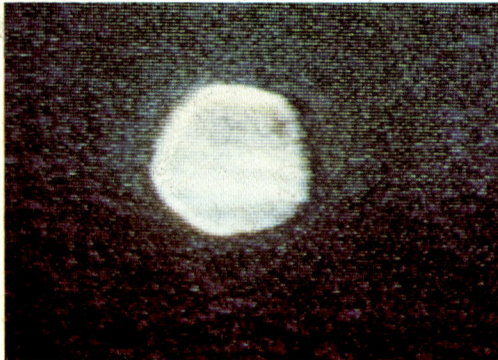

different regions of the sky; because the television crew were so vague about the position of the lights relative to the aircraft as they were filming them, it was impossible to make a positive identification.

One of the most exciting aspects of the incident is that it appears to offer independent instrumental evidence of the sighting both on film and radar. But even here there are problems. Although both ground radar and the Argosy's own radar picked up unidentified traces, the number of UFOs the television crew claimed to have seen – about eight – conflicts with the 11 reported by ground radar. And the crew actually filmed only one object. The radar controller at Wellington, Ken Bigham, was dismissive about the whole affair:

I managed to plot three of the echoes for 20 minutes or so before they faded

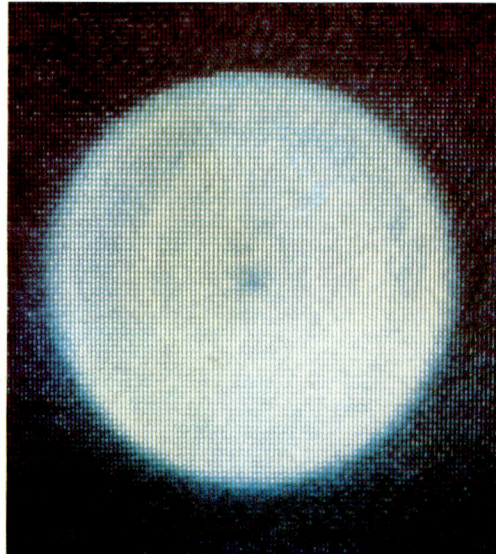

Alongside the 'official' Virgin Mary exists another, 'unofficial' Virgin. As RICHARD LEIGH and MICHAEL BAIGENT show, this other Madonna – black, mysterious and all-powerful – is quite unlike her chaste counterpart

UNTIL THE LATE 18th century, the pilgrim to Chartres traditionally participated in a complex, intriguing and not conventionally Christian ritual. Having prayed in the abbey and heard mass in the cathedral, he descended through a northern passageway to an ancient subterranean crypt beneath the church. Here he paid his pious respects to Notre Dame de Sous-Terre, 'Our Lady of the Underworld' – a black ebony statue of a seated woman holding a child on her knees. On the statue's head, there was a crown: on its pedestal, a Roman inscription – 'Virgini Paritures', 'the Virgin who will give birth'. Having completed his devotions, the pilgrim was blessed with water drawn from a sacred

This Black Madonna in the cathedral of Chartres is the Virgin of the Pillar. The original stone column on which the figure stood was much worn away 'by the bites and licks of its fervent worshippers'

well flowing into the crypt. He was also permitted to drink of this water. Continuing his underground journey or procession, he at last emerged by a southern passage.

At Montserrat, in Spain – where there is a particularly vigorous cult of the Virgin – a statue similar to the one at Chartres is especially venerated. Montserrat is a shrine for newly-married couples, and the statue it contains is deemed to preside over marriage, sexuality and fertility. According to traditional legends, prayers to this statue are believed to ward off sterility.

At Crotone, a promontory overlooking the Gulf of Taranto in Italy, there was once a temple dedicated to Hera Lacinia, the Roman goddess of moonlight who protects women, especially in childbirth. Her function was especially sexual: the bringer of fertility, governing the cycle of birth – conception, pregnancy, labour and delivery. Crotone's church, like those at Chartres and

Virgins with a pagan past

Black Madonnas

Left: the Black Madonna at Tarragona Cathedral, Spain, is a copy of the famous one at Montserrat in Catalonia. Though not officially recognised by the Church, Black Madonnas have enthusiastic followers and are credited with supernatural powers

Montserrat, houses a black statue of a woman. This statue, too, has become a centre for pilgrims. On the second Sunday of May, the statue is carried from the cathedral at Crotone to the Church of Our Lady of Capo Colonne on the promontory. At night, it is returned by sea in a procession of torchlit fishing boats – whose crews hope thereby to earn the statue's protection.

To the Roman Catholic Church, these three statues are officially regarded as Madonnas like any other, and no special status or significance is accorded them. But to the local people, and to pilgrims who visit them, they have a significance and power that goes far beyond that accorded them by the Catholic Church.

These statues are generally known as 'Black Madonnas'. In addition to the three already mentioned, there are at least 35 others, scattered not only throughout Europe, but as far away as Mexico. Among the most important Black Madonna sites are Einsiedeln in Switzerland, Rocamadour, Dijon, Avioth and Le Puy in France, Orval on the border of Luxembourg and France,

Loreto, Florence, Venice and Rome in Italy.

The statues, as their names suggests, are all black – made of stone, ebony or Lebanese cedar. They are robed in sumptuously rich apparel and, on festal occasions, are often decked with precious stones. All of them are crowned. To their worshippers they are regarded as the 'Queen of Heaven' and are attended by an image of the moon and/or stars – a belief that pre-dates Christianity and goes back to the pagan worship of female deity. All of them are depicted holding a child, usually on the left knee. They have all become the object of pilgrimage, and are believed to possess miraculous powers, especially of healing and fertility. The older ones have a curiously Eastern quality – Byzantine or Egyptian. And all present embarrassment for the Roman Catholic Church. Many – like that at Chartres – were destroyed during the French Revolution. Many others, especially during the last century and a half, were officially replaced by more conventional statues of the Virgin – statues which are *not* black. And many of the originally Black Madonnas have, over the centuries, been purposely painted over with whitewash.

Black Madonnas are surrounded by legend and are said to have appeared in miraculous circumstances. The Black Madonna at Tindari, Sicily, for example, is said to have been washed ashore in a casket. At Loreto, a 'strange building' containing the Black Madonna is said to have appeared suddenly, overnight, on 10 May 1291 – an event that the parish priest claimed to have been told of in a dream.

The Black Madonna of Montserrat was supposedly discovered by shepherds in a cave after they had been led to it by nocturnal celestial lights and angelic choirs. At Avioth, the Black Madonna is reputed to have suddenly materialised in a thorn bush. At Le Puy, she is said first to have appeared in a vision and commanded that a church be built

This Black Madonna at Einsiedeln, Switzerland, demonstrates the degree of veneration in which these unusual statues are held – richly adorned as it is with gold and jewels

on the site in her honour. The plan for the building is said to have been outlined by a fall of snow in midsummer and its consecration, a century or so later, was allegedly attended by celestial lights and choirs.

The Madonna, and the Black Madonna in particular, first assumed a crucial position in Christendom during the Middle Ages and the period of the Crusades. In large part this was due to the influence of Saint Bernard, the famous Abbot of Clairvaux, who probably did more than any other individual to propagate the cult of the Virgin. Saint Bernard himself is said to have experienced his most dramatic religious illumination from the Black Madonna of Chatillon. While he was reciting the Ave Marias before her, she reportedly pressed her breast, whereupon three drops of milk fell into the monk's open mouth.

A modern psychologist might well find Saint Bernard a suitable case for treatment, but the fact remains, however, that under his auspices the Virgin, whom he called the Queen of Heaven, assumed a hitherto unprecedented significance in Christendom. She became the official patroness of the Knights Templar and, later, of their German equivalent, the Teutonic Order. She figured on chivalric banners and standards, knights took the field in her honour, their battle cry often consisting solely of her name. In a sense she absorbed the whole of the Christian Trinity – Father, Son and Holy Ghost. And as 'Bride of God', the Virgin effectively displaced the Trinity.

In the text of the Mass of the Immaculate Conception of the Virgin, there is the following statement:

The Lord possessed me at the beginning of His ways. I existed before He formed any creature. I existed from all eternity, before the earth was created....

While the Virgin was sometimes referred to as the 'Bride of God', she was also known as 'Mother of God'. In this capacity, she virtually displaced God Himself. For some medieval Catholic writers it was the Virgin, not God, who created the world. The whole of existence depended upon her. According to one writer: 'At the command of Mary, all obey, even God.' She was frequently equated with the Holy Ghost – symbolised, like the Virgin, by a dove. And indeed, the Holy Ghost is regarded as feminine in Hebrew and was also considered to be such by the early Christian church.

During the Middle Ages, then, Christianity – particularly in the popular mind – centred primarily on the Virgin. It became, in effect, a matriarchal rather than a patriarchal religion – a religion orientated more around the feminine principle than around the masculine. God the Father ceased to dominate the popular mind. Jesus, the Son, became increasingly feminine in character, with emphasis placed upon his meekness, gentleness and passivity. The Virgin became the mediator between God and Man; the

Left: a stained-glass window in St Mary's Church, Shrewsbury, showing St Bernard (1090–1153) administering to the poor. It was after a visitation from the Virgin Mary that St Bernard described her as the 'Mother of God'

Top right: the medieval religious and military order of Teutonic Knights adopted the Virgin as their patroness

Below right: the Knights Templar professed a strict code of conduct dedicated, like the Virgin Mary, to a life of chastity, humility and poverty

The cult of the Virgin Mary

Mary, Mother of God plays a key role in the Roman Catholic Church. She is believed to possess miraculous powers and to have ascended into Heaven without having suffered bodily corruption. She is also believed to be a living person who intervenes directly in the affairs of Man. While these beliefs have come to be specifically Christian, they can be seen as originating in pagan beliefs stretching back 10,000 years before the birth of Christ. And it is these beliefs that mark the beginnings of the cult of the Virgin Mary and the origins of the Black Madonnas.

Long before the appearance of male gods, primitive man is supposed to have worshipped a female Creator. This Goddess, because she came before the male was believed to have been virgin. The cycle of birth was shrouded in mystery. Since sex did not always lead to birth, it

Madonna and Child – the bunch of lilies in her hand symbolises purity

was believed that birth could occur without sex: by swallowing a blade of grass, for example, or standing against the wind. The Goddess alone controlled the mysterious cycle of fertility, conception and birth.

To survive the shocks suffered after the sacking of Rome in 410, the early Church, it has been suggested, grafted on to Mary, mother of Christ, attributes hitherto accorded to the Goddess. Both were known as the 'Queen of Heaven', as 'Protectress' and Virgin. In place of the Christian concept of the all-male Trinity, Father, Son and Holy Ghost, the Church now emphasised the place of Mary, the female principle. In doing so they struck a chord in the popular imagination which had always held the female, in some sense, higher than the male. Mary fulfilled this role in a way the Trinity never could and indeed as 'Mother of God' became even more powerful than God Himself.

guardian goddess of all Western Europe.

The great Gothic cathedrals became her temples and palaces. Between 1170 and 1270, no less than 80 cathedrals to 'Our Lady' and 500 churches were erected in France alone. A significant number of these edifices were erected on sites already hallowed by the presence not merely of a Madonna statue, but of a Black Madonna. While it cannot be proved definitely, it has been argued that *all* the major cathedrals to Our Lady were situated on Black Madonna sites.

Yet the Church of Rome, as we have seen, appears to have been rather embarrassed by the Black Madonna statues – embarrassed and distinctly reticent. Officially it refused to distinguish them from the more conventional 'white' Madonnas. At the same time, however, many of them were white-washed or, as in the case of the Black Madonna of Avioth, painted a flesh colour. And elaborate attempts were made to rationalise the statues' blackness. Some of these rationalisations were plausible enough. The wood, in some cases, might well have been blackened by smoke or age. In some cases, the silver in which the statues were often swaddled might well have oxidised, thus darkening the wood. But the fact remains that most of the statues were carved originally from ebony – a black wood – or from black stone. In other words, they were *intended* to be black from the very beginning. This would seem to be confirmed by the fact that Black Madonnas have been

produced in modern times and they are *deliberately* black as the Black Madonna installed at Orvel, for example.

It has been suggested that the worship or devotion accorded the Black Madonnas was never strictly orthodox, never truly in accord with established Catholic dogma. And indeed, many beliefs associated with Black Madonnas are not only non-Christian in both nature and origin – they are clearly pagan in character. Many of the Black Madonnas are associated with sexuality, procreation and fertility – hardly traditional qualities attributed to the Virgin Mary. The Black Madonna of Montserrat is honoured at festivals by a circular (orgiastic) ritual dance, of unmistakably pagan derivation. Other Black Madonnas, like the one at Chartres, are identified as 'Queen of the Underworld'. Others still, are explicitly associated with the moon, or with the planet Venus. Again, such associations do not agree with the traditional image of Jesus' pure and immaculate virgin mother. Nor, for that matter, does the 'Feast of Fools' – a notoriously licentious festival observed in France until the 17th century. If the Black Madonnas represent the Virgin Mary, they must also, quite clearly, represent something else.

Like the pagan Goddess who preceded her, the Black Madonna was both harlot and nun as we reveal on page 110

Clues from clairvoyance

The uncanny ability that we call clairvoyance takes many forms, from a vague awareness of a distant event to a vivid revelation. Though not always reliable, clairvoyance has provided startling and unexpected clues in crime cases, as ROY STEMMAN recounts in this survey

ONE DAY in late October 1978, seven-year-old Carl Carter disappeared from his Los Angeles home. The police were baffled; they did not know whether he had been kidnapped, or had simply wandered off and got lost.

It was then that a retired police officer suggested that a local psychic – who is known only by the name of Joan – might be able to help. Within hours of her involvement, the case had changed from a lost child investigation to one of triple murder.

The psychic told the police that the boy was dead and she described the man she thought was responsible for his murder. Joan tried drawing his portrait and a police artist was called in to make a more accurate sketch of the suspect, based on her description. When the drawing was shown to Carl's parents his father said at once, 'That looks like Butch.'

Within an hour, Harold Ray 'Butch' Memro was arrested and by the end of the day he had confessed to strangling Carl, and to murdering two other boys two years earlier.

Psychics often volunteer their services to the police and there are countless stories of people whose extra-sensory powers have given them glimpses of crimes. But all too often the accuracy of their statements cannot be verified until after the criminals have been caught by conventional means. In other words, ESP seldom leads the police to a culprit as it appears to have done in the Memro case.

It has to be remembered that, for every impressive case reported in the press, there are probably a hundred or more where volunteered 'psychic' help only leads the police on a wild goose chase. Following the mysterious disappearance of schoolgirl Genette Tate in August 1978, for example, the Devon police received calls from over 200 mediums and other people interested in psychic detection who believed their paranormal powers could produce useful clues.

The definition of clairvoyance is 'extra-sensory knowledge about material objects or events which is not obtained from another person's mind' – in other words, not simple telepathy. It can take many different forms, ranging from a vague awareness of a distant event to a vision in which scenes unfold

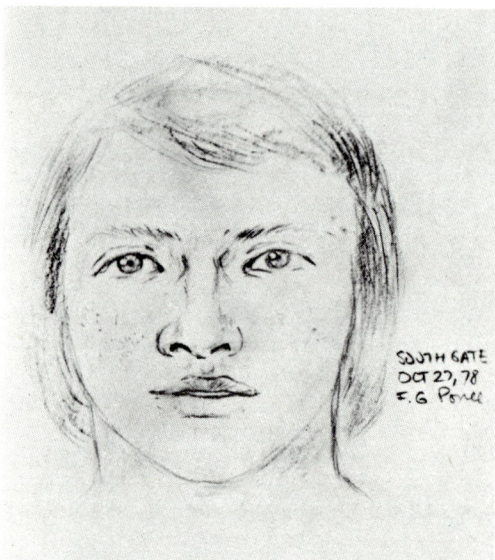

SOUTH GATE
OCT 27, 78
F. G Powell

Left: late in 1978 Los Angeles police called in a local psychic, Joan (top), to help solve the case of a small boy's mysterious disappearance. The psychic told the police the boy was dead and, on the basis of her description, a police artist was able to make a sketch of the murderer (centre). The victim's parents immediately recognised the man in the picture as 'Butch' Memro (bottom), who was quickly arrested and confessed to the crime

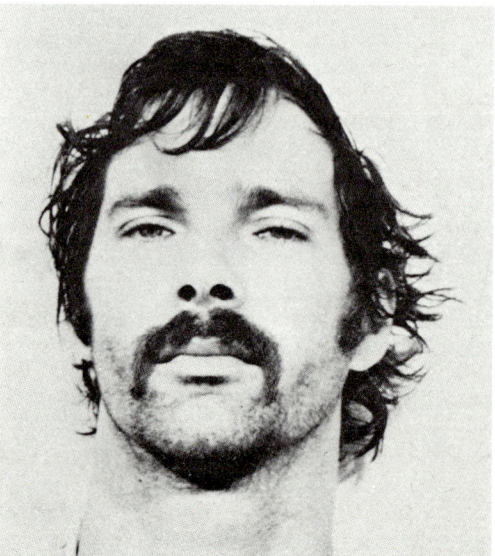

Croesus tests the oracles

In ancient times clairvoyants were known as oracles and their visions were subject to as much scrutiny as they are today. Two and a half thousand years ago Croesus, the fabulously rich king of Lydia, conducted a fascinating psychic experiment to test the powers of seven oracles, six Greek and one Egyptian. According to the historian Herodotus, the king was becoming increasingly alarmed at the power of the Persians and decided to consult an oracle as to what course of action he should take. But which one could he trust? He decided to test them.

He sent out seven messengers, one to each oracle, instructing them that on the hundredth day each should ask his oracle, 'What is King Croesus, son of Alyattes, now doing?' Their answers were to be written down and brought back to the King. Only one of the answers – the most accurate – remains on record. The oracle at Delphi – the Pythoness, as she was called – induced her prophetic trances by sitting over a volcanic fault and inhaling the fumes while chewing mulberry leaves. The moment the Lydian messenger entered her sanctuary, she answered him, without even hearing his question, in verse:

I can count the sands, and I can
    measure the ocean;
I have ears for the silent and know
    what the dumb man
    meaneth;
Lo! on my sense there striketh the
    smell of a shell-covered
    tortoise,
Boiling now on a fire, with the flesh
    of a lamb in a cauldron –
Brass is the vessel below, and brass
    the cover above it.

After sending his messengers to the oracles, the king set about deciding on what would be the most improbable thing anyone could conceive of him doing. On the appointed day he took a lamb and a tortoise, cut them to pieces with his own hands, and boiled them together in a brass cauldron covered with a brass lid.

Not surprisingly, the clairvoyance of the oracle at Delphi got her the job as psychic adviser to the king.

---

vividly before the eyes of the clairvoyant.

For ordinary people, clairvoyance is most likely to occur in stressful situations or when people or places connected with them are in danger. A well authenticated instance concerns the 18th-century Swedish scientist and seer, Emanuel Swedenborg, investigated and recorded by the distinguished German philosopher Immanuel Kant. On one occasion Swedenborg arrived in Gothenburg from England at around 4 p.m. on a Saturday. Soon he became restless and disturbed and left his friends to go for a walk outside.

On his return, he described a vision he had had of a fire which, he said, had broken out just three doors away from his home, 300 miles (480 kilometres) away. A fierce blaze was raging, he said, and he continued to be disturbed until 8 p.m. when he announced that the fire had been extinguished. News of this clairvoyant vision spread rapidly through the city and Swedenborg was asked to give a first-hand account to the Governor of Gothenburg. It was not until a royal messenger arrived in Gothenburg on the following Monday that the events of Swedenborg's vision were confirmed.

The pioneer of ESP research, Dr J. Rhine, and his colleagues at Duke University, decided in the 1930s to investigate clairvoyance. They had earlier conducted successful telepathy tests in which one person concentrated on a symbol while someone else, in another room, tried to read his mind; the symbols of a pack of Zener cards were generally used. The Duke University investigators decided to see what would happen if, instead of looking at the cards, the agent simply shuffled them and then removed them one at a time from the pack, face

Below: Emanuel Swedenborg (1688–1772), the Swedish scientist, philosopher and theologian, who was well known during his lifetime as a clairvoyant

down. The subject of the experiment had to use clairvoyance, instead of telepathy, to guess their running order. (The agent could then note down the order of the cards by going through the pack after the experiment.)

In one series of experiments in which J. Pratt was the experimenter and Hubert Pearce the subject, Pearce scored 558 correct responses out of a total of 1850 guesses. If chance alone had been at work, he should have scored only 370 correct answers. On this basis, the odds against Pearce's score were calculated as 22,000 million to one.

Not everyone is impressed with laboratory results. One criticism that has been levelled at the Pearce-Pratt experiments is that Pearce was unsupervised while making his guesses. Professor C. E. M. Hansel, a non-believer in ESP, has argued that, under the circumstances, the results cannot be taken seriously. It was possible, after all, for Pearce to have sneaked out of the building after the experiment and peered through the window of the room Dr Pratt was in to see what cards

he was turning over. He could have noted them down or memorised them, then dashed back to his room to compile a running order with enough mistakes to make it look genuine.

Another psychical researcher, Professor Ian Stevenson, has subsequently investigated the theory and asserted that it would have been physically impossible for Pearce to have cheated in this way, since the cards would not have been visible through the window.

But even where the methodology of clairvoyant research is beyond criticism, the statistical nature of the results leaves many people unimpressed. For them, individual cases of spectacular clairvoyance are more impressive than repeated card-guessing tests

that produce above-average results.

The clairvoyance of Polish engineer Stephan Ossowiecki attracted the attention of top psychical researchers in the early 1900s. Holding a sealed envelope or a folded piece of paper, he could often describe its contents or give the name of the signatory.

During an international conference on psychical research held in Warsaw in 1923, Ossowiecki's powers were put to the test. An English investigator, Dr Eric Dingwall, sketched a flag with a bottle etched in its upper left-hand corner. He then wrote the date, 22 August 1923, beneath his drawing and sealed it in a package consisting of three envelopes, one within the next. Dingwall sent the package from England to Baron Albert von Schrenck-Notzing in Warsaw.

Some important research into clairvoyance was carried out at Duke University, USA (top) during the 1930s. The experiments used Zener cards as targets: the agent, Dr Pratt (above left) sat in either room A or room B and withdrew cards one at a time, face down, from a pack while the subject, Hubert Pearce (above right) sat in room C and tried to name the cards as they were drawn from the pack. He was spectacularly successful: the odds against his results were 22,000 million to one

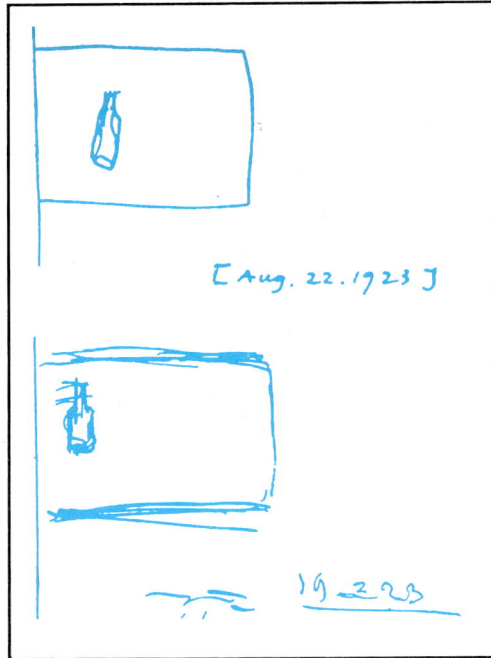

Polish engineer Stephan Ossowiecki (far left, pictured with his wife) had extraordinary clairvoyant powers. His abilities were tested in an experiment: an English investigator sketched a flag with a bottle on it, wrote the date beneath it and sent it in a sealed package to a noted Polish psychic researcher, Baron von Schrenck-Notzing (below), in Warsaw. The Baron handed the sealed envelope to Ossowiecki and asked him for his impressions.

Ossowiecki immediately realised that the Baron had not written the message. Then he suddenly grabbed a pen and agitatedly began to draw what he 'saw' inside the envelope. His drawing (left) is startlingly similar to the original

Baron von Schrenck-Notzing was a well-known pathologist of the day, who was also a noted psychical investigator. Neither the Baron, nor the two other researchers involved in the experiment knew what was inside the envelope. They simply gave it to Ossowiecki without explanation and asked for his impressions.

The Polish clairvoyant told them that the Baron had not written the message; there were several envelopes, something greenish – cardboard – and a little bottle. Then he grabbed a pen and, in an agitated manner, drew an almost identical replica of the target. He also wrote '1923' and said something was written before it, but he was unable to say what it was. This test left Dingwall and the other researchers in no doubt that Ossowiecki had paranormal powers.

Measuring the soul

The ability to pick up impressions from objects was investigated as early as 1949 by J. Rhodes Buchanan, a physician in Ohio, USA. He found that some people he tested were able to identify medicines hidden in sealed envelopes or give accurate descriptions of the writers of letters. He coined the word *psychometry* – which means, in Greek, 'measure of the soul' – to describe the ability.

One of the most detailed studies of clairvoyance and psychometry was carried out, from 1919 onwards, by a German physician, Dr Gustav Pagenstecher, who practised medicine in Mexico for 40 years. One day Senora Maria Reyes Zierold consulted Dr Pagenstecher, complaining of insomnia. He decided to treat her by hypnosis. While in trance, she told him she could see his daughter listening at the door. To his surprise, when he opened the door the child was there just as the patient had claimed. With her permission he set about investigating Senora Zierold's paranormal vision and soon discovered that, if an object was put in her hand while she was in trance, she was able to give a vivid description of events connected with it.

Once, for example, she was handed a piece of string. She began describing a battlefield on a cold, foggy day, with groups of men and continuous rifle fire. 'Quite of a sudden,' she said, 'I see coming through the air and moving with great rapidity a big ball of fire . . . which drops just in the middle of the 15 men, tearing them to pieces.' The string had originally been attached to a German soldier's dog tag (identity disc). The psychic had reported with startling accuracy a scene that the man described as 'the first great impression I received of the war.'

In an attempt to discover whether some element of telepathy was involved, or whether Senora Zierold was a genuine clairvoyant the American Society for Psychical Research sent its research officer, Walter Prince, to conduct tests with her. One experiment he carried out involved two identical pieces of silk ribbon, enclosed in identical boxes. He mixed them up so that even he did not know which was which. Holding one box, Senora Zierold described a Mexican church and dancing Indians. The other gave her impressions of a French ribbon factory. She was absolutely right: one piece had come direct from the manufacturers, the other from a church altar.

With many outstanding cases of clairvoyance on record, it is not surprising to find possessors of these abilities being consulted in particularly baffling crime cases. The consolation for criminals is that few clairvoyants are as spectacularly successful or as reliable as Ossowiecki or Zierold!

What are premonitions, and can people really see into the future? See page 110

Above: this photograph was taken by a coastguard, R. Alpert, at 9.35 a.m. on 16 July 1952 from the control tower at Salem Air Base in Massachusetts, USA. The objects were reported to be moving at great speed. They appear much brighter in the photograph than they actually were because the aperture of the camera was set for the brightness of the surrounding landscape and consequently the UFOs themselves are overexposed.

But is the photograph genuine? The images are unlikely to have been caused by lens flares, as these almost always appear in straight lines. But it is reported that the picture was taken through a laboratory window – and sceptics have suggested that the objects could actually be reflections of lights inside the laboratory. Photographic experts, however, point out that reflected lights are rarely as opaque as these.

Right: this picture, published here for the first time, was taken by London photographer Anwar Hussein in the Spanish Pyrenees in July 1978. After finishing filming one day, he found he had left one of his lenses at the top of a mountain. The next morning, about 9 o'clock, he returned to look for it. Mr Hussein found the lens and took some pictures; his camera was set on motor-drive. At the time he noticed nothing unusual – except the brightness of the light and the uncanny quietness. Back in London, he sent the film to be developed – and received a worried telephone call from the lab, who pointed out the 'object' on the film and thought it must be a fault that had appeared during developing. On examination, however, the emulsion was found to be undamaged. This is typical of many of the best UFO pictures, which are often of objects that go unnoticed at the time of filming.

Above and left: early in January 1958 a survey ship of the Brazilian Navy, the *Almirante Saldanha*, set off from Rio de Janeiro bound for the rocky island of Trindade, where the Navy had an oceanographic station. Among those on board was Almiro Barauna, a specialist in underwater photography.

Just before the ship was due to set sail on the return journey at 12.15 p.m. on 16 January 1958, a retired Air Force officer, Captain Viegas, who was on deck with other officers and technicians, called to Barauna that there was a bright object in the sky. Barauna located it and watched the moving object until it was silhouetted against some cloud. Then he shot two photographs. The UFO then disappeared behind the main peak of the island for a few seconds. When it reappeared it was flying in the opposite direction. Barauna took a third photograph, then a fourth and fifth, but these last two were wasted shots because the photographer was jostled by the other people aboard the ship, who were by now extremely excited. The UFO appeared briefly to halt its passage away from the island, and Barauna took his last picture of the object as it moved swiftly away.

The photographer said the object was silent, dark grey in colour, and was apparently surrounded by a greenish vapour or mist.

Barauna developed his film on board ship in the presence of the skipper, Commander Bacellar. (As there was no photographic paper on board, prints were made when the ship had returned to Rio.) Barauna said that in the urgency and excitement of the sighting, he did not think to check the settings of his camera and the pictures were consequently over-exposed.

Back in Rio de Janeiro, the Brazilian Navy examined the negatives. They found them to be genuine, and any possibility of a hoax was eliminated. Based on Barauna's account, the naval authorities set up a mock re-run of the incident, and were able to compute the speed of the object as about 550 to 600 mph (900 to 1000 km/h). The diameter of the Saturn-shaped UFO was estimated at around 40 yards (37 metres). At least 100 people had seen the UFO — and the photographs seem to be unimpeachable.

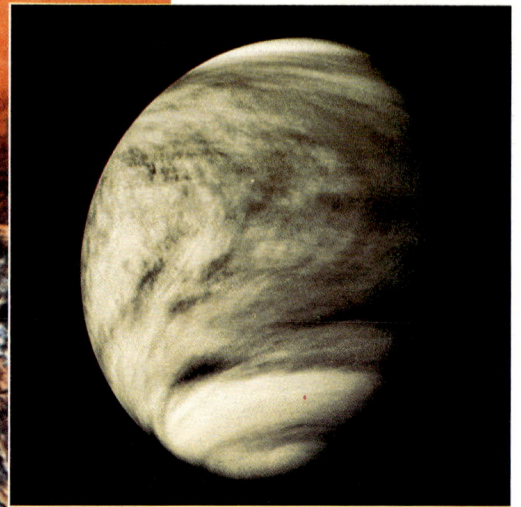

Above: the planet Venus, 26 million miles (48 million kilometres) from Earth

Left: an artist's impression of the surface of Venus, based on television pictures. With a surface temperature reaching 900°F (480°C) it is highly unlikely that anything could live on the planet

Below: Apollo 8 blasting off for the Moon. To reach planets beyond our Solar System would require a spacecraft powered by a vastly more efficient fuel

Spinning through space

Reports of UFOs describe a disc-shaped, highly manoeuvrable, immensely fast flying machine capable of feats that defy all known physical laws. TONY OSMAN believes that their existence should not be dismissed by conventional science. Here he describes how UFOs might work and the kind of civilisation that could produce them

THE WORD UFO – unidentified flying object – officially means simply something that has not been, or cannot be, accounted for by any of the known laws of physics. But the seemingly rational behaviour reported in many UFO sightings, as well as the accounts of meetings with humanoids, has led to the speculation that UFOs are, in fact, spacecraft bringing creatures from outer space.

If this is so, the spaceships must be able to cover immense distances. People who claim to have had contact with extra-terrestrials often say they have spoken with Venusians. But Venus is highly unlikely to be inhabited. Any intelligent life forms must be coming from still further away, and, even assuming that lifespans of creatures from other planets may be much longer than our own, it is clear that UFOs must be able to travel very fast indeed if they are not to take hundreds of years to travel between inhabited planets.

Reports of the movement of UFOs are remarkably consistent. Most people describe them as hovering and then taking off at very high speed, often executing manoeuvres that would be impossible in conventional aircraft. Even allowing for exaggeration by excited witnesses, the consistency of the reports

suggests the UFOs use a very powerful force to produce dramatic accelerations.

None of the rocket fuels we use at present can produce either the speed or acceleration observed in the UFOs, because they store only a small amount of energy for a given mass. Right from the beginning, rocket travel has been faced with the problem of enabling the rocket to carry enough fuel for its journey – it must lift the fuel, which can be very heavy if the journey is long, as well as itself and its occupants. The solution has been the multi-stage rocket: the initial acceleration is given by a rocket that is jettisoned when its fuel is used up and a second rocket takes over.

Space flights have always stretched our rocket technology to its limits – and, as everyone knows, our rockets and spacecraft do not accelerate very briskly away from the Earth. Although they eventually reach quite high speeds, they are nowhere near fast enough to reach planets outside our Solar System within a human lifetime.

If we assume UFOs are subject to the same laws of physics as we are, then, to operate on and near the Earth with the rapid accelerations and manoeuvres at high speeds that are often reported, they must be using a

Above: Professor Freeman Dyson, the American physicist who designed a nuclear-powered spacecraft as long ago as 1958

different source of energy from conventional chemical fuels. Their fuel must be highly compact, with a high energy yield for a small mass: the obvious source is nuclear fuel.

As long ago as 1958 – just after the Russians had launched the first man-made satellites into space – a brilliant theoretical physicist called Freeman Dyson embarked on a plan for a nuclear-powered spaceship. He had previously worked on the development of the atom bomb and had a comprehensive understanding of nuclear power. He assembled a group of scientists at La Jolla, southern California, to work with him; he called his scheme 'Project Orion'.

Project Orion was a serious attempt to build a spacecraft powered by nuclear explosions, and was intended as an alternative to the multi-stage rockets that Werner von Braun was proposing for space travel.

Freeman Dyson's ultimate aim was to build a spacecraft the size of a small city that would take a group of people to a distant comet on the edge of the solar system, where they would settle. This may have been only a pipe-dream, but the design was real enough.

The spacecraft was to be powered by hydrogen bombs. Essentially, his idea was to carry a number of hydrogen bombs aboard the spacecraft; these would be moved, one by one, to a position underneath the craft where they would be exploded. The base of the spacecraft would absorb the shock and the craft would be driven along. Obviously the spacecraft and the bomb system would have to be designed so that the craft was propelled along and not simply blown apart, but – in principle, at least – this was straightforward. However, Dyson was never able to test his ideas: he was prevented by public concern about the pollution of the atmosphere by radioactive fallout.

UFOs are often reported as disappearing rapidly – going off 'like a television set' and reappearing just as quickly. This aspect of the phenomenon has puzzled scientists for a long time and has led to suggestions that UFOs use some kind of 'anti-optic device' to prevent them being seen. There are, however, some simpler explanations that account for the majority of reports. UFOs 'disappearing' in the darkness of night could do so by simply switching off their lights; daytime discs could appear to vanish by turning themselves sideways on to the observer – it would be very difficult to pick out the thin edge of a disc against the sky. These explanations do not, of course, account for radarvisual sightings that suddenly vanish. But if a UFO disappeared behind a patch of disturbed air, a mirage-like effect could easily screen it both from sight and from radar detectors.

There are, however, cases on file for which none of these explanations seems credible. It seems that the phenomena involved can only be explained as products of a technology much further advanced than our own.

Just what kind of technology would we need to build a flying saucer? See page 88

Why saucers?

By far the majority of UFO reports describe the strange objects as disc- or cigar-shaped and it could be that most UFOs reported as cigar-shaped are in fact discs. Whether or not this is actually the case, the number of reports of saucer-shaped UFOs is overwhelming. There has been a great deal of speculation as to why this should be so – some people have suggested the mystical significance of the circle may have something to do with it – but there is a simple explanation.

On long inter-stellar voyages, a spacecraft will pass through vast regions of empty space – far from the regions of gravitational attraction of any major objects – where there is no wind resistance, no up or down, no east or west, nothing. The most logical shape for a vessel travelling in these circumstances is circular, for a circle is symmetrical about an infinite number of axes. The fact that most UFOs are disc-shaped rather than spherical can be explained as a design feature that allows spacecraft to operate at high speeds once they have entered the atmosphere of planets: by flying with their edges into the wind, they can cut down the effect of air resistance almost to zero.

Creatures from the void?

Some man-beasts seem to be impervious to bullets, while others appear to be able to vanish at will. What are these strange and terrifying creatures? In the final article of this series, JANET and COLIN BORD examine the evidence and present some astounding theories

THE BIGFOOT RIDDLE is not an easy one to solve. It is not simply a question of ascertaining whether or not the creature exists and, if it does, whether it is human or animal. Some reports, especially the more recent ones, have features that seem to deepen the mystery.

The average height of a bigfoot seems to be between 6 and 7 feet (1.8 and 2.1 metres), though much smaller ones are sometimes reported; these could be youngsters. However, much taller ones are occasionally reported. A 15-foot (4.5-metre) creature was seen by a USAF Staff Sergeant and two friends while they were camping at Belt Creek Canyon, Montana, in August 1977. They shot at it, but turned tail and drove away in their cars when it began to run towards them. Reports of fleeting sightings of this sort,

however, can never be taken at face value: size, for instance, is easily mistaken under conditions of stress.

Sometimes, however, an accurate calculation of height can be made. In April 1979, 16-year-old Tim Meissner saw a bigfoot twice in three days near his rural home in British Columbia. The first time, while fishing with friends at Dunn Lake near Barriere, he heard a high-pitched screech and saw on the lake's far shore a bigfoot with its arms raised. It ran away as the youths went to investigate. Hidden under branches and moss they found a deer with a broken neck.

Two days later, Tim Meissner returned with four friends, armed with a gun. They split up to search for the bigfoot. By an astonishing stroke of luck, Meissner saw it again. His first reaction was to shoot at the tall, black, hairy creature with glaring bright eyes and shoulders 4 feet (1.2 metres) wide. He seems to have hit it, since it went down on one knee, but then it got up and ran away at great speed. When Tim saw the bigfoot it was about 50 yards (45 metres) away, standing beside a tree. Later he returned to the tree and was able to estimate that the creature he had seen was about 9 feet (2.7 metres) tall.

The mystery deepens

Some bigfeet smell revolting. During a flurry of sightings around Little Eagle, South Dakota, in the autumn of 1977, one witness reported: 'It was like a stink of a dead person, long dead. It stayed in the air for maybe 10 to 15 minutes afterwards.' But by no means all bigfeet smell bad. It has been suggested, for example, that they can release the smell at will, perhaps to ensure that people keep their distance. Another strange feature is that some bigfeet have exceptionally large eyes which seem, uncannily, to glow. They are

Above: an alleged yeti scalp belonging to the Buddhist Pangboche monastery in the Himalayas of Nepal. Despite all the efforts of hunters, no unquestionably genuine yeti remains have been made available for research

Right: 16-year-old Tim Meissner (left) estimates the height of a bigfoot he saw and shot at near his home in British Columbia, Canada, in April 1979. The creature, about 9 feet (2.7 metres) tall, was standing beside this tree when Tim saw it

usually red, but sometimes yellow or green.

The footprint evidence is also puzzling. Five-toed prints are most commonly found, resembling large human feet. But sometimes the prints appear to have only two toes, or three, four or sometimes six. Perhaps this anomaly is explicable in terms of over-eager investigators misinterpreting less than perfect footprints.

A significant number of reports, many of them made by experienced huntsmen, tell of a disturbing phenomenon: some bigfeet are apparently completely unharmed by bullets.

There seem to be three possible explanations: the guns used are just not powerful

Left: these bones are claimed by the monks of Pangboche monastery to be the skeletal hand of a yeti. Although the hand seems small in comparison with the scalp (opposite), the remains can be taken as evidence to support the theory that the yeti is a form of ape – the hands of many ape species are relatively small

enough to tackle such a creature, or the witness in his excitement did not aim properly (although some shots were fired from very close range) – or bigfeet are not made of flesh and blood.

Bigfeet and UFOs?

If the theory that bigfeet are not composed of flesh and blood sounds incredible, there is some even more extraordinary evidence that tends to support it: the claim that some bigfeet are apparently able to disappear or dematerialise. A Pennsylvanian woman, confronted by one on her doorstep one night in February 1974, shot into its middle from a distance of 6 feet (1.8 metres). She was astounded to see it disappear in a flash of light! Other eye-witnesses have reported signs of insubstantiality in the bigfeet they have seen.

In the Pennsylvania case the witness's son-in-law, who came to help on hearing the shot, saw other bigfeet at the edge of nearby woods. He also saw a bright red flashing light hovering over the woods. There are a

number of other cases in which UFOs and bigfeet are reported as having been seen at the same time and in the same area. Coincidence? Or are they both part of the same phenomenon?

Another strange case involving a UFO took place on a farm near Greensburg, Pennsylvania, on the evening of 25 October 1973. When a large, bright red luminous ball was seen to come down in a field a 22-year-old farmer's son, pseudonym Stephen, went to investigate. He and two 10-year-old boys he took with him saw the shining object on or close to the ground. They also saw, near the ball, two tall, ape-like creatures with green glowing eyes and long, dark hair. The creatures began to approach them.

Stephen fired over their heads, but they kept walking towards the witnesses. So he fired three rounds straight into the largest creature, which raised its hand. The UFO disappeared and the bigfeet turned and slowly walked into the nearby woods.

Investigators were immediately called in, and although they saw neither UFO nor bigfeet, they found a glowing area where the UFO had been. Stephen subsequently went into a trance.

Rival killers

Bigfoot cases with such bizarre details are by no means widespread. They are generally reported in states far away from the traditional bigfoot territory in the north west of the continent. Some of the veteran bigfoot hunters and investigators are sceptical of apparent paranormal cases, possibly feeling that they do not wish to become involved in fringe eccentricities.

Those hunters who feel it is now their

life's work to convince the world of the existence of the bigfoot have a hard task for, despite the mass of data, few professional scientists or anthropologists will give their work a second glance. Certainly, if a bigfoot corpse was obtained, their case would, of course, be incontrovertible. Consequently there is rivalry – even open hostility – among those hunters who compete to be first to capture or kill one. So far they have been totally unsuccessful.

Even the rare cases of killed or captured man-beasts have not resulted in any corpses being made available for study. In 1917 Swiss geologist Francois de Loys shot a 5-foot (1.5-metre) animal on the borders of Columbia and Venezuela, which zoologist Dr Bernard Heuvelmans believes may have been an unknown type of spider monkey.

Of many reports from the USSR, the most recent tells of a man-beast captured and later killed in the mountains near Buinaksk in Daghestan. A Soviet army officer, Colonel Karapetyan, saw the creature while it was still alive and later remembered it vividly:

Above: this 'man-beast' was shot by Swiss geologist Francois de Loys on the borders of Columbia and Venezuela in 1917. It is now thought it may have been a kind of spider monkey

Above right: a drawing of the hairy man-beast captured and killed near Buinaksk in Daghestan, USSR, in 1941. The creature was seen alive by Colonel V. S. Karapetyan (right) but was never made available for scientific research

I can still see the creature as it stood before me, a male, naked and bare-footed. And it was doubtlessly a man, because its entire shape was human. The chest, back, and shoulders, however, were covered with shaggy hair of a dark brown colour . . . his height was above average – about 180 centimetres [6 feet]. He stood before me like a giant, his mighty chest thrust forward. . . His eyes told me nothing. They were dull and empty – the eyes of an animal. And he seemed to me like an animal and nothing more . . . this was no disguised person, but a wild man of some kind.

In December 1968 came a report from Minnesota, USA, of a bigfoot corpse frozen in a block of ice. Dr Heuvelmans and biologist Ivan T. Sanderson saw it and, despite the difficulties of examination, were convinced that the ice contained the fresh corpse of a hitherto unknown form of hominid. For various complex reasons, however, the corpse was never made available for proper examination.

There are several reasons why, despite the number of sightings, hunters are not able simply to go into the forest and kill a bigfoot. Bigfeet are reputed to possess intimate knowledge of the terrain they inhabit such that they can travel through it far quicker than a man and remain completely concealed. Given these alleged characteristics the prospect for the hunter of capturing or killing one remains remote.

Most of the time, all the intrepid bigfoot hunter can do is interview witnesses, examine footprints, and collect newspaper reports. Such work, carried out by dedicated enthusiasts all over the North American continent, has resulted in an accumulation of data and many intriguing theories about the nature of bigfeet – and indeed all man-beasts. Nevertheless, without high-quality photographs, a corpse or a skeleton, or even part of one, all that scientists can do is speculate about possible explanations.

Man, beast . . . or hologram?

All we know for certain is that large, human-like footprints have been found in large numbers in remote areas – and not all of them are likely to be fakes – and that well over 1000 people in North America alone have reported seeing tall, hairy man-beasts. The various theories that have been put forward to explain these facts apply equally well to man-beasts seen all over the world.

On the negative side, it has been suggested that all man-beast reports are hoaxes. This seems unlikely. Another suggestion is that people may be misidentifying known animals under poor viewing conditions. This explanation could account for some of the sightings, but by no means all of them. Yet another view is that it is simply a case of hallucination. People who have seen too many horror films have had hallucinations –

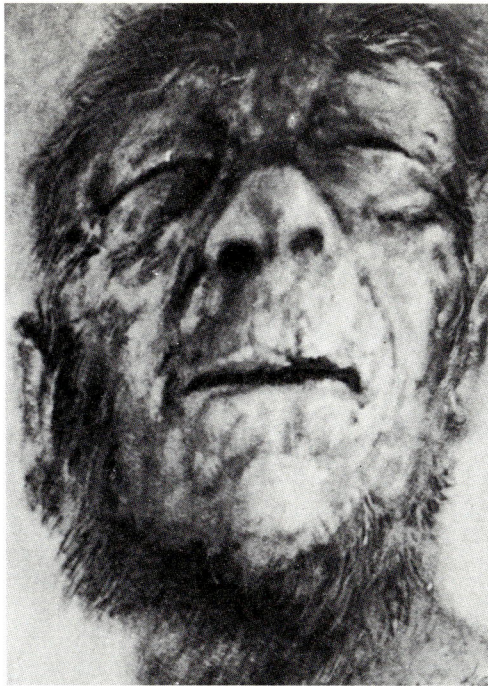

and claim to have seen something that simply is not there. May not man-beast sightings be a similar case? Such a theory does not, however, account for the footprints, which appear to be real enough.

A more sympathetic view is that the man-beasts may be some form of giant ape or perhaps an early form of man-like ape, *Gigantopithecus*. This seems possible, even likely in some parts of the world. Alternatively, man-beasts may really be men, pre-historic survivals that have managed to stay concealed against all the odds.

Some people have argued that man-beasts are some kind of paranormal phenomenon. They may come into being when certain types of energy are available (electrical, nuclear or psychic, for example). Bigfeet have sometimes been reported near energy sources. An even more remote possibility is that man-beasts come from UFOs, for reasons as yet unknown. Against this, it has been pointed out that if UFOs and man-beasts are both paranormal phenomena, they are just as likely to have been formed in the same way – which may explain why they sometimes appear close together in time and space. Finally, man-beasts could be holograms, three-dimensional images projected from space by an unknown intelligence. If so, who or what is doing it – and why?

Investigators differ in their interpretations of the data, and perhaps no one explanation can account for all the reported sightings. It is most likely that the term 'man-beasts' covers a wide range of phenomena that, for unknown reasons, appear – or seem to appear – in similar guises. Whatever the truth may be, the man-beast phenomenon is an extraordinary and complex one that requires a great deal more research before any firm conclusions can be drawn.

Left and below: sketches by biologist Ivan T. Sanderson of 'Bozo', a hairy man-beast seen frozen in a block of ice in Minnesota, USA, in December 1968. The owner apparently later replaced the corpse with a model – leaving only the evidence of Sanderson and zoologist Dr Bernard Heuvelmans, who had seen the original body, to prove it had ever existed

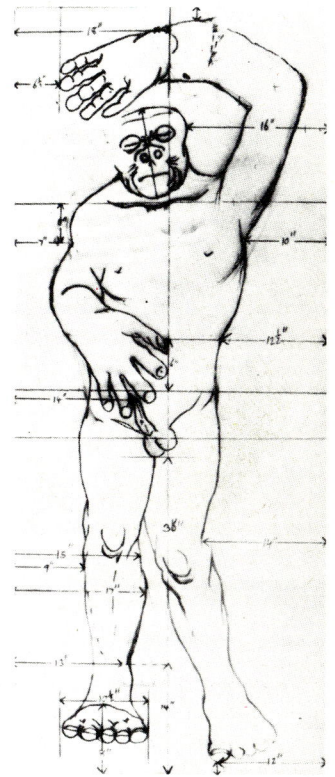

Further reading
Janet and Colin Bord, *Alien animals,* Paul Elek 1980
Janet and Colin Bord, *Bigfoot casebook,* Paul Elek 1981
Bernard Heuvelmans, *On the track of unknown animals,* Paladin 1970
John Napier, *Bigfoot,* Abacus 1976
Ivan T. Sanderson, *Abominable snowmen* Jove (New York) 1977
Ann B. Slate and Alan Berry, *Bigfoot,* Bantam (New York) 1976
Odette Tchernine, *The yeti,* Neville Spearman 1970

The case for Bridey Murphy

Have our lives been shaped not only by experiences and impressions gained since birth, but also by those from some other, previous existence? DAVID CHRISTIE-MURRAY discusses this vexed question and describes the remarkable case of an American, Mrs Virginia Tighe, who, under hypnosis, regressed over a hundred years to become an Irish woman – 'Bridey Murphy'

IN 1956 AND 1957, Emile Franckel conducted a series of live experiments for a Los Angeles television programme called *Adventures in Hypnotism*. Franckel's aim was to bring to the public's attention the possibility that individuals under hypnosis can relive previous lives. His attitude was sceptical: he believed that recollections of previous lives arose from promptings from the hypnotist or deep subconscious memory. Some of the experiences he was able to draw from his subjects, however, seemed unaccountable by this explanation. Since the hypnotist did not know his subjects, he could scarcely have induced their responses except by a series of coincidences too remarkable to be statistically acceptable as mere chance.

Yet Franckel was right to have remained sceptical. For although some of the results were so remarkable as to seem almost miraculous, hypnosis is a mental state that almost anyone may experience given the right circumstances and which almost everyone can produce in at least some subjects – provided, of course, that he has mastered a few simple techniques – techniques that should never be used merely as a party game nor for exhibition purposes, nor by anyone who is unaware of its dangers. This does not

mean that hypnosis is fully understood by the medical profession. The following cases illustrate some of the areas where our knowledge is still inadequate in explaining regression into previous lives under hypnosis.

We assume that the human personality consists of potentialities derived from a combination of factors – parents' genes, plus, perhaps, racial memories and other elements. If reincarnation is ever to be established as fact, these 'other elements' will include memories of previous lives.

What appears to happen under hypnosis is that the layers of experience we have all acquired during our lives – experiences that have pushed our memory of previous existences deep into the subconscious – comes to the surface. When the hypnotist suggests, for example, to a 30-year-old subject: 'It is now 1970. You are now 20—you are waking up on your 20th birthday. Tell me where you are, what is happening', the subject's life and development of the past 10 years are as if they had never been.

Practising hypnotists know that no two subjects ever behave exactly alike, for all human beings are unique in some way, and with many subjects there seems to be a 'shadow' personality—a fantasy personality

Below: King Richard II (1367–1400) and courtiers at Conway Castle, Wales. In 1906 a clergyman's daughter claimed, while under hypnosis, to have lived a previous life in the court of Richard II and to have known his mother, the 'Fair Maid of Kent'

that is only revealed sometimes in dreams or under hypnosis. And, the suggestion is, it is this 'fantasy personality' that is revealed, not recollection of a previous life.

How are we to distinguish between what may be mere fantasy and a true account of a previous life? As early as 1906 the Society for Psychical Research reported the case of an unnamed clergyman's daughter who, under hypnosis, recounted her life during the reign of Richard II. In that life she was no great lady herself – despite the claim by cynics that *all* cases of regression imagine themselves to be famous people – but an acquaintance of Maud, Countess of Salisbury, her friend Blanche Poynings, née Mowbray, and Richard's mother, 'Fair Maid of Kent'.

In this case, almost every historical fact stated under hypnosis was found to be true, as were details of the dress and food described by the girl. Moreover, she had no recollection of ever having read about either the period or the people.

Some early psychical researchers into hypnotic phenomena awoke their subjects and placed their hands on a planchette board, usually screened from the subjects' view, and proceeded to interrogate them. The planchette – it is claimed – wrote down true answers to the questions from knowledge in the subjects' subconscious minds. Under these conditions the girl revealed that she had just read an historical romance in which every person and fact, except for some minor details, had appeared, though she had devised a new setting for them.

If all cases were as straightforward as this, there would be no need for further investigation, and believers in reincarnation would have to look elsewhere for evidence. How complicated the majority of cases are, however, is shown by the celebrated case of

Bridey Murphy. This is no more remarkable than a hundred other cases of hypnotic regression, but was brought to the public's attention by a heated debate in a number of American newspapers and a film shown widely in English-speaking countries.

In a number of sessions from November 1952 to October 1953, Morey Bernstein, an amateur American hypnotist, regressed Mrs Virginia Tighe to a life in early 19th-century Ireland. Mrs Tighe, 29 years old at the time, a native of Maddison, Wisconsin, and resident in Chicago from the age of three until her marriage, had never visited Ireland, nor had much to do with Irish people (she

Right: Morey Bernstein, the American hypnotist, and Mrs Virginia Tighe. The account given by Mrs Tighe of her 'previous life' as 'Bridey Murphy' led Morey Bernstein to become a firm believer in reincarnation

Below: a view of Cork as it was in the mid 18th century. It was here that Mrs Tighe claimed she had previously been born as 'Bridey Murphy' in 1798

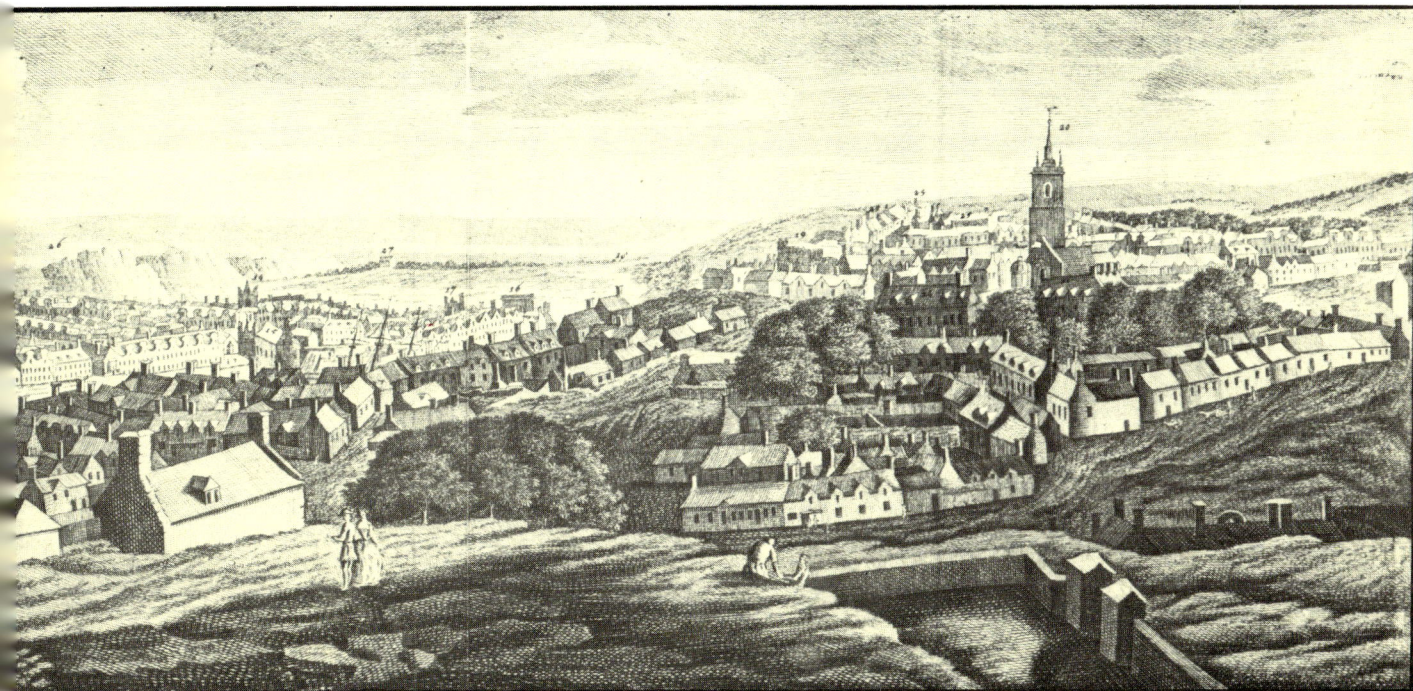

Right: kissing the Blarney Stone in the manner described by Mrs Tighe. Today, all one does is to lie on the back, hold on to two bars attached to the wall, lower the head and kiss the underside of the Stone. The earlier method, used at the time of 'Bridey Murphy', would not have been known by Mrs Tighe without her having done a great deal of research

Below: to counter the claim that he had in some way rigged his experiments, Morey Bernstein hypnotised Mrs Tighe only in the presence of two witnesses

Bottom: uillean pipes of the type 'Bridey Murphy' claims were played at her funeral in Cork in 1864

strongly denied allegations to the contrary, and the evidence supports her denials). Under hypnosis she began to speak with an Irish accent, said she was Bridget (Bridey) Murphy, daughter of Duncan and Kathleen Murphy, Protestants living at the Meadows, Cork. Her brother Duncan, born in 1796, married Aimée, daughter of Mrs Strayne, who was mistress of a day school attended by Bridey when she was 15.

In about 1818 she married a Catholic, Brian MacCarthy, whose relatives she named, and they travelled by carriage to Belfast through places she named but whose existence has never been found on any map.

The couple worshipped at Father John Gorman's St Theresa's Church. They shopped at stores that Bridey named, using coins correctly described for the period. In addition, Bridey produced a number of Irish words when asked, using some as they were used then, though their meaning had changed since: 'slip', for example, referring to a child's pinafore, not petticoat – the more common modern word. Bridey Murphy had read some Irish mythology, knew some Irish songs and was a good dancer of Irish jigs. At the end of one sitting, Mrs Tighe, aroused from her trance, yet not fully conscious,

KISSING THE BLARNEY STONE.

There is a Stone whoever kisses, / A clever spouter he'll sure turn out, or
Oh! he never misses to grow eloquent, / An out-and-outer to be let alone.
'Tis he may clamber to a lady's chamber / Don't hope to hinder him, or to bewilder him,
Or become a member of sweet Parliament. / Shure he's a Pilgrim from the Blarney Stone.

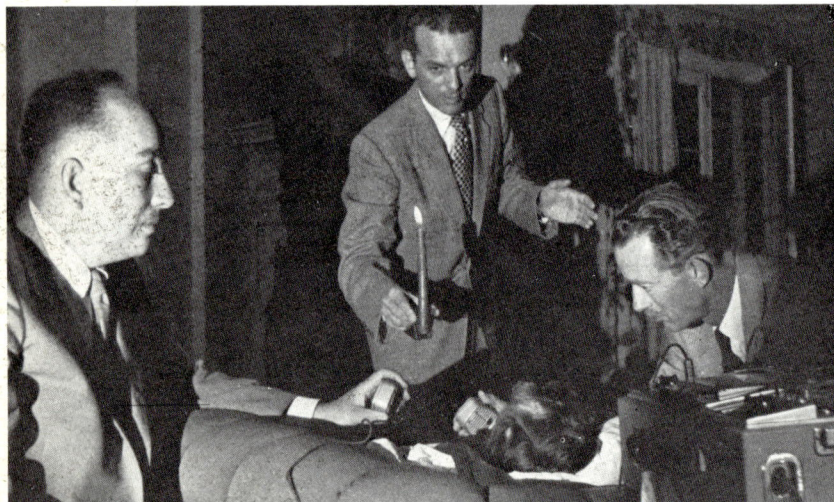

danced 'The Morning Jig', ending her performance with a stylised yawn. Her description of another dance was confirmed in detail by a lady whose parents had danced it. Another telling detail was that she described the correct procedure for kissing the Blarney Stone used in Bridey's day.

Bridey's story was investigated by the American magazine *Empire*. William Barker was commissioned by the magazine to spend three weeks in Ireland checking the facts 'Bridey' had given. His visit resulted in a 19,000-word report. Barker's account is typical of regression cases. Some facts were confirmed, others unconfirmed, others proved incorrect. Memories of insignificant detail proved true, while Bridey displayed total ignorance of other important events. Confirmation of facts proved impossible

in many instances. There was no possibility, for example, of confirming dates of birth, marriages and deaths, as no records were kept in Cork until 1864 and if the Murphy family kept records in a family Bible, a customary procedure, its whereabouts are not known. No information could be discovered concerning St Theresa's Church or Father Gorman in Belfast, but the two shops mentioned by Bridey, Carrigan and Farr, had both existed. Bridey had said that uillean pipes had been played at her funeral and these were found to have been customarily used at funerals because of their soft tone.

So the neutral enquirer is left puzzled. Where did Mrs Tighe learn about uillean pipes, kissing the Blarney Stone and the names of shops in Belfast whose existence was only confirmed after painstaking research? Why should she have created a vivid picture of life in Ireland at the beginning of the 19th century, if this was simply a creation of some part of her subconscious? From where did she – along with many other regressed subjects with no pretence at acting ability – draw the talent to dramatise so effectively a life in another age and another country?

Yet, if reincarnation is a fact, why should trivialities be remembered and great emotional experiences that one would have expected to have contributed to one's development in this life, be forgotten or go unmentioned? The questions are as bewildering as they are intriguing.

If we have lived past lives, why do we not remember them? See page 104

Cosmic construction: Building a black hole

In the not too distant future a fleet of 'cosmic bulldozers' could be crossing the Galaxy to build an artificial black hole, one light-year from the Sun. Such a task, says ADRIAN BERRY, is by no means impossible

A visit to distant parts of the Milky Way is inconceivable by any known means of travel. By building an artificial black hole, within range of a conventional spaceship from Earth, we may be able to traverse the Galaxy instantaneously

Inset above: despite the obstruction of dust clouds, astronomers are able to see enough of our Galaxy to realize it is spiral-shaped, like Coma Berenices

Inset left: the nearest known black hole is situated in Cygnus X-1, 6000 light-years away. An artificial black hole, however, could be built nearer to Earth, one light-year from the Sun

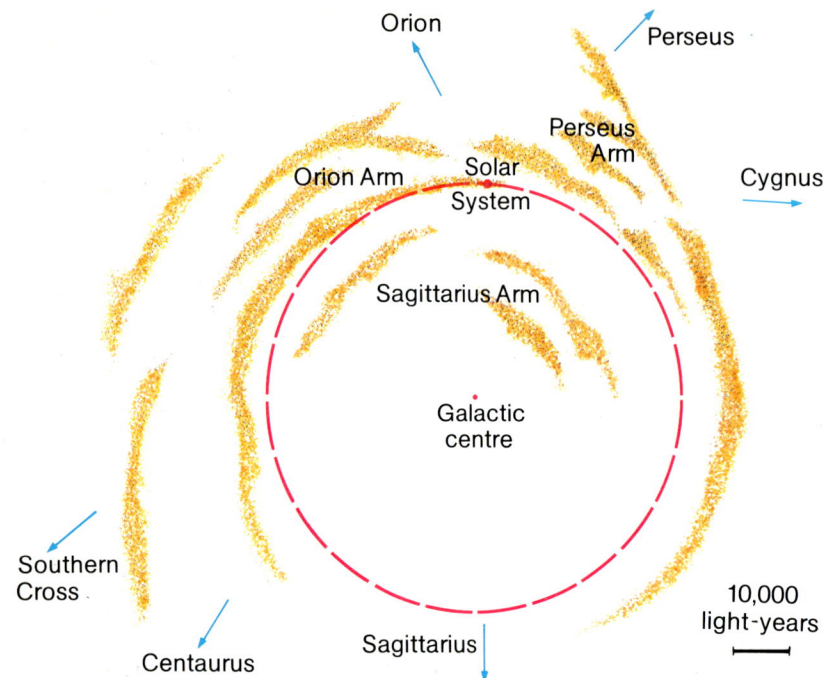

10,000 light-years

A JOURNEY TO our nearest star neighbour in the Milky Way would take over 4 years in a spaceship travelling close to the speed of light (670 million mph, 1000 million km/h). To reach more distant stars would take centuries – even assuming that we could construct a spaceship capable of travelling close to the speed of light.

We are thus presented with a problem that seems to place a severe restriction on our ability to journey to the stars. But the discovery of black holes has opened up the possibility of a totally new form of space travel: one in which a spaceship can disappear into a black hole and reappear almost instantly in another part of our Universe, without having passed any point in between. As we have seen in previous articles, the possibility of making such a journey is not ruled out by science, indeed it follows remorselessly from fundamental scientific principles. The problem that we have to overcome is a practical one – how are we to reach the nearest black hole?

Astronomers think that the nearest black hole lies some 6000 light-years away in the constellation of Cygnus. The distance a spaceship would have to cover to reach Cygnus is immense: 36,000 million million miles (58,000 million million kilometres). How is it ever going to be possible for us to cover such an incredible distance?

What I propose may, at a first consideration, be regarded as raving insanity. I suggest that we create an *artificial* black hole within our own Galaxy, through which we can travel to other parts of our Universe instantaneously.

The creation of a black hole, of course, requires far more energy than any human society could hope to generate unless it was helped by nature. But stealing energy from

Above: the Orion Arm contains vast quantities of iron, nickel and other raw materials. These could be used to construct an artificial black hole

Below: asteroids present the best and most accessible objects to convert into 'cosmic bulldozers'. A supercharged Bussard ramjet added to a hollowed-out asteroid would be able to scoop up material along a vast magnetic field

nature has been a common practice of science since the 17th century.

Within a sphere with a radius of one light-year round the Sun lies the belt of cosmic dust called the Arm of Orion. This dust is more than just debris, however. We know from the millions of tons of this material that has fallen to Earth that by far the greatest part is nickel and iron. It was from this material that our Sun was formed billions of years ago. Such material is ideal for constructing a black hole because it is capable, in certain circumstances, of being moved great distances by the field of a magnet.

The problem facing our descendants, however, will be how to transform this material into a manageable form that can then be magnetised.

Fortunately there is an answer to this problem. If hydrogen, the interstellar hydrogen that exists in relatively high densities inside the Arm of Orion, could be heated up until it becomes plasma, it would respond to a magnetic field. Plasma, the fourth state of matter beyond the three states of solid, liquid and gas, is matter whose electrons have been stripped away from the atoms. All substances become plasma when heated to about 40,000°F (22,000°C).

How might our descendants heat up interstellar hydrogen? The answer is quite simple: they could do it by shining very intense laser beams directly at the hydrogen. This will cause the hydrogen to undergo a rapid increase in temperature until it reaches the point at which it ionises (its electrons separate from its atoms) and becomes plasma.

A large fleet of spaceships acting as magnetic scoops will have to move through the Orion Arm, pushing iron, nickel, hydrogen plasma and other ionised interstellar material before them. And to achieve this ionisation,

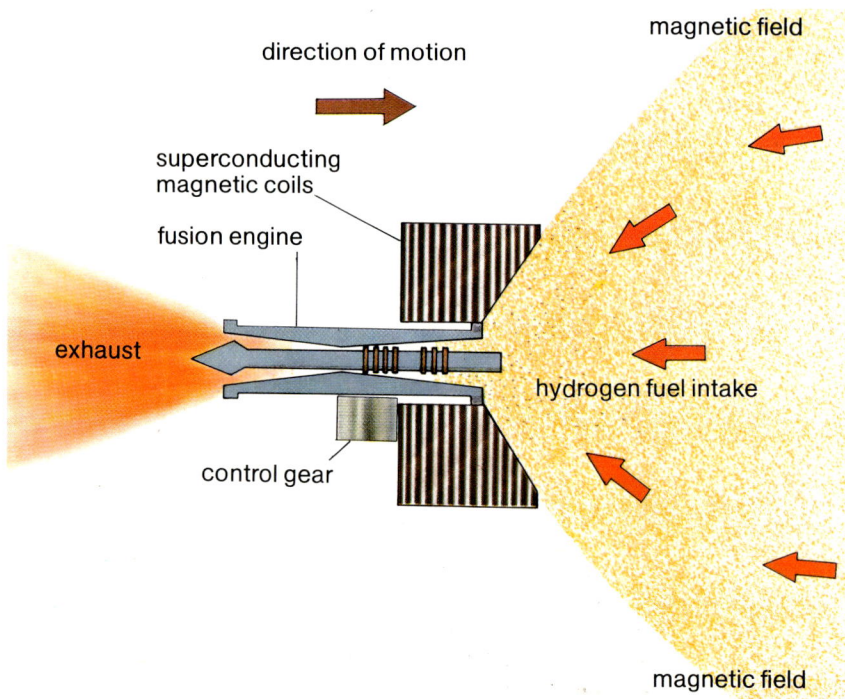

direction of motion

magnetic field

superconducting magnetic coils

fusion engine

exhaust

control gear

hydrogen fuel intake

magnetic field

each scoop-vehicle will bombard the interstellar medium with the most powerful laser beams that the scientists of that distant age will have been able to devise.

Using magnetic fields in space as giant interstellar bulldozers to accumulate matter will be a difficult task, but in essence it is much simpler than achieving a fusion reaction inside a closed container, as scientists are now trying to do. The idea of a magnetic scoop in space has been thought of before, but for a different purpose. The concept will be familiar to people who have considered the feasibility of interstellar travel; I do not mean those few who have discussed instantaneous journeys, but the many who have long brooded on the problem of how to accelerate to a speed close to that of light.

As Robert Bussard pointed out in 1960, even with the most efficient means of propulsion yet conceived, no spaceship would be able to achieve the speed of light because it would need to carry millions of times its own

material can be used as fuel. The rest of it piles up in front of the vehicle. Acceleration becomes increasingly more difficult, for the ramjet engine is expending energy pushing its way through the plasma (which the ramjet itself has accumulated) that it ought to be expending on accelerating the ship. So a simple ramjet engine could never succeed in accelerating a ship to anything more than a low percentage of the speed of light.

But a low percentage of the speed of light will be perfectly suitable for the purpose of accumulating matter and bulldozing it forward. Ships will be launched into interstellar space with no other purpose but to collect the material for constructing a black hole.

Some further practical questions must now be discussed. What kinds of ships will be needed? Where would they be constructed? And above all, how much interstellar material could they accumulate and drive before them in how short a time?

Between the orbits of Jupiter and Mars is

The Asteroid Belt, as the diagram shows, is well within range of a spaceship from Earth. Space probes, for example, have already reached Jupiter – beyond the Asteroid Belt

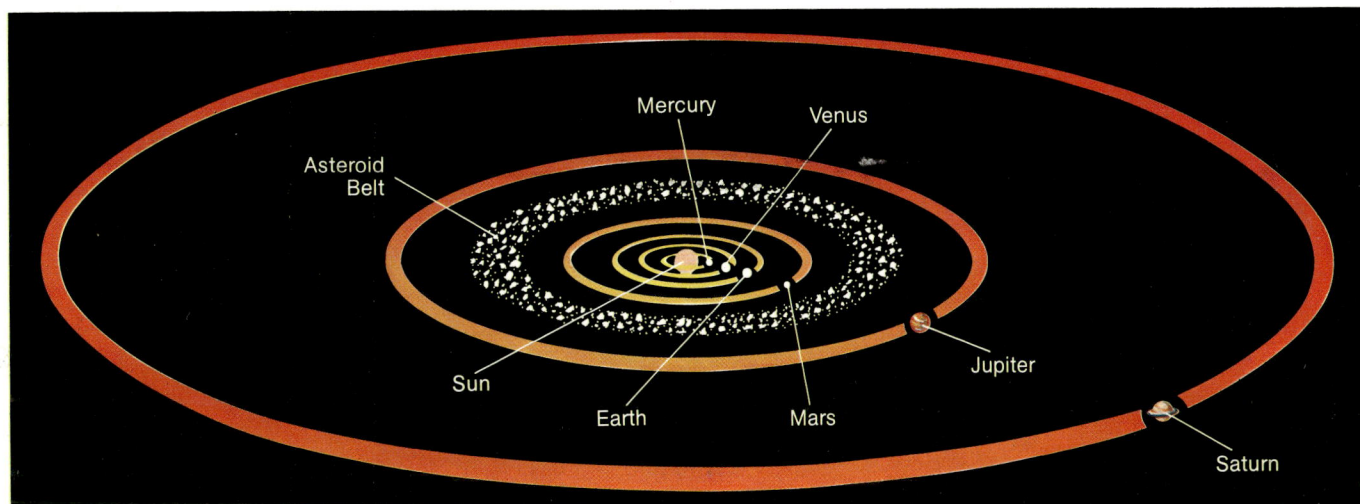

weight in fuel. Bussard worked out a possible solution to this problem, which is known as the Bussard 'ramjet'.

This ramjet would operate on a similar principle to the air-breathing jet aircraft engine, which sucks in air in the front and expels it in the rear. Bussard's ramjet, to be used on an interstellar spaceship, would carry in front of it huge magnetic fields, thousands of miles in radius, which would scoop up particles of ionised hydrogen as it passed through space. The collected hydrogen would enter the fuel tanks and power the spaceship through a fusion engine. It would be possible to construct a black hole of 10 Solar masses about one light-year from the Sun, using the same basic method as that of Bussard's ramjet.

But the ramjet system, as envisaged by Bussard, is inherently inefficient in the sense that it would fail to achieve its aim, namely to accelerate a ship to a speed close to that of light. The reason is obvious. According to engineers who have studied the problem, only about 1 per cent of the interstellar

a great ring of tiny planets known as the Asteroid Belt. Numbering about 50,000, these lumps of rock range from Ceres, the largest, which is about 430 miles (690 kilometres) across, to much smaller fragments a few hundred yards in diameter. Some of these medium-sized asteroids can be adapted to serve as magnetic ramjets.

Asteroids have often been proposed as raw material for space engineering works. Being of extremely low mass compared with planets, they will be much easier to explore and redesign.

We can now envisage perhaps a thousand gigantic unmanned spaceships – redesigned asteroids – accelerating out of the Solar System in slightly different directions as they follow a rigid mathematical plan. They will be travelling, by different routes, to a point one light-year from the Sun, on a direct line with the central regions of the Galaxy, where the black hole is to be constructed.

Once through the black hole, how will our astronaut get back again? See page 118

Mysteries of the human bonfire

Medical men and scientists have long doubted that spontaneous human combustion actually occurs. But the facts stubbornly refuse to fit their conventional explanations. BOB RICKARD suggests that behind the mysterious burning lies a rare and complex series of events

DEATHS THAT APPEAR to have been caused by spontaneous human combustion (SHC) have always been an embarrassment to the medical profession. The refusal to believe in SHC is not the result of a deliberate conspiracy to suppress the evidence, however. Rather there has been a turning away, a wish not to think about such an outrage of accepted medical and scentific knowledge.

If SHC is mentioned at all, it is only to be dismissed as a belief mistakenly held by the uninformed, or as a superstition lingering from less enlightened times. J. L. Casper, for example, in his *Handbook of the practice of forensic medicine*, complained: 'It is sad to think that in an earnest scientific work, in this year of grace 1861, we must still treat of the fable of "spontaneous combustion".' And opinion today is hardly less compromising. Dr Gavin Thurston, the coroner for Inner West London, has said that 'no such phenomenon as spontaneous combustion exists, or has ever occurred'.

At the same time, those scientists and doctors who have examined the effects closely, acknowledge that there have been cases of death by burning that are genuinely inexplicable. But since SHC officially does not exist, some other reason has had to be found for the same effects. And so the notion of

'preternatural combustibility' was born.

The next step was to identify the causes of such a combustibility – and, in any given case, to discover its source of ignition. So, in the middle of the 19th century, a typical SHC victim was thought to be almost certainly a drinker and a smoker; most likely an elderly, solitary, corpulent woman of sedentary habits. Alcohol was both the physical and the moral cause of conflagration. Horrific tales circulated about divine punishment for inebriation, in which the lambent and inextinguishable flames were but a foretaste of the everlasting hellfire to come. Boineau, a French priest, reported the 1749 case of an 80-year-old woman reduced to a carbonised skeleton as she sat sipping brandy. As Baron Justus von Liebig noted sarcastically, 'The chair, which of course had not sinned, did not burn.'

Liebig, in fact, sceptical of SHC though he was, utterly discredited the notion that there was any connection between the phenomenon and drinking. Liebig showed conclusively that alcohol-saturated flesh will burn only until the alcohol is used up; and fatty tissue behaves in the same way – when it can be set alight.

In his 1965 article in *Medicine, science and the law*, Dr D. J. Gee, a lecturer in forensic

Top: Only the legs remain of Mrs E.M., a widow who died on 29 January 1958. Was she burnt by the fire in the grate, or did she combust of her own accord?

Above: Dr Gavin Thurston, who has firmly stated that SHC has never taken place

medicine at Leeds University, described his own experiments following his examination of a charred corpse in 1963. Dr Gee successfully set light to small quantities of fat, but the burning could be sustained only by placing the sample in a strong draught. Even this resulted in no more than a slow smouldering, not the spectacular blaze typical of SHC. However, this has only made it necessary for investigators of what would otherwise be admitted as cases of SHC to look for the 'explanatory' sustaining draught, and prompted some writers to highlight victims who were found in or near a fireplace, where there would be such an updraught.

The readiness with which coroners have adopted these suggestions seems to indicate a strong desire to terminate the proceedings as quickly, conveniently and 'reasonably' as possible, rather than admit a bizarre and frightening mystery. Some verdicts are far from satisfactory. Consider the case of Grace Pett, a fishwife of Ipswich, who was found on the morning of 10 April 1744, lying on the floor near the grate, and burning 'like a block of wood . . . with a glowing fire without flame'. After the fire was put out, Grace was seen to be 'like a heap of charcoal covered with white ashes'. That Grace was a regular smoker, and had the previous evening 'drunk plentifully of gin' in welcoming a daughter

home from Gibraltar, were sufficient for the advocates of temperance and preternatural combustibility.

There are several details in this case, however, that afford these apologists no comfort. According to the account in Sir David Brewster's *Natural magic* (1842) there had been no fire at all in the grate, and a candle, in use that fateful evening, had burnt down safely overnight in its candlestick. And worse: 'The clothes of a child on one side of her, and a paper screen on the other were untouched', and the wooden floor beneath her burning body 'was neither singed nor discoloured'.

Can we, in the 20th century, offer an alternative explanation for SHC besides 'preternatural combustibility'? The savants of the 19th century can be forgiven for thinking only in terms of conventional fire. But since the admirable Liebig's day the physical and medical sciences have made enormous progress. Today we know of many forms of death that can penetrate a man's body silently and invisibly. Military research into 'radiation weapons' has supplemented nuclear radiation with beamed ultrasound, x-ray lasers, microwave projectors and other horrors, all of which can cook a man inside his clothes. But the spirit of Liebig exhorts us to be rigorous: even if we credit the idea of an

Sir David Brewster, whose account of one fire death bears all the marks of a case of SHC. The coroner, however, thought otherwise

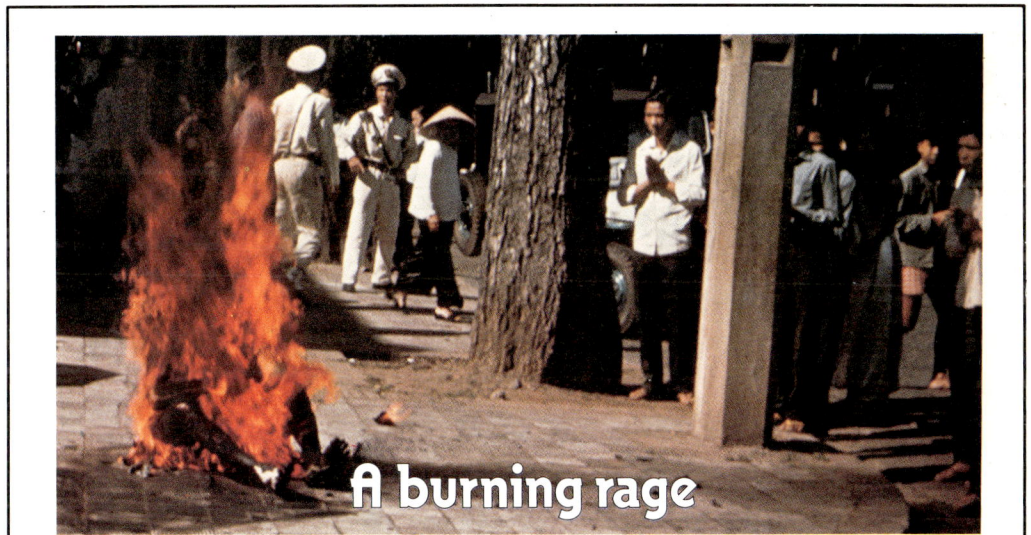

A burning rage

Reviewing the cases of SHC in his book *Mysterious fires and lights* (1967), veteran Fortean Vincent Gaddis noted that a high proportion of victims had apparently given up on life. 'Some were alcoholics, and alcoholism is a form of escape from reality . . . Most were elderly with lowered resistance and perhaps tired of life. Many were invalids or poverty-stricken, dying in rest homes or almshouses. Many led idle, sedentary lives.' Charles Fort and his successors have also observed a significant number of 'no-hopers' among SHC victims. In *Fire from heaven* Michael Harrison suggests that

there are several kinds of SHC, one of which is self-induced by people who are depressed, lonely, deprived, frightened and perhaps resentful. Harrison wonders if normally controlled reserves of physical and psychical energy are not suddenly released in a fatal conflagration, as a kind of 'psychic suicide'.

Suicide by fire has always had symbolic overtones, and has been used to make a political gesture. That a massive build-up of rage or despair may result in a spontaneous blaze is appealing, but it is highly conjectural. Besides, it would account for only some cases.

ubiquitous madman recently on the loose with a death ray, we still have to account for the instances from the past.

There are in fact a number of theories that might account for SHC, though not all are equally attractive. Among the least likely are the 'psychic suicide' theory (see box), and the proposition that people whose clothes are set alight catch fire themselves.

This was the suggestion in the case of Phyllis Newcombe. At midnight on 27 August 1938 she and her fiancé were leaving the dance floor of a Chelmsford ballroom, when she suddenly screamed. Her crinoline dress had become a mass of flames. It was put out with some difficulty – and too late, for Phyllis died in hospital a few hours later. At the inquest it was suggested that a discarded cigarette had set the dress alight. The material flamed when a lighter was put to it, but failed to catch fire when lit cigarettes were thrown at it. The coroner expressed his puzzlement and gave a verdict of accidental death. Puzzled he might have been, since in any case external fires cannot produce burns as extensive as those in SHC cases unless large quantities of fuel and oxygen are supplied over a considerable period of time. Even when these conditions are met, the body is burnt from the outside *in*. But there are many cases of SHC in which the burning takes place *within* the flesh, and the clothes or surroundings remain unharmed.

Another somewhat unsatisfactory thesis is the 'corrosive liquid' theory, and it likewise attempts to explain *away* certain cases of death by fire. Nevertheless this was the reason suggested for the death of Madge Knight. At about 3.30 a.m. on 19 November

The scorching of a slim lady

Photographic evidence of bizarre burning deaths is very rare and not readily accessible even to the dedicated and bona fide researcher. The charred remains shown here are of 'a slim lady, 85 years old, who was in good health' when she was consumed by flames in November 1963. The case was investigated by Dr D. J. Gee. Because of extensive damage to the body (but to little else) it was assumed that the victim had been in a state of unusual combustibility, and was set alight by an ember or a spark – a theory that would accord with the results of Dr Gee's experiments and the theory of preternatural combustibility.

Conflagration of a clergyman

While away from his parish in Stockcross, Newbury, England, the Reverend Mr Adams burned to death in a hotel room in New York, in 1876, apparently as a result of spontaneous combustion. In *Fire from heaven*, Michael Harrison remarks that 'ecclesiastics, as a class' seem strangely vulnerable to SHC and other paranormal heat phenomena.

1943 she was asleep alone in the spare room of her house in Aldingbourne, Sussex. She awoke feeling as if she were on fire. Her screams brought her husband and others who were sharing the house.

Madge was naked under the bedclothes, but she was in agony because extensive burning had removed most of the skin from her back. A doctor administered morphine, and, bemused, called in a Harley Street specialist. The specialist later told the coroner that he thought the burns must have been caused by a corrosive liquid because there was no sign of fire on the sheets or anywhere else in the room, and no smell of burning. Madge was repeatedly questioned but could not, or would not, say what had happened before she died in hospital in Chichester, on 6 December.

The lack of any sign of fire in many cases has led some researchers to theorise about substances that can burn without flame. In Madge Knight's case, no trace of any corrosive chemical could be found, nor any possible container for it. The notion that Madge hid the evidence before crawling into bed is too absurd to contemplate.

Perhaps the most fruitful clue to the

nature of the phenomenon came in 1975, with Livingstone Gearhart's article in the Fortean journal *Pursuit*. He had discovered that a significant number of SHC cases took place on or near a peak in the geomagnetic flux. The strength of the Earth's magnetic field rises and falls quite dramatically in relation to solar activity. Global averages of the daily figures are gathered for astronomers and geophysicists, and these show a distinct correlation between the incidence of SHC and high geomagnetic readings. This seems to indicate that SHC may be the result of a very complex chain of events, in which there is an interaction between certain astronomical conditions and the state of an individual's body. These in turn form the preconditions for the 'ball lightning' theory.

Ball lightning has been offered as one possible culprit for Mrs Reeser's demise. And hers is not the only case. According to an article in *Fate* (April 1961) by the Reverend Winogene Savage, a friend's brother awoke one morning to his wife's screams. Rushing to their living room he found her on the floor, ablaze, with a strange fireball hovering over her blackened form. With the help of neighbours and several buckets of water the flames were put out; but the lady later died, and her husband suffered burns from his ministrations. Witnesses noted that although the wife's clothes had been burnt off, there was no scorching on the rug where she had collapsed, and no other sign of fire damage in the room.

Death from natural causes
Maxwell Cade and Delphine Davis include this account in their 1969 study of ball lightning, *Taming of the thunderbolts*, and note its similarity to the records of spontaneous human combustion. They review the theories of several physicists who suggest that the huge energies of ball lightning could, in certain circumstances, manifest short radio waves of the kind used in microwave ovens. And they speculate:

If this theory is correct . . . it is possible for victims to be burned to death, not merely within their clothes, but even within their skin, either by the proximity of a lightning ball or by having a ball form within their body, or just by the action of the intense radio-frequency field which, in the absence of their body, would have formed a lightning ball at that place.

As it is a natural phenomenon, and because ball lightning is notoriously capricious, it is the best candidate so far for the cause of SHC cases, whether ancient or modern. It would also account for the victims being fried from the inside out. Microwave diathermy can heat different materials at different rates, and this may explain the curious phenomenon of selective burning that is associated with SHC.

Not one of these theories can account by

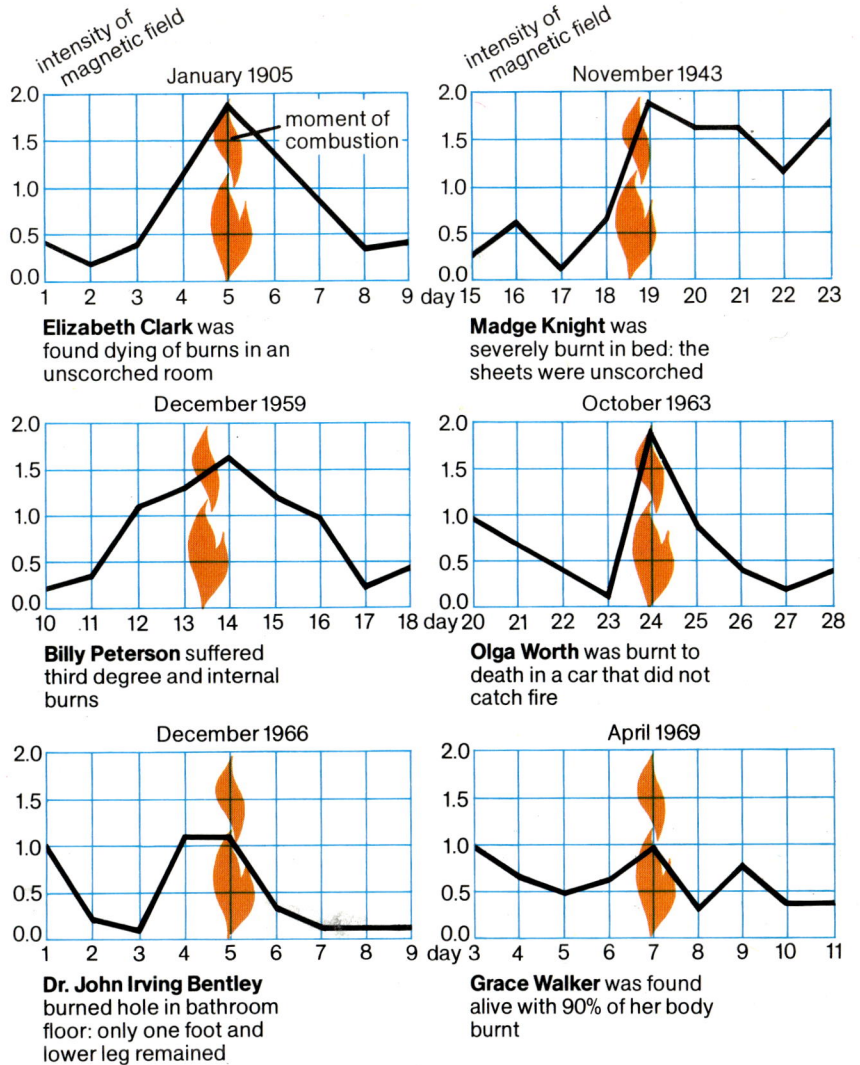

January 1905

moment of combustion

Elizabeth Clark was found dying of burns in an unscorched room

November 1943

Madge Knight was severely burnt in bed: the sheets were unscorched

December 1959

Billy Peterson suffered third degree and internal burns

October 1963

Olga Worth was burnt to death in a car that did not catch fire

December 1966

Dr. John Irving Bentley burned hole in bathroom floor: only one foot and lower leg remained

April 1969

Grace Walker was found alive with 90% of her body burnt

itself for the bizarre varieties of burning that have been authoritatively recorded. The fact that SHC occurs infrequently (if not so rarely as some writers claim) also suggests that it requires special circumstances to come about, and depends on the correct conjunction of many necessary factors. Some we can guess at; others remain unknown. But we can at least offer the following synthesis.

Age and sex seem less important than the victim's psychic and physiological state. We may imagine a lonely, sedentary person, incapacitated by illness or injury, or psychically by despair, fear, depression and perhaps resentment. This incapacity may psychosomatically affect the body and its metabolism, causing an imbalance of phosphagens and erratic behaviour in the body's heat-regulating mechanisms. Normally, this state would pass unnoticed. But imagine that it should happen a few days after intense sunspot activity, with a magnetic storm pushing up the value of the geomagnetic field to abnormal heights for the victim's locality. Now all that is needed is a trigger: a cosmic ray, a natural burst of low-frequency energy, or a lightning ball. And then we have a human bonfire.

The force of the Earth's magnetism is surprisingly uneven. It is unequally distributed around the globe, and fluctuates in intensity (measured in gausses). These six charts show the curious relationship between a high reading on the geomagnetic scale and the incidence of SHC

Further reading
Maxwell Cade and Delphine Davis, *Taming of the thunderbolts*, Abelard-Schuman 1969
Charles Fort, *Complete books*, Dover (New York) 1976
Vincent Gaddis, *Mysterious fires and lights*, Dell (New York) 1968
Michael Harrison, *Fire from heaven*, Pan 1977
Francis Hitching, *The world atlas of mysteries*, Pan 1979

On an H-bomb to the stars

Harnessing the awesome energy of the H-bomb and using the pressure exerted by sunlight – 'solar sailing' – are two revolutionary ideas in space travel research. Even so, says TONY OSMAN, alien technology may be far more sophisticated than anything we can imagine

THE UFO SIGHTINGS of the past 30 years have caught the imaginations of aircraft designers – as well as hoaxers – throughout the world. Sometimes the results have been elaborate hoaxes, but some serious research has also been done, and prototype models of some saucer-shaped aircraft have actually been made. Designed to operate within the Earth's atmosphere, they are powered by traditional chemical fuels. Some are large-scale passenger or freight vehicles, others small craft that might one day replace helicopters and introduce the flying car.

Designers have been researching revolutionary new power sources and planning craft capable of space travel. Many theories have been advanced as to how UFOs might fly, and some of these may one day be of use in designing long-distance spacecraft. Among the wilder ideas are the use of anti-gravity, time warps to cut the journey time between distant planets, or even 'gravitic propulsion' – in which the spacecraft, by some unspecified means, would generate its own gravitational field which it would then literally *fall* into. The spacecraft could travel in any direction by projecting its gravitational field in front of it.

One of the exciting new ideas for space travel, which has actually reached the drawing board and will soon be tried out, is solar sailing. Sunlight exerts a pressure and in space this pressure could be used to power a spacecraft. It would have to be lifted from the surface of the Earth using normal rocket power, but once in space it could unfurl giant reflecting sails. Because the fuel would not have to be carried inside the spacecraft, there would be no limit to the distance it could travel. None of the UFO reports on record describe craft with solar sails, but this is hardly surprising – they are not suitable for use within the Earth's atmosphere, where most UFOs are seen. If we, or the inhabitants of other planets, wish to travel long distances, solar sailing could well be the way to go.

British Rail has gone one step further than most inventors of new spacecraft and has actually patented a design. The complete specification was filed with the Patent Office in London on 10 March 1972.

The 'space vehicle', as described and illustrated in the patent, is saucer-shaped with windows round the edge – like so many of the classic 'flying saucers' reported in UFO sightings. It is powered by a controlled

Below left: farmer Dick Jennings examines a 'flying saucer' he found in a field near Chippenham in Wiltshire on 4 September 1967, while a policeman looks on. It was one of six found in a straight line from Somerset to Kent – all of which proved to be fakes

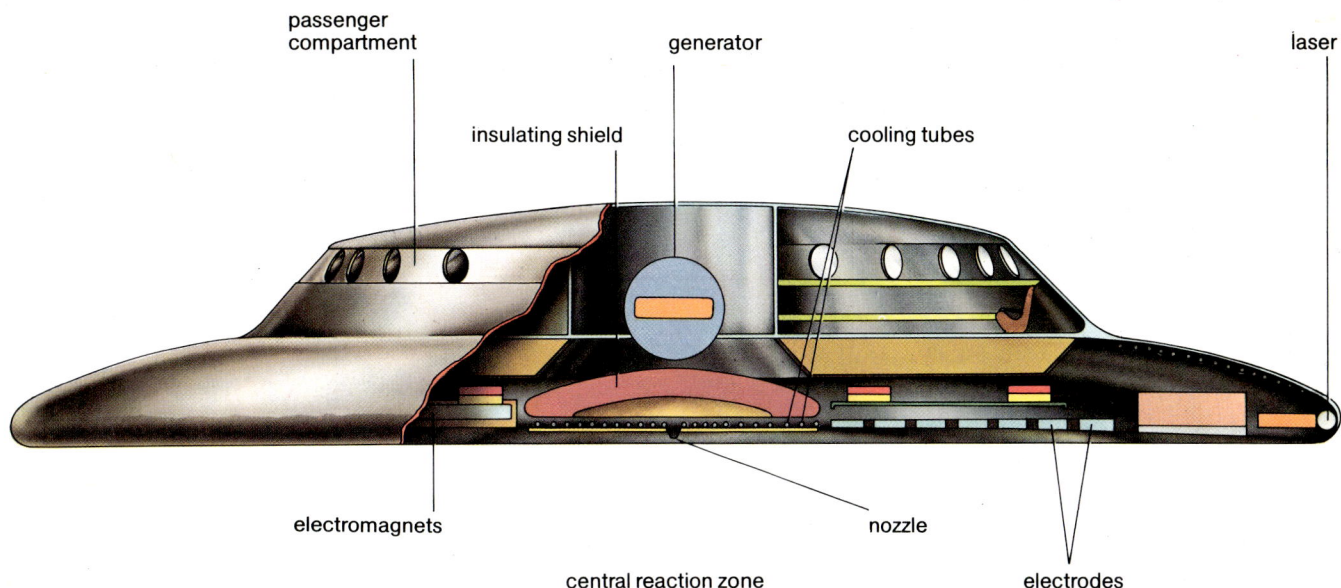

passenger compartment · generator · laser · insulating shield · cooling tubes · electromagnets · central reaction zone · nozzle · electrodes

thermonuclear reaction – a hydrogen bomb. Controlled in this sense means that the reaction goes on more or less continuously rather than in a series of single explosions.

In a thermonuclear reaction two atoms of hydrogen, or some other light element, are forced to combine to form a different and heavier element such as helium. This reaction produces nuclear radiation plus a very large amount of energy. For British Rail's purposes the radiation is very important: it consists of an enormous number of electrically charged particles, driven powerfully outwards by the energy of the thermonuclear reaction just as hot gases are driven away from a normal rocket by the energy of the

burning. The particles that travel away from the spacecraft can be carefully directed using powerful electro-magnets to give a strong thrust as well as to steer the spacecraft. Electrodes can be placed in the stream of particles to collect energy to run the equipment inside the spacecraft.

A fusion reaction demands an enormous amount of concentrated energy to start it off. The hydrogen bomb uses an atom bomb to trigger the reaction; in the British Rail spacecraft, the initial energy comes from one or more pulsed laser beams focused onto a central reaction zone. A nozzle leading to this area fills it with the vehicle fuel, which is either hydrogen or one of its isotopes. The rest of the spacecraft is protected from the explosions as well as from the radiation from the stream of nuclear particles produced by the reaction by a thick, rigid disc above the reaction zone. The frequency of the explosions is designed to be greater than 1000 per second to avoid structural vibration within the vehicle. The initial pulses of electricity to run the lasers come from a generator mounted centrally on top of the protective disc.

British Rail's patent contains no details of the size of the spacecraft, its crew or its power to fuel ratio – but in theory the possibilities are unlimited. Because the fuel the craft uses has an enormous amount of energy in proportion to its mass, it could carry enough fuel to travel vast distances into outer space. We do not yet have the technology that would enable us to manufacture such a spacecraft. We don't know what technology might have been developed by civilisations on planets other than ours and it is possible that their spacecraft are powered by fuels we know nothing about. But we do know that visitors from other parts of space *could* reach us in spacecraft similar to the one envisaged by British Rail.

Above: after the high–speed train – the space vehicle? In British Rail's patented design for a spacecraft, the power comes from a controlled nuclear fusion reaction – the same kind of reaction as produces the immense destructive energy of a hydrogen bomb (opposite)

Left: a prototype of a giant 'flying saucer' that could completely revolutionise air transport. Designed by a British firm, Airship Industries, this Skyship will be able to hold as many as 105 transport aircraft and cruise at about 100 miles per hour (160 km/h) at an altitude of 5000 feet (1520 metres)

Further reading
Leonard G. Cramp, *Piece for a jigsaw*, Summerton 1966
Leonard G. Cramp, *Space, gravity and the flying saucer*, T Werner Laurie 1954
Harry Harrison and Malcolm Edwards, *Spacecraft in fact and fiction*, Orbis 1979

Monsters of the deep

For thousands of years, sightings of strange sea monsters have been reported around the world. Here, JANET and COLIN BORD argue that the ocean depths contain many creatures as yet unknown to science, and that these reports should not be discounted as wild imaginings

WITH MORE THAN 60 per cent of the Earth's surface covered with water, it is hardly surprising that sightings of giant underwater monsters have been reported since antiquity. Even today, marine biologists, who have long been aware of the vast unexplored depths of the Earth's oceans, cautiously accept that the numerous reports of sea monster sightings seem to provide evidence that many creatures, at present unknown and unclassified, may be living in the dark and hidden waters.

The Biblical beast of evil, the leviathan ('the twisting serpent . . . the dragon that is in the sea') is mentioned in the Old Testament five times, and from the Norsemen to the Aborigines in Australia, from the Chinese to the American Indians, ancient mythologies speak of giant sea serpents.

Many of the early reports of sea monsters were collected by Scandinavian ecclesiastics. Archbishop Olaf Mansson, now better known as Olaus Magnus, who was exiled to Rome after the Swedish Reformation in the early 16th century, published a natural history of the northern lands in 1555 that contained reports of sea serpents. He described a sea serpent 200 feet (60 metres) long and 20 feet (6 metres) thick that would eat calves, lambs and hogs, and would even pluck men from boats. Archbishop Magnus also stated that the monster's appearance foretold disasters such as wars.

Interestingly, Magnus described the sea serpent as being black, having hair hanging from its neck (or mane), shining eyes, and putting its 'head on high like a pillar'. These characteristics also appear in recent sighting reports, suggesting that Olaus Magnus was writing about originally factual reports that had become distorted and embroidered with much retelling.

Two hundred years later historians were still recording sightings of sea serpents, though the clergy still maintained that these were sightings of the beast of evil. On 6 July 1734 a sea monster appeared off the coast of Greenland, and was reported by a Norwegian missionary, Hans Egede. In 1741 he wrote that its body was as bulky as a ship and was three or four times as long, and that it leapt from the water and plunged back again.

Another 18th-century writer on the mystery of the sea serpent was the Bishop of Bergen, Erik Pontoppidan. After detailed enquiry he found that hardly a year went by without some sea serpent sightings along the Scandinavian coastline and he published his findings in 1752.

A year earlier Bishop Pontoppidan had arranged for a letter from Captain Lorenz von Ferry to be read to the Bergen Court of Justice, in which was described a sea serpent that the Captain and his crew had seen in 1746 while rowing ashore to Molde in Norway. He said it had a grey head like a

Above: the eminent British naturalist, Sir Joseph Banks (1743–1820). In 1820 he affirmed his 'full faith in the existence of our Serpent in the Sea'

Right: when the crew of a French ship were saved from death at the hands of a frightful monster, they gave a painting of the event, in thanksgiving for their deliverance, to a church in St Malo. The original disappeared, but the French naturalist, Denys de Montfort, had a copy made in the 1790s (shown here), as he felt it confirmed the existence of giant sea monsters

horse, large black eyes, a black mouth and a long white mane. Behind the head seven or eight coils could be seen above the water. Captain von Ferry fired at it and it sank below the water and did not reappear. Two of his seamen, who had also been witnesses, swore on oath that the contents of the report were true.

During the 18th century, the increasing importance attached to rational scientific analysis resulted in mariners' reports of monstrous sea beasts being discounted, then openly derided. A Norwegian scientist, Peter Ascanius, stated that sailors who saw a line of humps in the water were not viewing a huge water beast, but were in fact seeing a line of leaping dolphins. This doubtful explanation has since become a favourite standby for debunkers of sea monster reports.

However, perhaps surprisingly, naturalists who took the time to study the reports almost invariably pronounced in favour of the sea serpent's existence. These included Sir Joseph Banks, a leading British scientist in the early 19th century who sailed round the world with Captain Cook, and Thomas

Huxley, who in 1893 wrote that there was no reason why snake-like reptiles 50 feet (15 metres) or more in length should not be found in the sea.

American marine biologists of repute at this time agreed that the sea could very well contain unknown species of monstrous creatures and a curator of the London Zoological Gardens, A. D. Bartlett, wrote in 1877 that it was unwise to disregard the evidence from so many different sources.

Constantin Samuel Rafinesque was a brilliant and controversial naturalist, who made a tremendous contribution to the

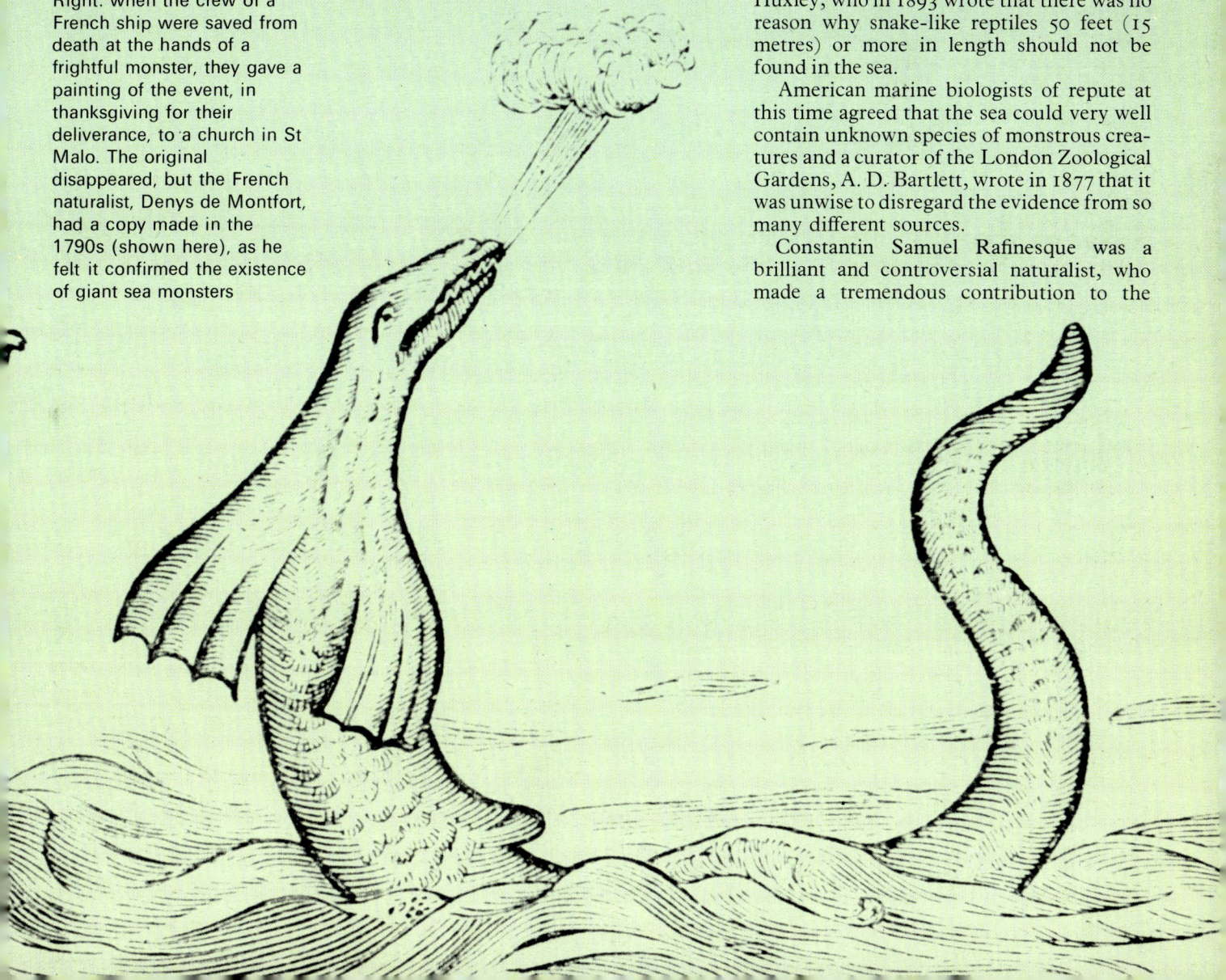

Sea monsters

knowledge of American flora and fauna. Born in 1783, he emigrated to America from Europe in 1815 where he became Professor of Natural Sciences at Transylvania University, in Kentucky. Among his wide range of interests was the sea serpent, of whose existence he was fully convinced.

During the first half of the 19th century there were a great many sightings of sea serpents along the north-east American coast, centred on the fishing port of Gloucester, in Massachusetts. Rafinesque examined the reports and decided that they fell into four groups, to which he gave the generic name of *Megophias*, or 'big snake'.

However, there were many opponents of scientists who were investigating the unexplained phenomenon of sea monsters. Among the more vociferous was Sir Richard Owen, an influential but conservative scientist of the 19th century, whom Darwin called 'one of my chief enemies'.

In 1848 Owen conducted a correspondence of some acerbity with Captain Peter M'Quhae, through the columns of *The Times*. Their debate concerned the 60-foot (18-metre) sea serpent that the Captain and his crew had seen in the southern Atlantic from the deck of HMS *Daedalus* on 6 August that year. Although Owen used the sceptic's customary ploy of interpreting the report to fit his own preconceptions (in this case his identification was a sealion), Captain M'Quhae would have none of it and firmly maintained that he had seen a sea serpent.

Antoon Cornelis Oudemans was a Dutch biologist who came from a family of scientists. Born in 1858, he studied biology at Utrecht and became an authority on mites and ticks. He also brought his scientific skills to bear on the problem of the sea monster.

Throughout his long life (he died in 1943) Oudemans collected many sighting reports and continued to speculate on the place of the

sea monster in nature. His book, *The great sea serpent*, published in 1892, is based on 187 sighting reports and was a courageous work in the contemporary sceptical climate, but it is marred by his preconception that there is only one kind of unknown sea monster, closely related to the seal family.

As one would expect, sea monsters have long been a part of mariners' tales. Some reports have undoubtedly been exaggerated, but many others that made their way into ships' logs are strangely consistent.

In May 1901, when the officers on the bridge of the steamer *Grangense* in the western Atlantic saw a monstrous crocodile-like creature with 6-inch (15-centimetre) long teeth, splashing about on the surface, the Captain refused to note the encounter in the ship's log, saying: 'They will say we were all drunk, and I'll thank you, Mister, not to mention it to our agents at Para or Manaus.'

But there were others who were perhaps less careful of their reputation, such as

Left: Thomas Huxley (1825–1895) was another noted British scientist who pronounced in favour of giant sea serpents

Below: on 6 August 1848, Captain M'Quhae and six members of the crew of HMS *Daedalus* sighted a 60-foot (18-metre) serpent in the southern Atlantic. When an illustrated report of the encounter appeared in the British press, it caused a fierce controversy

Bottom: one of the sea monsters described by Archbishop Olaus Magnus and illustrated in his history of Scandinavia, which was published in 1555

Despite scathing criticism from 19th-century scientists, sightings of sea monsters continued to be reported. The painting above shows a monster sinking a ship off the coast of Massachusetts in 1819, an area where giant sea creatures seemed to thrive

Lieutenant George Sandford who, as captain of the merchant ship *Lady Combermere*, in 1820 reported seeing in mid-Atlantic a serpent 60 to 100 feet (18 to 30 metres) long, spouting water like a whale. On 15 May 1833 four British Army officers and a military store-keeper were out for a day's fishing when they saw an 80-foot (24-metre) long serpent swim by, not more than 200 yards (180 metres) away. This was at Mahone Bay, 40 miles (65 kilometres) west of Halifax, Nova Scotia, and so convinced were they of the importance of their sighting that they all signed a statement and added:

> There could be no mistake, no delusion, and we were all perfectly satisfied that we had been favoured with a view of the 'true and veritable sea-serpent', which had been generally considered to have existed only in the brain of some Yankee skipper, and treated as a tale not much entitled to belief.

Another sighting of the crocodile-like type of sea monster was made by the captain and crew of the *Eagle* on 23 March 1830, a few hours before they docked at Charleston, South Carolina. Captain Deland sailed his schooner to within 25 yards (22 metres) of the basking creature and fired a musket at its head. When the bullet hit, the monster dived beneath the ship and struck it several times with its tail, blows strong enough to damage the craft if not to sink her.

Another military man who had a close-up view of an unknown monster from the depths was Major H. W. J. Senior of the Bengal Staff Corps. He was travelling on the *City of Baltimore* in the Gulf of Aden on 28 January 1879 and saw 500 yards (450 metres) from the ship a head with a 2-foot (60-centimetre) diameter neck protrude from the water to a height of 20 or 30 feet (6 or 9 metres). The creature was moving so rapidly he was unable to focus his field glasses upon it as it rose up, opened its mouth wide and closed it again before submerging, only to reappear a few moments later. No body was visible, but Major Senior described the head as of a bulldog-like appearance. His report was also signed by other witnesses.

In the 100 years since this sighting, sea monsters have continued to surface before startled onlookers. The intrepid trans–Atlantic rower Captain John Ridgway saw a monster just before midnight on 25 July 1966. His companion, Sergeant Chay Blyth, who has since became a world-famous yachtsman, was asleep. As Ridgway rowed he heard a swishing noise and a 35-foot (10-metre) long sea serpent outlined in phosphorescence, 'as if a string of neon lights were hanging from it', came swimming towards the boat. It dived underneath and did not reappear on the other side.

Are all sea monsters from one 'family'? Why do they remain a mystery? See page 121

An ocean giant

Many zoologists believe the kraken – the legendary Norwegian sea monster – probably refers to the giant squids of the genus *Architeuthis*. These creatures inhabit the depths of the ocean and can grow to lengths of over 60 feet (18 metres). The sperm whale is the only animal brave enough to tackle these monsters and fierce battles take place between them.

The giant squid shown here was stranded at Ranheim, Norway, in 1954. Though not the largest specimen known to science, its overall length was 30 feet (9 metres).

Reading between the lines

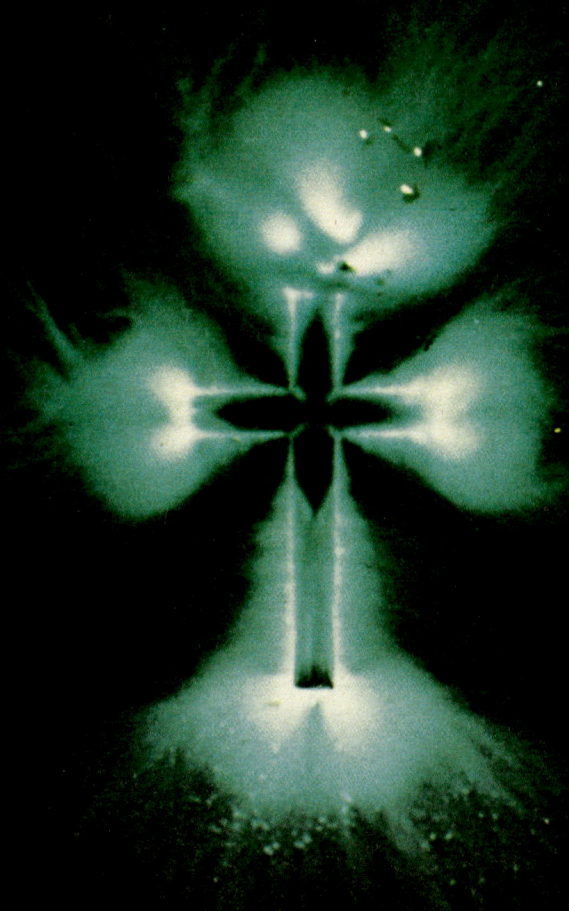

Can Kirlian photographs reveal the early stages of cancer?
Does a disturbed 'corona' indicate stress and anxiety? What else
can Kirlian photography detect? BRIAN SNELLGROVE investigates

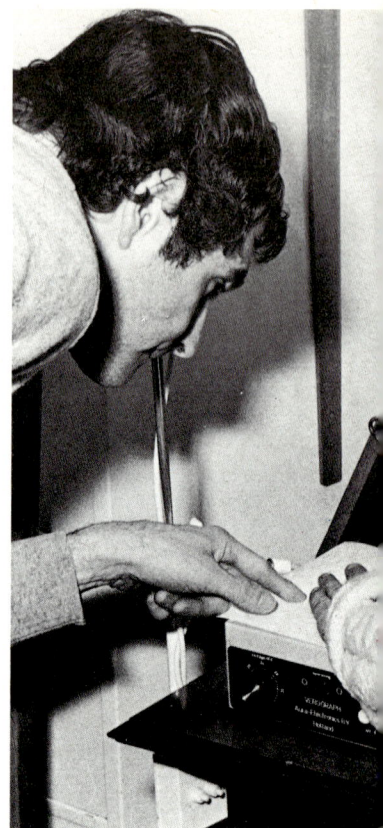

Left: the bright glow
surrounding this gold cross
is attributed to the influence
of the wearer's 'aura'. Gold is
able to retain the 'aura'
indefinitely

Above: the author, Brian
Snellgrove (left), operating
a Kirlian machine. The
regularity of the corona
produced by the subject's
hand can provide information
about his personality
and state of health

WHEN RUSSIAN SCIENTISTS announced the discovery of an 'energy body' composed of 'bioplasma' existing quite separately from the physical body, few scientists in the West were prepared to take them seriously. What evidence was there, they asked, to substantiate such a claim?

And the question, despite much scientific investigation, still awaits a conclusive answer. What the Russians believed to be the 'energy body' turned out to be the curious corona shown by Kirlian photography to surround almost all living things. But, as sceptics in the West asked: what exactly is the strange corona effect that Kirlian photography is able to capture on film? Does it really constitute, as some have claimed, positive scientific evidence for the existence of an 'energy body'? Is the corona effect, perhaps, a picture of the 'aura' that has been described by mystics and clairvoyants? Or is there some

other, perfectly ordinary, explanation?

Recent research has been concerned to show that whatever Kirlian photographs may mean, they can be used to achieve practical benefits in medical diagnosis and insights into the human mind. For example, a relationship has been found to exist between the various patterns of Kirlian photographs of the human hand and the physical and psychological condition of the subject.

The left hemisphere of the brain corresponds to the right hand, and radiations from it detected by Kirlian photography provide clues to the logical ability of the subject. The intuitive potential of the subject can also be discovered by a reading of the corona effect of the left hand, which correlates with the right hemisphere of the brain. Both hands in a state of balance show a well-balanced personality.

Characteristics that can be recognised by

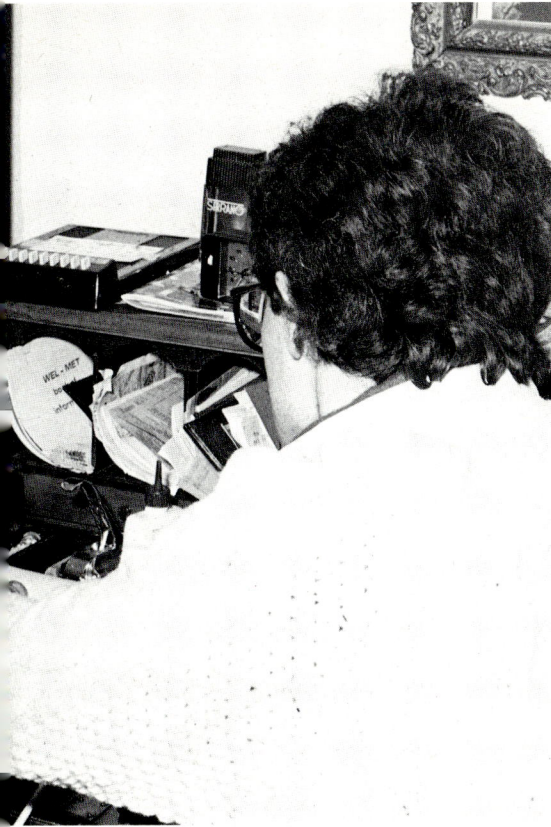

this method of analysis – characteristics that the subject himself may not realise he possesses – include healing ability, creative potential and qualities of leadership. Kirlian photographs are also said to show the nature and extent of conflicts arising from professional and emotional life and also the existence of physical tension.

Initial investigations into the diagnostic possibilities of Kirlian photography have revealed a wide range of possibilities. Studies on rats carried out by Dr Thelma Moss and Dr Margaret Armstrong of the University of Rochester, New York, indicate that marked changes occur in the corona discharge of the tails of cancerous rats as compared to those of non-cancerous rats. Similar corona patterns have been found in cancerous plants and in the fingertips of cancerous humans. Virtually all areas of the body photographed by the Kirlian method have yielded some information about the physical and mental condition of the subject. However, areas where the clearest corona pictures are obtained are the hands and feet.

The basic equipment used in Kirlian photography is simple, and consists of a high voltage 'Tesla coil', which is connected to a metal plate, and which is insulated from the subject by a non-conductive layer. A sheet of light-sensitive material – bromide paper or film, for example – is placed between subject and machine.

The Kirlian machine radiates a high-voltage, high-frequency field. The 'energy body' of the hand or object to be photographed repels the field and causes a pattern

of interference to be established. This 'energy body', or whatever it is that creates the pattern, varies. When the 'energy body' is in a balanced condition a regular interference pattern is produced when the field of the machine and that of the subject interact. When there is an imbalance in the field of the subject, irregularities appear in the corona. And it is these irregularities, as research has shown, that can often be correlated to some physical or mental ailment.

Energy of the soul?

Despite the quite beneficial results that have been achieved, Kirlian photography is still beset with many theoretical and practical difficulties. Perhaps the most controversial area of Kirlian photography centres on the interpretation of results.

There are at present four broad views taken of Kirlian photography. According to the cynical view, the so-called Kirlian effect is merely the result of normal discharge between the subject, film and the machine. Any accurate diagnosis produced is purely coincidental and is due solely to the intuition of the researcher. Accepting that Kirlian photography can monitor physical symptoms such as the activity of the sweat glands and temperature, more sympathetic critics say that it still needs to be shown that these changes reflect changes in the physical or psychological state of the subject before proper diagnosis can be made.

Parapsychologists, however, insist that although purely physical causes, such as sweat, may play a part in the production of

Above: a Kirlian picture of a slice of wholewheat bread. Russian experts on nutrition are said to have used the Kirlian process in improving the quality of grain and other foodstuffs

Kirlian photography

Right: a photograph of a healthy geranium leaf taken with a conventional camera

Far right: the same leaf photographed by the Kirlian method. The corona surrounding the body of the leaf can be seen quite clearly

Below right: a Kirlian photograph of the same geranium leaf taken after the leaf has died. The corona effect has almost completely disappeared, leaving only the image of the leaf

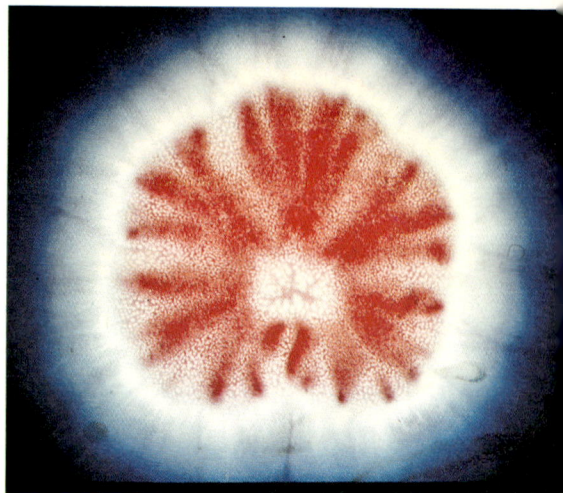

Below: the strong corona surrounding the foot of this subject suggests good health. But notice the absence of the corona around the big toe. This indicates that the subject is suffering from a headache. By massaging the toe, it is claimed, the headache will be eased

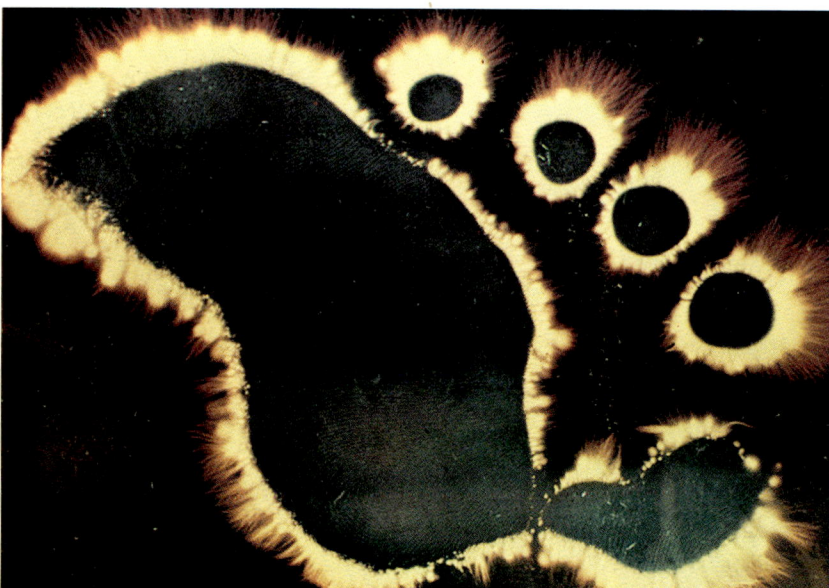

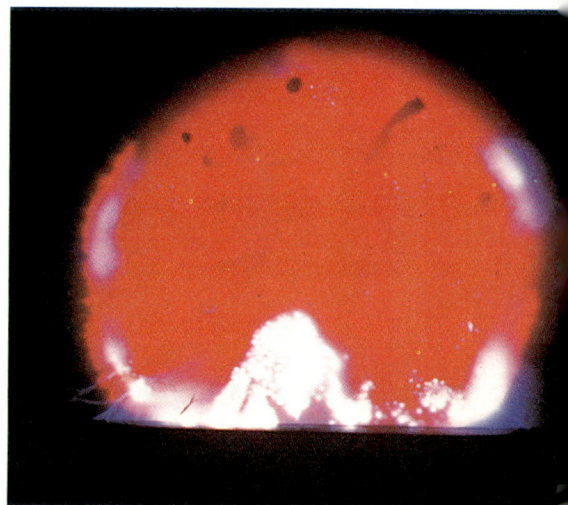

the corona effect, these causes by themselves do not provide a full explanation. According to parapsychologists, Kirlian photography can only be fully understood if the existence of an 'energy body', 'aura', 'bioplasmic body' or some other 'paranormal' phenomenon is accepted.

The most radical interpretation is that of the 'enthusiast' who claims that Kirlian photography has nothing to do with such mundane physical causes such as sweat. It shows, quite clearly, the energies of the soul. The colours and shapes revealed by Kirlian photography are what mystics and clairvoyants have been talking about for centuries.

Before being able to say which of these four competing views is most likely to be correct, there are a number of factors that the serious researcher has to take into account. The Kirlian machine used must conform to a certain standard to ensure that skin resistance, sweat, and other physical manifestations do not interfere with the corona. The subject being investigated must be relaxed. It has been found that when the majority of people try consciously to project their 'aura', the result is a weaker and more irregular radiation. A similar effect is caused by anxiety or fear on the part of the subject. But, on the other hand, the researcher must be experienced enough to be able to distinguish between cases where the result is caused by anxiety, sweat, or some other temporary physical manifestation owing to nervousness, and those effects that indicate deeper physical or psychological significance.

There are, in addition, six areas where the Kirlian photographer needs to exercise caution if he is to avoid the more common criticisms levelled against Kirlian photography.

The area to be photographed needs to be chosen with care. A fingertip when photographed alone presents a different image from that of the finger when photographed as part of the hand. When photographing a single fingertip only the most acute abnormalities show up, so fingertip photography does have a limited usefulness in medical diagnosis. But for psychological diagnosis the larger the area photographed, the better the diagnosis.

There is a temptation to correlate the colours of the corona with an emotional state. The colour cast, however, depends solely on the type of film used. Ektakrome 35 mm film, for example, produces reds or yellows, while

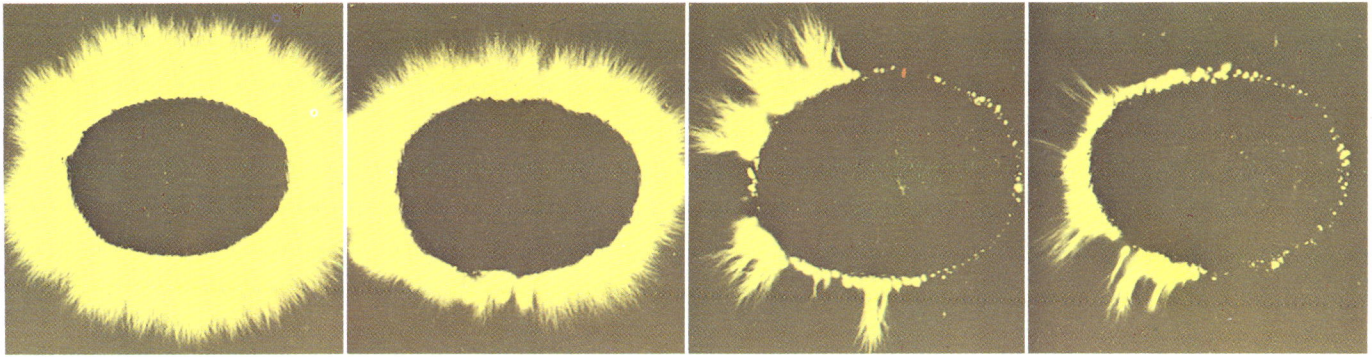

1   2   3   4

Above: a series of four Kirlian photographs of the same fingertips, taken at different times of the day. 1: 9.15 a.m., just after breakfast. Note the strong corona. 2: at 12.30 p.m., before lunch – the corona is noticeably weaker. 3: by 3.45 p.m., after only a sandwich for lunch, the subject's corona has faded considerably. 4: at 7 p.m., before dinner

Left: the 'spiky' nature of the streamers surrounding these hands is typical of tense subjects and indicates a lack of emotional flow. A well-balanced personality, on the other hand, has a softer, more regular corona

Polaroid film produces a red outer corona with a white inner band. Resin-coated paper produces blue and little else. The colours themselves are not important. What is important is the regularity and extent of any colour effects and what stimuli causes them.

Operator effect also needs to be taken into account. The ability of the mind to cause structural and emotional changes in both living and inanimate objects has been observed on many occasions. An aggressive attitude on the part of observers can inhibit the performance of ESP subjects; voltage patterns of wired-up plants change when disharmonious thoughts are projected. In order to exclude any possible effect of this nature, the operator should stand at least 4 feet (1.5 metres) away from the subject in a relaxed and open frame of mind.

Excessive voltage produces an artificially bright corona and the researcher needs to be able to recognise voltage and waveform characteristics. The golden rule is to use the minimum voltage required to produce a readable pattern.

The energy body takes time – sometimes a matter of days – to settle down after therapy. Results can also be misleading when photographing a subject after, for example, a session of meditation. In many cases the corona will have completely disappeared.

Too long or too short an exposure time can also produce misleading results. There appear to be slow cycles of activity that can be missed if exposure time is too short. For fingertip photographs, one second is sufficient; for the whole hand, two seconds.

In recent years Kirlian photography has been used successfully in a number of applications. In a study commissioned by a commercial firm in the USA, for example, Dr Thelma Moss was able to predict the incidence of germination of soya bean seeds with almost 100 per cent accuracy. The implications for agriculture are immense. Other areas where Kirlian methods of interpretation might be used include personnel selection and evaluation by employers of prospective employees, compatibility assessment and the estimation of the effect of parental conflict, particularly on children. When used in conjunction with acupuncture, counselling or homeopathy, Kirlian photography can produce accurate medical diagnoses.

While the practical benefits of Kirlian photography have been clearly shown, doubt remains as to whether it proves the existence of the 'aura'. There seems to be a 'flow of energy' surrounding almost all living things. But *what* that energy is remains unknown.

Further reading
Walter Benjamin, *Beyond the body*, Routledge and Kegan Paul 1974
Henry Gris and William Dick, *The new Soviet psychic discoveries*, Sphere 1980
Stanley Krippner and David Rubin, *The Kirlian aura* Doubleday Anchor (New York) 1974
Thelma Moss, *The probability of the impossible*, Paladin 1979
Sylvan Muldoon and Hereward Carrington, *The projection of the astral body*, Weiser (New York) 1969
Brian and Marita Snellgrove *The unseen self*, Kirlian Aura Diagnosis 1979

Silently, out of the night sky

SCIENTISTS GENERALLY consider UFOs that give responses on radar scopes the most reliable for their purposes. The first sighting described below took place at Caselle Airport in Turin, Italy, and is one of the most well-documented radar–visual sightings on record, while the second, at Ivinghoe, Bedfordshire, had only one witness, but its authenticity is vouched for by his sheer terror.

One of the most spectacular UFO waves lasted for five months in the winter of 1973 to 1974. It was heralded by the impressive sighting at Turin in November 1973—an

CHARLES BOWEN continues his series of UFO sightings with an examination of two very different – but equally convincing – cases

event of profound significance for the science of ufology. It attracted the attention of Jean-Claude Bourret, a top reporter from the French radio station France-Inter, who broadcast a series of programmes about UFOs culminating in a startling and important interview with the then Minister of Defence, Monsieur Robert Galley.

The Ivinghoe incident, which took place 11 years earlier in 1962, shows a fascinating aspect common to many UFO reports—electromagnetic effects on electrical and mechanical equipment such as car radios.

'Sudden vast jumps to and fro'

Radar-visual: Caselle airport, Turin, Italy, 30 November 1973

On 30 November 1973 Riccardo Marano was preparing to land his Piper Navajo at Caselle Airport when he was advised by control that there was an unidentified object at a height of about 4000 feet (1200 metres) above the runway, close to where he was due to land. Control had the object on its radar screens and gave Marano permission to approach it to see what it was. As he neared his target, control reported that it was moving and was heading for the Suza Valley. Accordingly, Marano changed course to follow it – and suddenly control announced that the target had disappeared from its radar.

At that moment Marano received a message from another aircraft: the UFO was behind him at about 12,000 feet (3600 metres). Marano's Navajo was then flying at about 10,000 feet (3000 metres). He began to turn – and saw in front of him what appeared to be a bright white luminous sphere, which was emitting light of all colours of the spectrum. The light pulsated from bright to dim, but never went out completely. As he closed on the UFO, Marano reported that it was 'flying in a most irregular fashion, making fantastic lateral deviations and sudden vast

jumps to and fro'. Taking advantage of a moment when the object was below him, Marano put his plane into a dive, accelerating to a speed of over 250 mph (400 km/h) – but he could not catch up with the UFO. When he gave up the chase, it was heading southeastwards. He estimated its speed at about 550 mph (900 km/h).

Two other pilots confirmed the presence of the object. They were Comandante Tranquillo, who had just taken off in his Alitalia DC-9, and Comandante Mezzalani, who was bringing his Alitalia DC-9 in from Paris. Comandante Tranquillo advised control that he dared not approach the 'shining object giving out flashes' and thereupon adjusted his course.

Comandante Mezzalani observed the object as he was touching down. He said it was large and bright, yet dimmer than a star or an artificial satellite.

There was another very reliable witness, none other than the commander of the neighbouring Caselle military airfield, Colonello Rustichelli, who stated that he had observed the UFO on his radar screen. It was, he said, something solid, which lit up like an aircraft on his radar, giving the same sort of return as would a DC-9. He said it looked like a star, but when he got it on his radar it stayed firm. Soon afterwards it headed off westwards.

A curious event, which may or may not be

Below: Monsieur Robert Galley in his historic interview with reporter Jean-Claude Bourret of the French radio station France-Inter on 21 February 1974. M. Galley admitted that the French government had been secretly studying UFOs for 20 years

connected with the UFO sightings described above, took place earlier on the same evening. At 5.00 p.m. Signor Franco Contin, an amateur photographer, saw an extremely bright object in the sky. At first he thought it was a star, but when he saw it begin to move about, he realised it must be something else. A slightly misshapen luminous globe, it was white at first and then suddenly turned deep orange. Signor Contin fetched his camera and took a total of eight photographs. These show an enormous object, oval in shape and brightly luminous.

The Turin sighting was remarkable not only because it was followed by a world-wide wave of UFO reports, but also because it attracted the attention of two very important people. The first of these was M. Jean-Claude Bourret of the French radio and television service ORTF, chief reporter of the radio station France-Inter, who was so impressed by the report of the sighting that he made a series of 39 radio programmes devoted to UFO research, which were broadcast between January 1973 and March 1974.

The other person whose interest was aroused by the Turin incident was Monsieur Robert Galley, Minister of Defence for France, who granted an exclusive interview to M. Bourret, which was broadcast on 21 February 1974.

This interview was of immense importance for the science of ufology – for in it a serving Minister of Defence admitted, not only that UFOs exist, but also that in 1954 his government had set up a secret section devoted to their study within the Ministry of Defence. M. Galley spoke of the massive nature of the UFO phenomenon, of the many detailed eyewitness reports he had read and of the volume of reports received from the Air Force in the early days of the project – in which, he said, 'the general agreement was quite disturbing'. Since 1970, UFO research in France has been in the hands of the *Centre National d'Etudes Spatiales* (The national centre for space studies), which evaluates reports of UFO sightings from both the Air Force and the Gendarmerie. Unfortunately, however, the French UFO group has no contact with international military groups.

M. Galley also admitted that 'it is certain that there are things that we do not understand and that are at present relatively inexplicable. I will indeed say that it is undeniable that there are things today that have not been explained or that have been incorrectly explained'.

This startling interview was immediately given wide coverage in the French papers, including *France-Soir*, *Le Parisien Libéré*, *L'Aurore* and *Le Figaro* and all the big provincial papers. It was soon reported in German, Spanish, Swiss, Italian, Brazilian and American newspapers – but not in the British press, or on radio or television. In his English translation of Jean-Claude Bourret's book *The crack in the universe* Gordon Creighton describes his unsuccessful attempts to convince the BBC that the interview was important enough to warrant a mention on one of its radio science programmes. He suggests that the scant and biased reporting of the UFO phenomenon by the British media may be the result of an official debunking attitude on the part of the authorities. Their methods are different from those used in the USA; indeed, says Mr Creighton,

> quieter and more subtle techniques of ridicule and denigration, plus, no doubt, the occasional discreet telephone call to the newspaper that has offended by printing a serious looking UFO report, have yielded far better results than the CIA's methods.

This scepticism on the part of the authorities no doubt accounts for the fact that very little serious scientific research is carried out into UFOs in Britain. Amateur UFO societies can do little more than monitor sightings. Suppression of information can only be harmful to research, and it is disturbing to think there may be many UFO sightings we simply never hear about.

'Like a halo round the moon'

Close encounter of the second kind: Ivinghoe, Bedfordshire, England, 9 February 1962

Mr Ronald Wildman, a delivery driver for the Vauxhall Motor Company, left his home in Luton, Bedfordshire, at 3.00 a.m. on 9 February 1962 to drive a new estate car from the factory to Swansea. He had passed Dunstable, and was on the Ivinghoe road approaching a set of crossroads at Tringford, when he saw an oval-shaped object ahead of him on the road. It was white with black markings at regular intervals around the perimeter. It appeared to be 20 to 30 feet (6 to 10 metres) above the road, and was at least 40 feet (12 metres) wide. Mr Wildman drove straight towards the object, but when he was 20 yards (18 metres) from it the power of the car's engine began to fade until he was going at just 20 mph (30 km/h). Putting his foot flat down on the accelerator did not help; neither did changing down through the gears. Mr Wildman noticed, however, that his headlights stayed on. For some 200 yards (180 metres) as he drove down the road, the UFO stayed about 20 feet (6 metres) ahead of, and above, him.

Suddenly a white haze appeared around the perimeter of the object – it was 'like a halo round the moon', said Mr Wildman – and it veered off to the right at high speed. As it went, it brushed particles of frost from the trees onto the windscreen of the Vauxhall.

In an interview, Mr Wildman recalled that his headlights were reflected from the object when it was closest to the road, and in his opinion this showed it was solid.

After the UFO had disappeared, the car's engine returned to normal working and the witness, by now panic-stricken, drove as hard as he could to Aylesbury where he reported the affair to the police. They noted the distraught condition of the driver.

The credibility of sightings with only one witness rests on the trustworthiness of the person concerned. Mr Wildman's report was checked by three investigators from *Flying Saucer Review*, who were extremely impressed by Mr Wildman's obvious sincerity. They were convinced his sighting had been genuine, not a hallucination.

Interference with electrical equipment such as televisions, car radios and headlights is a common feature of UFO reports. It has been suggested that this phenomenon may result from electromagnetic fields created by UFOs along their surfaces in order to minimise the effects of air resistance. Whatever the cause, this phenomenon can be one of the most frightening aspects of a UFO incident.

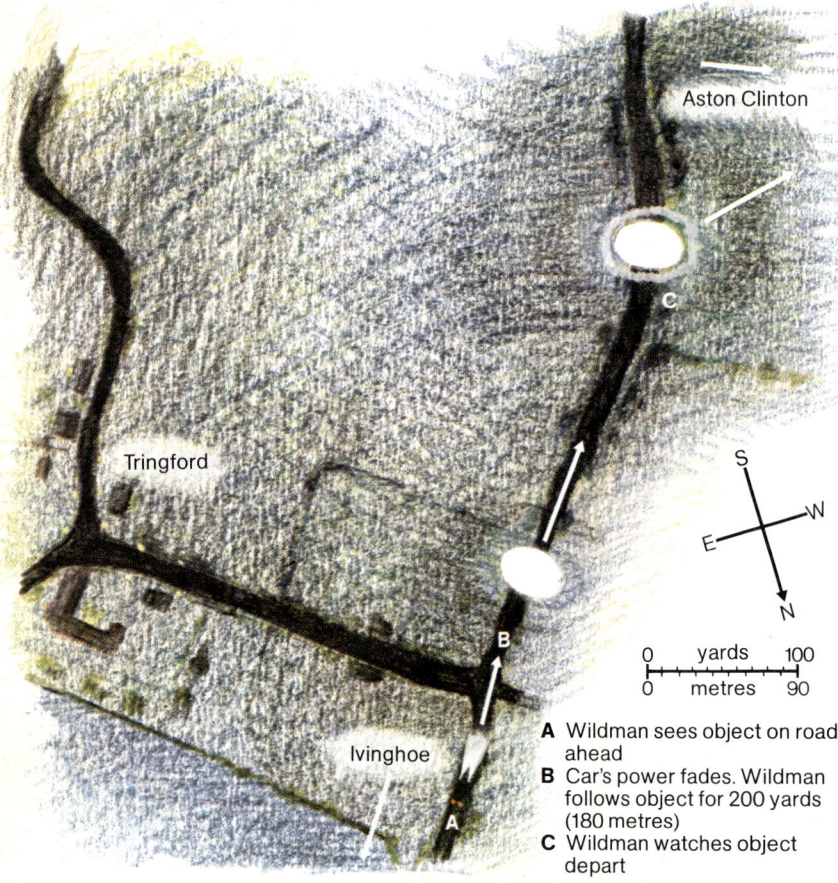

Aston Clinton

Tringford

Ivinghoe

A Wildman sees object on road ahead
B Car's power fades. Wildman follows object for 200 yards (180 metres)
C Wildman watches object depart

Many people have suddenly found themselves in the peculiar position of existing outside their own bodies, looking at the world from some detached, external point. JENNY DAWSON describes the circumstances in which such out-of-the-body experiences take place

The disembodied self

ASTRAL PROJECTION, ESP projection and spontaneous projection are just some of the terms that refer to the same phenomenon – an out-of-the-body experience (OOBE). This is an experience in which a person leaves his physical body and appears to view the external world from a position that is completely divorced from his material body. It has been widely reported in both psychic and medical journals and it appears to be a relatively common experience.

The circumstances in which an OOBE occurs vary considerably. Stress seems to be a significant factor and many people have reported experiencing the sensation of leaving their bodies when undergoing an operation, after an accident or when seriously ill. But there are numerous cases of people who were asleep or going about everyday tasks, such as shopping or gardening, when the experience occurred.

From accounts given by those who have had an OOBE, the general sensation is at first indistinguishable from the ordinary physical

state, except for a feeling of buoyancy and positive well-being. Some subjects have mentioned that their 'phantom' or 'astral' body seemed to remain attached to their physical body by a thin cord, enabling them to return to their normal state.

The word 'astral' is used to describe a second body within the physical one. It is an exact copy of the flesh and blood version, but is made of finer material and has a luminous appearance. It is apparently capable of separating itself from the physical body and travelling about, passing through solid objects. The astral body exists in what is called the astral plane, which includes the everyday world, but extends beyond it. It is also said to survive death.

References to the astral body abound in ancient literature. Ancient Indian writings tell of eight *siddhis* (supernormal powers) that can be acquired through meditation. The sixth *siddhi* is 'flying in the sky', presumably indicating astral projection. A religious belief common to some cultures is that

The ancient Egyptians thought of the astral body, or *ba*, as a bird with a human face. At death, the bird would leave the physical body, but hover close to it

Out-of-the-body experiences

Left: in his second Epistle to the Corinthians, St Paul refers to a man who had had an out-of-the-body experience

Below: the great mystic poet and painter William Blake portrays the reunion of the soul and the physical body in this illustration of Robert Blair's poem, *The grave*, published in 1813

medieval scholars wrote of the soul as the *anima divina* or *anima humana*. Dante's *Purgatorio* (canto 25), written in the 14th century, says that after death the soul 'around it beams its own creative power, like to its living form in shape and size . . . the circumambient air adopts the shape the soul imposes on it.'

One of the few men whose ability to travel astrally was acknowledged by the Roman Catholic Church was St Anthony of Padua (1195–1231). St Anthony was a Portuguese Franciscan friar who won a great reputation as a preacher in southern France and Italy. He is the patron saint of the poor and is often called upon for the return of lost property.

It is said of St Anthony that one day in 1226, when he was preaching in a church in Limoges, he suddenly remembered that he was supposed to be reading a lesson at another church on the other side of town. St Anthony stopped his sermon, pulled his hood over his head and knelt silently for several minutes. During that time, monks in the other church saw the saint suddenly appear in their midst, read the lesson, then

the *shaman* (a kind of priest-doctor) is able to leave his body at will and escort the souls of the dead to the land of tribal ancestors.

It appears from drawings that the ancient Egyptians believed that the astral plane was entered by 10 gates and seven doors. They thought of the soul or astral body as a bird, independent of gravity (a puny soul was symbolised as a mouse!).

Among the many Biblical references to astral projection, St Paul describes a man he knew who 'whether in the body or out of the body, God knoweth, was caught up into paradise and heard unspeakable words, which it is not lawful for a man to utter' (2 Corinthians 12:3).

Widespread beliefs

The modern idea that it is wrong to awaken a sleepwalker may be traced back to the primitive belief that to do so would prevent the soul, or astral body, from returning. Even more frightening is the belief, common in Haiti, that the soul can be stolen by evil beings and its owner subsequently enslaved – the zombies of Haiti are deemed to be bodies without souls.

In 1978, Dean Shiels, Associate Professor at the University of Wisconsin, USA, published the results of his cross-cultural study of beliefs in OOBEs. He had collected data from nearly 70 non-Western cultures and this revealed that the belief in OOBE occurred in about 95 per cent of them. Despite the need for further research, Professor Shiels remarked that 'the near-universality of OOBE beliefs and the *consistency* of the beliefs is striking.'

The notion of the astral body has a continuous history in the West, too –

The near-death experience

Many people have experienced an OOBE for the first time through being involved in a serious accident. In 1964 David Taylor and a friend were spending the last few weeks of their tour of East Africa in northern Tanzania, when they had a serious collision with a lorry. David nearly died as a result of his injuries.

'We had been driving through the game park and had just turned on to the main road to Moshi. It was dusk and I was sitting half-asleep in the passenger seat.

'I was suddenly woken by my friend, who was delighted to see the first vehicle we had come across in six hours, driving down towards us. Either my friend or the other driver must have been half-asleep, too, for within seconds the two vehicles drove smack into each other.

'As the two vehicles collided, I suddenly found that I was watching the scene from several yards up in the air, as if I were suspended above the road. I saw our own Land-Rover colliding with a large lorry. I watched as I was thrown from the Land-Rover and my friend then climbed out unhurt and came back to examine my body. I also saw the lorry drive off. I remember thinking that I looked a terrible mess lying there on the road and could well be dead.

'The next thing I knew was coming to in Moshi Hospital. I had been unconscious for two days with serious injuries. I told my friend what I had seen and he confirmed that it was indeed a lorry that had run into us and that it had driven on. I had only been saved because another car had come down the road soon afterwards and taken me to the hospital.

'The whole experience, even after all these years, has left me completely unafraid of death.'

Below left: the astral body lying above the physical body at the start of an OOBE. The 'cord' that connects the two bodies has been mentioned by some subjects as the means by which they can return to a normal state

Bottom: St Anthony of Padua's ability to leave his physical body enabled him to preach to two congregations at once

just as suddenly disappear again. St Anthony returned to his kneeling body and continued his sermon.

During recent centuries, many notable writers have described their own experiences of spontaneous projection or those of colleagues, among them Walter de la Mare, T. E. Lawrence, Jack London and Guy de Maupassant. Ernest Hemingway experienced the sensation of quitting his body when he was hit by shrapnel during the First World War. He later described it as

. . . my soul or something coming right out of my body, like you'd pull a silk handkerchief out of a pocket by one corner. It flew around and then came back and went in again, and I wasn't dead any more.

The phenomenon of OOBE raises considerable problems for philosophers and psychologists. Many sceptics maintain that any suggestion of an OOBE should be dismissed as an hallucination or delusion. But people who have had such experiences are adamant that they have, indeed, taken place. Even when unconscious at the time of the experience, some people have later described what was going on around them and those present have confirmed their accounts. Subjects who experience this phenomenon are fully aware that they are in an out-of-the-body state.

Many subjects who have had an OOBE while on the operating table or after a serious accident say that the experience has profoundly changed their view of life and dispelled any fears about dying. An interesting theory on this type of projection, or 'near-death experience' (NDE) has been put forward by Doctor Carl Sagan, director of the Laboratory for Planetary Studies in New York. He describes the phenomenon of NDE in these terms:

Every human being has already had an experience like that of travellers who return from the land of death; the sensation of flight and the emergence from darkness into light; an experience in which the heroic figure may be dimly perceived, bathed in radiance and glory. There is only one common experience that matches this description. It is called birth.

In times of mortal danger or acute emotional stress, perhaps one is able to retrieve these memories of birth and, once again, leave the darkness – the suffering body – and rise towards freedom and the light.

Do out-of-body experiences provide evidence for life after death? See page 144

Remembrance of things past

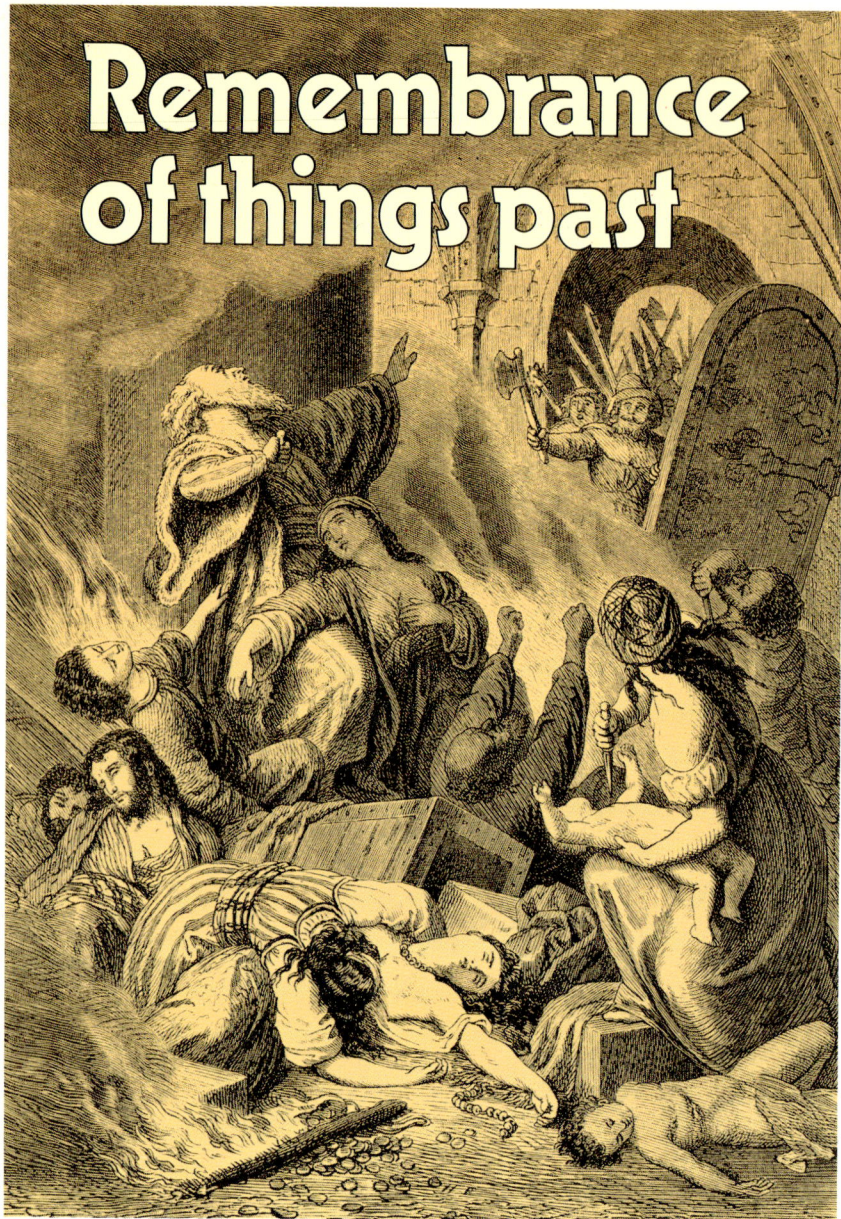

Believers in reincarnation find the details of everyday life recalled under hypnosis are proof of previous lives. DAVID CHRISTIE-MURRAY discusses whether these are more important than a knowledge of major historical events

The Jews of York met a violent end as a result of persecution by Christians, in the massacre of 1190. One of Arnall Bloxham's subjects, Jane Evans, regressed to previous life of Rebecca, one of the Jews who was murdered

IF THERE WERE a place in the *Guinness book of records* for the greatest number of past lives one individual was able to recollect, it would probably go to a patient of Dr Blanche Baker of San Francisco. This patient, born in Utah of Scots-English-American ancestry, boasted a total of 47 previous lives – 23 as a man, 24 as a woman. Historical details revealed by this patient were later found, it is claimed, to be accurate.

But the recollection of past lives aroused in Dr Baker's patients resulted not from a direct suggestion that they should return to previous existences, but by a light, hypnotic free association technique first used in 1950. Under this form of hypnosis, Dr Baker's patients experienced scenes of violence,

death and curious personal relationships, in which the senses of sight, smell, taste and touch played important parts, accompanied sometimes by physical pain and acute emotional anguish.

The feeling of pain and grief experienced by many patients under hypnotic regression answers in many ways the oft-asked question, 'If we have lived before, why do we not remember past lives?' There would seem to be a natural tendency for the mind to suppress memories of events or scenes that have caused pain and distress. So it would not be surprising for people to forget or positively wish to forget previous lives that were painful or unpleasant. And under hypnotic regression it is those events that have caused extreme physical and mental pain in previous lives that are often the most vivid memories recalled.

Traumas from the past
Take the case, for example, of Jane Winthrop, a name assumed by another of Dr Baker's patients. Under hypnosis, Jane became Mary Dunlap, a settler in 18th-century Massachusetts who lost her husband, Allan. 'Certainly,' said Jane Winthrop, 'I have never consciously known such overpowering grief as I relived each time I spoke of Allan's death,' adding: 'That which comes from any of us must be first within us.'

Here Jane Winthrop touches upon an important element in the belief in reincarnation. Just as in this life much of what we are is the result of forgotten or unconscious schooling and instruction, so, our present selves, reincarnationists believe, are similarly made up of experiences from previous lives, which we have also forgotten. As in this life a neurosis may be caused by a childhood trauma and cured by its being uncovered under hypnosis and brought to the patient's conscious memory, so a trauma from a past life may be revealed and its discovery heal the present-life neurosis it has caused.

Whatever the explanation of former 'lives', the vividness of them and the emotions they arouse are convincing to those undergoing the experience and to some observers as well. Yet vividness and conviction do not in themselves guarantee truth. Barbara Larson, a university graduate, a teacher until her marriage and mother of three, was hypnotised in middle age and became Sam Sneed (1853–96), a cocky young gambler and cardsharp. Sneed's whole career was portrayed from a 19-year-old gamester, swaggering across America, hopping trains one jump ahead of the lawmen of the towns in which he played, through salesman and entrepreneur to solid citizen, selling advertising and writing editorials for the Sacramento *Bee*. Shot by a Frank Jordan, whom he had accused of corruption, he was buried in Sacramento cemetery.

Such a bare narrative cannot do justice to the intense vividness of the regression;

Above: part of the Ontario landscape in Canada that Joanne McIver claimed to recognise from her previous life, some 100 years before, as Susan Ganier

Right: a model of Eboracum, the Roman city of York. This was the home of Livonia, one of the previous lives of Jane Evans

Below: Arnall Bloxham, a distinguished British hypnotherapist, has tape recorded over 400 cases of regression. Some of his subjects have regressed to as many as 14 quite separate former lives spread out over many centuries

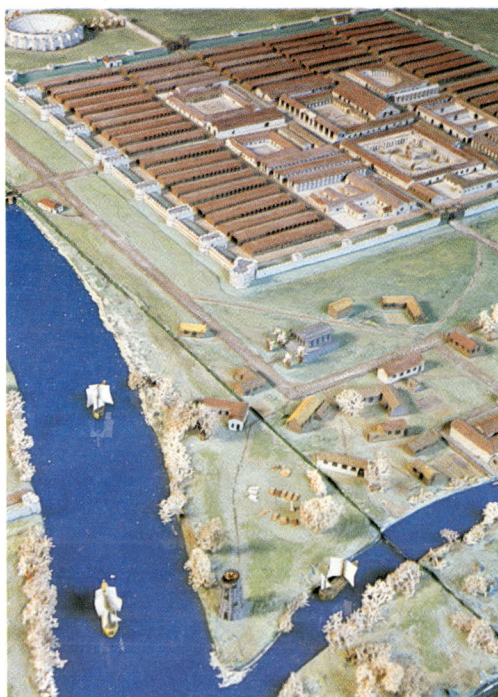

the source of her fantasy – if it was one.

More probable was the study by Jess Stearn, published in 1969, of Joanne McIver's previous life as Susan Ganier. Joanne, who lived at Orillia, some 80 miles (129 kilometres) north of Toronto, was regressed by her father during her teens, and produced some half dozen former lives, of which five were fragmentary compared with that of Susan Ganier. Her story was that she was born about 1835 in St Vincent Township, Ontario, some 90 miles (145 kilometres) from Sydenham Township, later Owen Sound, near where the McIvers live today. Susan married Thomas Marrow, a tenant farmer, in July 1849, the ceremony being conducted by an itinerant preacher called McEachern, and they settled at Massie village. Thomas was killed in an accident in 1863, and Susan died after a completely uneventful existence as farmer's wife and widow, in 1903.

The search for proof

Though 19th-century provincial records of births and deaths are incomplete, some confirmation of the Ganier story was found. Ganier's farm was shown on a contemporary map issued by the Ontario Department of Lands and Forests. Massie exists, though it does not appear on most maps, and a Vail's Point, mentioned by Susan, also exists. The tombstone of her close friend, Mrs Speedie, a postmistress, who died in 1909, can still be seen in Annan, a nearby village. Arthur Eagles, an octogenarian in 1969, remembered the Ganier family, knew Susan Marrow, whom he used to drive as an old lady into Owen Sound, and recalled that his parents had told him that Thomas and she were man and wife. The Toronto Department of Public Records confirmed the existence of people previously named by Joanne: Mrs Speedie, Robert MacGregor, the blacksmith in Massie, Joshua Milligan, storekeeper, and William Brown, miller.

Susan's knowledge of details of contemporary life was correct. Sugar came in packages at 10 cents a box, saddles cost from $7.50 to $12, oranges were greatly prized and a Democrat was a kind of wagon, peculiar to that time and place (this last item, however, seems known generally to Canadians). Joanne claimed to recognise places known to Susan, including the churchyard, a barn and her old home, and identified a well where none had been known to exist. At one period during the investigation she felt herself to be Susan Ganier, as if she were moving in two worlds simultaneously, with confusion of memories of past and present lives. When regressed her voice changed from its normal huskiness to a lighter, musical treble, and the depth of her emotions under hypnosis, especially her joy after marrying Tommy, her recreation of scenes delineating her relationships and the vivid pictures she gave of the Canadian wilderness were beyond acting or

as one observer wrote: 'To watch the transformation of swaggering Sam Sneed into a charming, attractive Californian matron was an astonishing experience. For two hours I had been so caught up with the life of this Personality Kid that I felt I knew him better than most of my friends, because this seemed to be the inner man speaking. Those who have since heard the tape recording capture this same intensity of feeling, and roar with laughter at his broad sallies.'

Yet there is no evidence that Sam ever lived, and many errors were discovered in his story. Mrs Larson, rehypnotised and challenged in Sam's person about the proved errors, insisted his story was true. It is a principle of hypnotic theory that subjects under hypnosis do not lie if specifically told to tell the truth. One would have expected Sam to lie, and in this he was 'true' to his character. What the hypnotist does not seem to have done is to have hypnotised Mrs Larson in her own person and asked her for

The medieval home (above left) of a wealthy merchant prince, Jacques Coeur (inset), at Bourges in the Loire Valley, where Jane Evans lived as Alison, a teenage servant. Under hypnosis, Mrs Evans gave a remarkably accurate description of life in France at the time of Charles VII

any impression given by reading books.

The majority of the 400 regressions achieved by hypnotherapist Arnall Bloxham were of lives as uneventful as that described by Susan Ganier. Some, however, detailed in Jeffrey Iverson's books, *More lives than one?* (1976) and featured in broadcasts and on television, are intensely dramatic. One of the best known of his subjects is Jane Evans, who has been regressed to six previous lives.

First she was Livonia, living in AD 286, wife of Titus, tutor to Constantine, later Roman Emperor, son of Constantius and Helena, living at Eboracum (York). Livonia and Titus were converted to Christianity by a woodcarver named Albanus and died violently in Diocletian's reign. Professor Brian Hartley, an expert on Roman Britain, stated that Livonia knew 'some quite remarkable historical facts, and numerous published works would have to be consulted if anyone tried to prepare the outline of such a story.'

Where the facts could be checked, most of them proved correct. It was possible that Constantius could have been Governor of Britain from AD 283 to 290 because historians know nothing of these 'missing' years of his life. Hartley, however, questioned some details such as Livonia's statement that Roman ladies rode on horseback.

Mrs Evans' second life as Rebecca, a Jewess, showed an entirely different personality. She was massacred in 1190 with many other Jews in the crypt of St Mary's Church, Castlegate, York, where no crypt was known, until it was discovered in 1975, several years after the regression. Professor Barrie Dobson, author of a book on the massacre, commented that Jane's story was true to what was known of the events and the times, that much of the detail was impressively

accurate, that disputed facts could well be true and some could have been known only to professional historians. There are some anachronisms where memories of the present life and a previous life may have become confused. But Rebecca's terror when the murderers enter the crypt is, as usual, beyond acting.

Her third life, as Alison, the teenage servant of a French merchant prince, Jacques Coeur, has been criticised on the grounds that all the facts about Coeur are readily available to British readers. Mrs Evans' knowledge included a description of the merchant's mansion at Bourges in the Loire Valley with its courtyard and style of architecture in the year 1450. She also showed a detailed knowledge of medieval French history and the life of her master, though she omitted obvious facts such as he was married and had five children.

Yet if Jane Evans' knowledge had been gained only from books she would have known these facts, and, if she had been faking, would have produced them. She

Left: one of Mrs Evans' brief regressions was as lady-in-waiting to Catherine of Aragon (1486–1536), when the young princess was about to depart from Spain in 1501 to marry Prince Arthur, eldest son of Henry VII of England

Below left: Queen Anne, who reigned from 1702 to 1714, with her son William, Duke of Gloucester. In her fifth life, Mrs Evans was a London sewing-girl, Anne Tasker, who referred to the death of the young prince, though she inaccurately described him as the Queen's only son

referred to the king, Charles VII, by his nickname of 'Heron Legs' – his thin shanks looked ridiculous in yellow tights – gossiped about his mistress, Agnes Sorrel, and other personalities, and repeated the rumour that Louis, the Dauphin, had murdered his wife. Alison also mentioned a golden 'apple' containing jewels, listed as a 'grenade' (that is, pomegranate) in a catalogue of items confiscated by the Treasury from Coeur.

Mrs Evans' fourth remembered incarnation was as Anna, lady-in-waiting to Catherine of Aragon at the time she was about to leave for England to marry Henry VII's son, Arthur. She again gave correct

historical details but revealed nothing remarkable. Nor did she reveal much in her fifth life, as Anne Tasker, a London sewing-girl in Queen Anne's time at the turn of the 17th and 18th centuries. She made one reference, however, which illustrates a difficulty for researchers in this field. She referred to the death of William, the Queen's 'only child', an allusion which critics fasten upon as an obvious inaccuracy. Yet it is true in the sense that Anne's son, upon whom all her hopes rested, was her only *remaining* child. Hit or miss?

Mrs Evans' last incarnation before her present life was as Sister Grace, born in 19th-century Des Moines, Iowa, and a member of an enclosed order. The nun has not been identified, because no registration of birth in Iowa was required until the 1920s and although censuses existed, they were not accurate. All that is known is that Sister Grace showed a knowledge of contemporary events that Jane seemingly did not have.

It is reasonable to expect that Mrs Evans would have spoken the languages of her incarnations, and a considerable research has been carried out on paranormal speaking in foreign tongues. However, most subjects, when regressed to previous lives in other lands, do not adopt the language of the time or the country. When Arnall Bloxham was asked if any of his subjects spoke in a foreign tongue, he replied no, for if they had he would not have understood them. But his subjects pronounced the names of cities and people correctly according to the pronunciation of the country (not Munich, for example, but 'München').

On page 126, we look at the phenomenon of speaking in a foreign tongue (xenolalia)

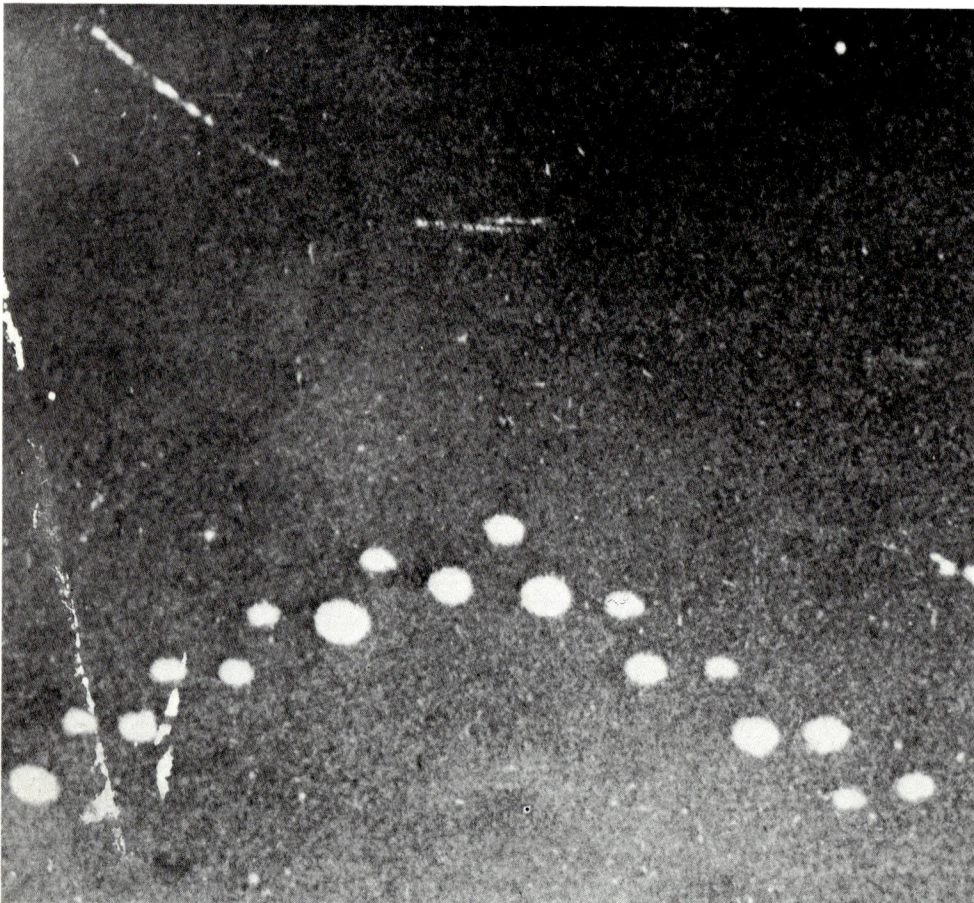

Above: this impressive photograph was taken during the Gemini XII space mission on 12 November 1966. Analysis has shown that the UFO that appears on the right of the picture is a distant object – but the NASA Photo Evaluation Lab claims this is actually rubbish that has been discarded from the Gemini XII spacecraft itself.

Left: at about 9.10 p.m. on 25 August 1951 a group of five professors and a post-graduate student were relaxing outside the house of Professor W. I. Robinson in Lubbock, Texas. Suddenly they saw a formation of bright lights flying rapidly across the sky. The professors estimated their speed at around 1800 miles per hour (2900 km/h) at a height of about one mile (1.5 kilometres). Sceptics claim that the lights were nothing more than reflections from the bellies of flying ducks – but if so, they would have been flying at more than 125 miles per hour (200 km/h) – which is far too fast for ducks!

Below: this UFO was observed by three witnesses near Saasfee, Switzerland, on 26 July 1975. It seemed to be metallic and was difficult to make out against the mountain fog, and was reported to be humming softly.

The photograph has been rigorously analysed by the American UFO organisation Ground Saucer Watch Inc., of Phoenix, Arizona. The techniques they use can reveal a number of details not immediately apparent from the photograph – including the time, to within an hour, at which the photograph was taken, the apparent size of the UFO, its distance from the camera, and any supporting threads or structures that may indicate a hoax.

The black-and-white picture (right) shows a computer digital image enhancement of the original. It passes the test.

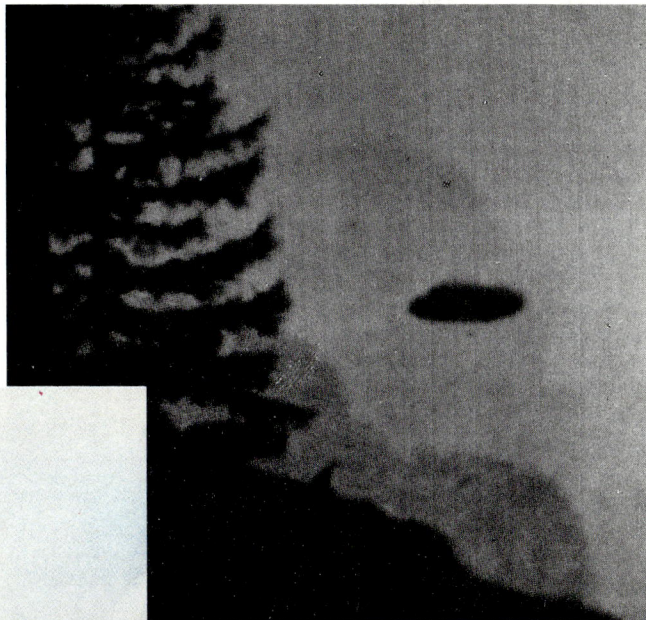

Below: another photograph that has passed GSW's computer tests, this was taken by Deputy Sheriff Strauch while on a hunting trip in Gibbon, Minnesota, USA on 21 October 1965. It shows a typical UFO – a bright, blurred, disc-shaped light – and illustrates the difficulty of taking accurate colour pictures of UFOs in poor light conditions; the strange colour of the sky makes it possible to deduce that the original object was probably red, another feature that links it with other UFO sightings.

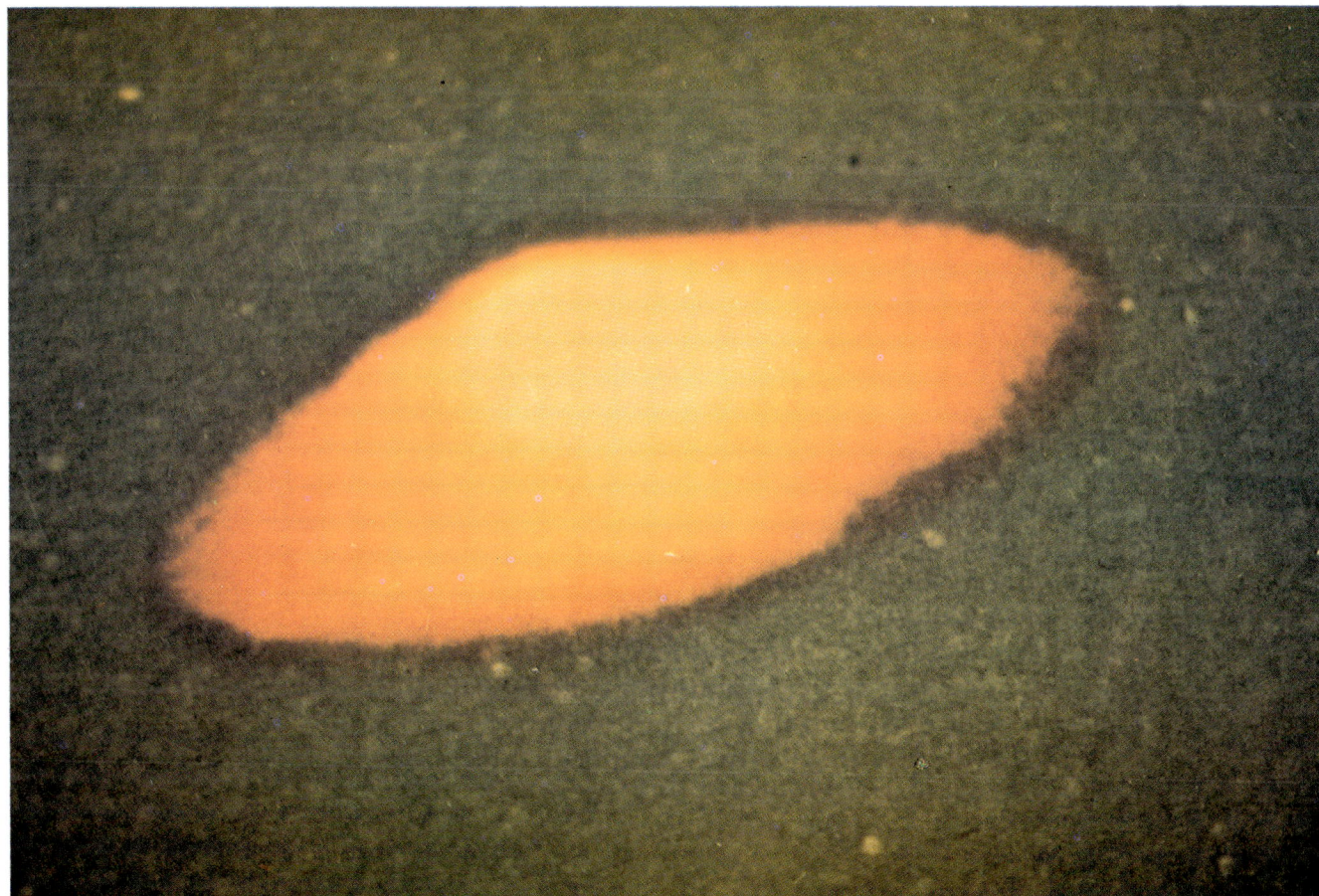

The sinking of the Titanic, the assassinations of the Kennedy brothers and the Aberfan disaster – all these have been subjects of premonitions. ROY STEMMAN describes some spectacular successes achieved by those with the fascinating gift of precognition

The warning voice

AT 5 O'CLOCK one morning in 1979 a knock at her apartment door woke Helen Tillotson from a deep sleep. She heard her mother calling, 'Helen, are you there? Let me in!' Helen hurried to the door to find out what was wrong. Her mother, Mrs Marjorie Tillotson, who lived in a Philadelphia apartment block across the street, demanded to know why Helen had been knocking on *her* door minutes earlier.

Helen, 26, assured her mother that she had retired at 11 o'clock the previous night and had not woken up until she heard her mother knocking at the door. 'But I *saw* you. I *spoke* to you,' said Mrs Tillotson. She said Helen had told her to follow her home immediately without asking questions.

Suddenly there was a loud noise from outside. Both women rushed to the window: across the street a gas leak in Mrs Tillotson's block had caused an explosion, and her apartment was gutted. 'If she had been asleep there at the time,' said a fire chief, 'I doubt whether she would have got out alive.'

Had Helen been sleep-walking? Or did her mother have a psychic vision? Whatever the explanation, either mother or daughter had apparently sensed the danger of an explosion, and saved Mrs Tillotson's life. Such incidents are known as premonitions; although they are rare, enough cases have been documented to suggest that some people are able to catch a glimpse of the future.

Early in 1979 Spanish hotel executive Jaime Castell had a dream in which a voice told him he would never see his unborn child, which was due in three months. Convinced that he would die, Castell took out a £50,000 insurance policy – payable only on his death, with no benefits if he lived. Weeks later, as he drove from work at a steady 50 mph (80 km/h), another car travelling in the opposite direction at over 100 mph (160 km/h) went out of control, hit a safety barrier, somersaulted and landed on top of Castell's car. The drivers of both cars were killed instantly.

After paying the £50,000 to Castell's widow, a spokesman for the insurance company said that a death occurring so soon after such a specific policy was taken out would normally have to be investigated thoroughly. 'But this incredible accident rules out any suspicion. A fraction of a second either way and he would have escaped.'

Sometimes a number of people have dreadful forebodings of the same event. Many of them have no direct connection with the tragedy they foresee, but some, like Eryl Mai Jones, become its victims. On 20 October 1966, this nine-year-old Welsh girl told her mother she had dreamed that when she had gone to school it was not there. 'Something black had come down all over it,' she said. Next day she went to school in Aberfan – and half a million tons of coal waste slithered down onto the mining village, killing Eryl and 139 others – most of them children.

After the disaster, many people claimed to have had premonitions about it. They were investigated by a London psychiatrist, Dr John Barker, who narrowed them down to 60 he felt were genuine. He was so impressed by the evidence for premonitions of the tragedy that he helped set up the British Premonitions Bureau, to record and monitor predictions. It was hoped the Bureau could be used

Above: the terrible events of 21 October 1966, when the entire Welsh mining village of Aberfan was obliterated by coal waste, were foreseen by many people. Among them was nine-year-old Eryl Mai Jones (inset), who became one of the victims

Far right: the Titanic, the 'safest ocean liner ever built', which sank on her maiden voyage in 1912. Journalist W.T. Stead (right), one of the many who drowned, had published a strangely prophetic story a few years earlier about a similar tragedy

to give early warning of similar disasters and enable lives to be saved. Unfortunately it has not yet proved to be of very much practical use.

A similar attempt to harness predictions is now in operation in the United States. An earthquake is expected on the San Andreas fault in the near future and it is hoped it will be possible to predict its date by monitoring premonitions so that a mass evacuation can be made before the event.

When Dr Barker analysed the Aberfan premonitions he noticed that there was a gradual build-up during the week before the Welsh tip buried the school, reaching a peak on the night before the tragedy. Two Californian premonition bureaux – one at Monterey, south of San Francisco, the other at Berkeley – are now sifting through predictions from members of the public in the hope of detecting a similar pattern.

Sceptics often point out that information about premonitions is published only after the event, and that the vast majority of such predictions are discarded when they are found to be wrong. This may be true in many cases, but there are exceptions.

Prophet arrested

A Scottish newspaper, the *Dundee Courier & Advertiser*, carried a story on 6 December 1978, headlined 'Prophet didn't have a ticket'. It told of the appearance of Edward Pearson, 43, at Perth Sheriff Court, charged with travelling on the train from Inverness to Perth on 4 December without paying the proper fare.

Pearson – described as 'an unemployed Welsh prophet' – was said to have been on his way to see the Minister of the Environment to warn him about an earthquake that would hit Glasgow in the near future. The *Courier's* readers doubtless found it very amusing. But they were not so amused by the earthquake that shook them in their beds three weeks later, causing damage to buildings in Glasgow and other parts of Scotland. Earth-

quakes in Britain are rare. Prophets who predict them are even rarer.

The most remarkable prophecy ever made must surely be the story of the *Titanic*, the great ocean liner which sank on her maiden voyage in 1912 with terrible loss of life. In 1898 a novel by a struggling writer, Morgan Robertson, predicted the disaster with uncanny accuracy.

Robertson's story told of a 70,000-tonne vessel, the safest ocean liner in the world, which hit an iceberg in the Atlantic on her maiden voyage. She sank and most of her 2500 passengers were lost because, incredibly, the liner had only 24 lifeboats – less than half the number needed to save all the passengers and crew on board.

On April 14, 1912, the real-life tragedy occurred as the 66,000-tonne *Titanic* was making her maiden voyage across the Atlantic. She, too, hit an iceberg; she, too, sank. And, like the liner in the novel, she did not have enough lifeboats – only 20, in fact – and there was terrible loss of life. Of the 2224 people on board the luxury liner, 1513 perished in the icy waters. Robertson even came close to getting the vessel's name right – he called it the SS *Titan*.

Another work of fiction about a similar tragedy had appeared in a London newspaper some years earlier. The editor was a distinguished journalist, W. T. Stead, who added a prophetic note to the end of the story: 'This is exactly what might take place, and what will take place, if liners are sent to sea short of boats.' By an ironic twist of fate, Stead was one of the passengers on the *Titanic* who died for that very reason.

Such cases are rare, however, and for every prediction that is fulfilled there are perhaps a thousand that are not. In 1979 the Mind Science Foundation of San Antonio, Texas, USA, came up with a novel experiment to test how accurately people could predict an event. The American Skylab space station had begun to fall out of orbit and, although it was known for certain that it

would eventually fall to Earth, scientists did not know when this would occur or where it would land. The Foundation invited people known to have psychic powers – and anyone else who wanted to participate – to predict the date of Skylab's fall and the spot on Earth where its remains would land. It called the exercise Project Chicken Little, and over 200 people responded to the appeal. Their predictions were analysed and published before Skylab fell – and they were virtually all wrong: very few came close to the date of Skylab's return (11 June) and even fewer guessed that it would land in Australia.

Bombs and assassinations

While experiments to prove that the future can be predicted have not been very successful, some individuals nevertheless seem to excel at prophecy. Nostradamus, for example, the 16th-century seer, made many prophecies that have apparently come true. Not everyone agrees with their interpretation, however. Take this one, for example:

Near the harbour and in two cities will be two scourges, the like of which have never been seen. Hunger, plague within, people thrown out by the sword will cry for help from the great immortal God.

What does it predict? Nostradamus's followers say it is a prediction of the atom bomb attacks on Nagasaki and Hiroshima in 1945. But no one could have used his prophecy to foretell the events. In other words, it is hindsight that gives credibility to Nostradamus' writings.

A modern seer is Jeane Dixon, who predicted the assassinations of President John F. Kennedy, his brother Robert Kennedy, and civil rights leader Martin Luther King. Her premonition of the American president's murder came 11 years before the event and before he had even become President.

A devout woman, she had gone to St

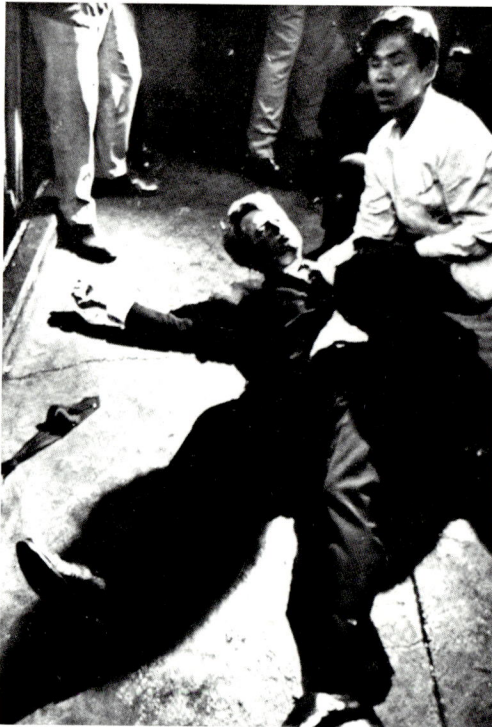

Matthew's Cathedral in Washington one morning in 1952 to pray, and was standing before a statue of the Virgin Mary when she had a vision of the White House. The numerals 1 – 9 – 6 – 0 appeared above it against a dark cloud. A young, blue-eyed man stood at the door. A voice told her that a Democrat, who would be inaugurated as President in 1960, would be assassinated while in office.

She predicted his brother's death in 1968 – in an even more startling way – while addressing a convention at the Ambassador Hotel, Los Angeles. She invited questions from the floor and one woman asked if Robert Kennedy would become president. Suddenly, Jeane Dixon saw a black curtain fall between her and the audience, and she

Above: Nostradamus, the 16th-century seer, is credited with having prophesied the atom bomb attacks on Nagasaki and Hiroshima (above left) in 1945. But his writings are couched in such general terms that it is difficult to tell precisely what they predict

Below: Jeane Dixon, the modern American seer who predicted the assassinations of President John F. Kennedy, his brother Robert Kennedy (left) and civil rights leader Martin Luther King

told the questioner: 'No, he will not. He will never be President of the United States because of a tragedy right here in this hotel.'

A week later Robert Kennedy was gunned down in the Ambassador Hotel.

But even Jeane Dixon doesn't get all her predictions right. In fact, even the best seers claim no more than a 70 per cent success rate, and sceptics argue that it appears so high only because their predictions are vague.

Sceptics, of course, will argue that it is impossible to look into the future. Many of them feel that, until the existence of pre-cognition is proved in the laboratory, it cannot be taken seriously. But, although it may not be easy to look ahead at will, there remain on record some extraordinary stories of premonition that are difficult to explain according to the laws of conventional science – unless there is something wrong with our concept of space and time.

A first-class example of this is the experience of Mark Twain. Before he became a famous writer – and while he was still known by the name Sam Clemens – he worked as an apprentice pilot on a steamboat, the *Pennsylvania*, which plied the Mississippi river. His younger brother Henry worked as a clerk on the same boat. Sam went to visit his sister in St Louis, and, while he was there, he had a vivid dream. He saw a metal coffin

resting on two chairs. In it was his brother and, resting on his chest, a bouquet of white flowers with a crimson one in the middle.

A few days later, back on the boat, Sam had an argument with the chief pilot of the *Pennsylvania* and was transferred to another boat, the *Lacey*. His brother stayed aboard the *Pennsylvania*, which was travelling up the river two days ahead of the *Lacey*. When Sam reached Greenville, Mississippi, he was told that the *Pennsylvania* had blown up just outside Memphis with the loss of 150 lives. His brother Henry, however, was still alive, though badly scalded, and Sam spent six days and nights with him until he died. Exhausted, he fell into a deep sleep; when he awoke, his brother's body had been removed from the room, so he went to find it.

He found it just as he had seen it in the dream. Henry was in a metal coffin, which was resting on two chairs. But there was one detail which was missing – the flowers. As Sam watched, an elderly woman entered the room carrying a bouquet of white flowers with a single red rose in the centre. She placed them on Henry's body and left.

Mark Twain's glimpse of the future was fulfilled in every detail.

How could ESP be put to practical use? Science seeks the answers: see page 134

Samuel Clemens (1835–1910), better known as the writer Mark Twain, who had a remarkable premonition about his brother's death in a steamboat accident on the Mississippi River

A nightmare comes true

On the evening of Friday, 26 May 1979 the world was shocked to learn that an American Airlines DC-10 airliner had crashed – a mass of flames and twisted wreckage – on take-off from Chicago's O'Hare International Airport. The lives of 273 people were lost in the worst disaster in the history of flying in the United States.

In Cincinnati, Ohio, 23-year-old office manager David Booth sat slumped in horrified disbelief in front of his television. For 10 consecutive nights before the disaster he had had the same terrible nightmare. First, he heard the sound of engines failing, then looked on helplessly as a huge American Airlines aeroplane swerved sharply, rolled over and crashed to the ground in a mass of red and orange flames. Not only did he see the crash and hear the explosion, he also felt the heat of the flames. Each time he awoke in terror and was obsessed all day by the memory of the hideous dream. He was sure it was a premonition: 'There was never any doubt to me that something was going to happen,' he said. 'It wasn't like a dream. It was like I was standing there watching the whole thing – like watching television.'

After several nights he could no longer keep his terrible premonition to himself and, on Tuesday, 22 May 1979, he telephoned the Federal Aviation

Authority at the Greater Cincinnati Airport. Then he called American Airlines and a psychiatrist at the University of Cincinnati. They listened sympathetically, but that didn't make David Booth feel any better. Three days later, almost out of his mind with worry, he heard the news of the DC-10 crash.

The Federal Aviation Authority had taken David Booth's call seriously enough to attempt – in vain – to match up the details of his nightmare with some known airport or aeroplane somewhere in the country. When they heard the news of the crash, the details tallied all too well. 'It was uncanny,' said Jack Barker, public affairs officer for the southern region of the FAA. 'There were differences, but there were many similarities. The greatest similarity was his calling [naming] the airline and the airplane . . . and that [the plane] came in inverted.' Booth had mentioned a 'three-engine aircraft' resembling a DC-10, and the crash site he described was similar to the airport at Chicago.

David Booth stopped having nightmares once the disaster had happened, but he continued to feel disturbed by the whole affair. 'How can you make sense of something like that?' he asked. 'There's no explanation for it. No meaning. No conclusion. It just doesn't make sense.'

The goddess behind the mask

Christianity did not suddenly usurp the old religions of Europe. Instead, the early Church worked subtly to take over gods and shrines that had existed for centuries before the birth of Christ. As a result, the Black Madonnas are a blend of paganism and purity and, as RICHARD LEIGH and MICHAEL BAIGENT show, are still surrounded by ambiguous associations that reach far back in time to ancient religious – and even demonic – beliefs

THE MEDIEVAL KINGS of France traditionally accorded a special significance to the Black Madonnas. This attitude was particularly evident in Louis IX, who ruled during the 13th century and is now known as Saint Louis. Saint Louis had always revered the Black Madonna at Le Puy. She does not appear to have been inordinately grateful, however, because Saint Louis, having launched a crusade against the Saracens of Egypt, was resoundingly defeated and captured along with his entire army. Nevertheless, he commanded considerable respect from the sultan who had vanquished him; and on his eventual release, the sultan offered him as a gift any object he might desire from the Egyptian treasury. The King selected a statue of what he called 'Our Lady and Child' – a Black Madonna, some 27 inches (69 centimetres) high, swathed in bandages and wearing a copper crown.

This statue had been part of the Islamic treasure for centuries – indeed, it had been highly venerated by the Saracens, who claimed it had been carved by the prophet Jeremiah. In 1254, Saint Louis carried the statue back to France, and installed it at Le Puy in place of the Black Madonna which had formerly been there. At least one of the present-day Black Madonnas is thus unequivocally Eastern in origin.

Harlot and nun

The Black Madonna Saint Louis obtained in Egypt, and many of the others as well, were originally pre-Christian Mother Goddesses. It is well known that the Middle East – from Egypt, through Palestine and Syria, to Persia – was influenced by such goddesses in pre-Christian times. These Mother Goddesses were worshipped under a number of names, but they were essentially the same figure. And their appeal was extraordinarily tenacious. Demeter, for example, was worshipped at Eleusis, Greece, as late as 1801; and when two Englishmen in that year removed her statue, a major riot ensued among the peasantry.

The Mother Goddess was an extremely complex figure. She was simultaneously good and evil, creative and destructive, beneficent and malevolent, light and dark. She embodied the myriad aspects of nature – storm, drought and famine as well as bountiful harvests and the fruits of the earth. At times, she could be cruelly chaste, at times shamelessly promiscuous – a combination of harlot and nun. In order to reflect her dual character, she was sometimes depicted with one side of her face black, the other white. Alternatively, she was sometimes clad in a black and white garment. And on at least one site, there were actually two statues, identical except that one was light and the other dark.

The ancient Mother Goddess was often associated with the Moon, which passes through a spectrum of phases, from dark to full. By virtue of the Moon's influence on

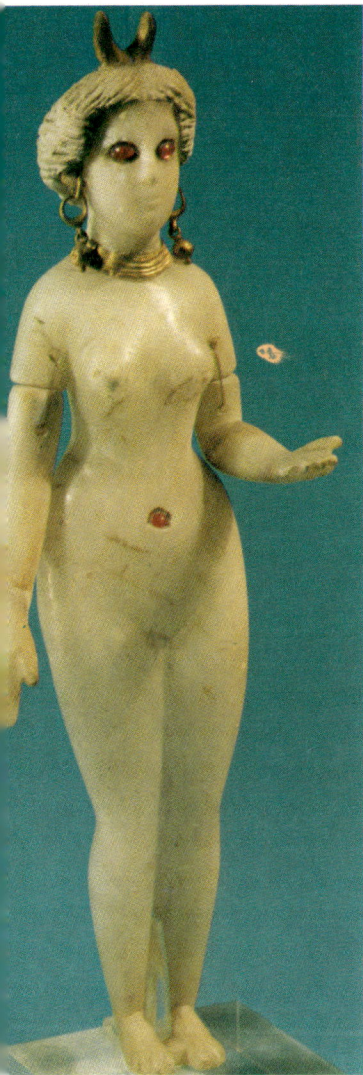

Above: for thousands of years the goddess Ishtar has been associated with the Moon, which can be seen crowning the head of this figurine from Babylon

Left: the Virgin of Jasna Góra, who was declared Queen of Poland in 1656. Legend says the painting was executed by St Luke. The silver cover was presented by a Polish military order for the 600th anniversary of the installation of the image in the monastery

Right: two statuettes from Saqquara, Egypt, both representing Isis with the infant Horus on her left arm

Far right: Astarte, mounted on the back of a lion. Like the Roman goddess Diana, she carries a bow and arrow

tides, the Mother Goddess was also associated with the sea and became patroness of mariners – who revered her as 'Star of the Sea' or 'Stella Maris'. This led to her being further associated with the Pole Star, and with Venus as well. Like the Moon, Venus possessed a dual aspect – that of Morning and Evening Star. The former of these aspects was regarded as sinister; this is reflected in Judaeo-Christian tradition, where the Morning Star is often linked with Lucifer.

The Mother Goddess was worshipped under a bewildering variety of names. In Egypt, for example, she was known as Isis – who was often depicted as black and holding her son, Horus, on her knee. There would seem to be little question that the Madonna obtained by Saint Louis from the Egyptian treasury was originally an Isis figure.

In northern Syria and in Babylon, the Mother Goddess was known as Ishtar – which was also the Babylonian name for the planet we call Venus. Like Isis, Ishtar was often depicted as black; and although she had beneficent aspects, many Babylonian myths – the *Epic of Gilgamesh*, for instance – stress the harmful side of her nature.

In Phoenicia, the Mother Goddess was known as Astarte, and it was in the guise of Astarte that she exercised perhaps her most profound influence on Western tradition. The Phoenicians, of course, were seafarers. In the course of their maritime movements – under the patronage of Stella Maris – they brought numerous images of Astarte to Western Europe, and these images subsequently became Black Madonnas. Like the later Christian Madonna, Astarte was often symbolised by a dove. Sometimes she was portrayed as half black, half white. Sometimes she was worshipped in the form of a triangular stone, which was occasionally white, but more often black and probably meteoric in origin. Astarte figures prominently in the Old Testament, where she is referred to as 'Queen of Heaven'.

In the chronicles that comprise the Old Testament, Astarte, the Queen of Heaven, appears as one of the primary adversaries or rivals of the God of Israel – the patriarchal God of Abraham and Moses. Indeed, the Israelites, on a number of occasions, defect from the God of Abraham and Moses and make their devotions to the Queen of Heaven. Jeremiah, for example, angrily condemns his people for falling away from God and *returning* to the worship of Astarte – implying that Astarte-worship was once the norm. The Old Testament tells us further that Solomon was a passionate devotee of the Queen of Heaven, to whom he erected altars on every high hill. It can be persuasively argued, in fact, that the *Song of songs* is not addressed to any mortal woman, but to Astarte. If this is true, the opening words of that famous text become particularly significant: 'I am black, but comely, O ye daughters of Jerusalem.'

We have already noted the importance of the Black Madonna to Saint Bernard. It is thus not surprising that, of all Biblical texts, the one to which Saint Bernard most frequently addressed himself was the *Song of songs*. He is said to have written more than three hundred sermons on it.

Needless to say, Astarte was vigorously condemned by both Jewish and Christian teachers. By the advent of the Christian era, in fact, she had been masculinised and turned into the arch-demon Ashtaroth, one of the most powerful of Satan's minions. And yet, as a Black Madonna, she continued to attract devotees – including a pillar of Christendom as august as Saint Bernard.

As we have noted, numerous Black Madonnas were undoubtedly carried to Europe by the Phoenicians. In subsequent centuries, the whole of the Mediterranean world – the world of the Mother Goddesses – fell under the sway of the Roman Empire. According to Imperial policy, the Roman army conscripted its recruits from one part of the Empire and dispatched them as garrisons to others. Thus, Roman conscripts from the Mediterranean were posted to northern Europe. Many of them brought their guardian deities with them.

There is reason to believe that the Mother

one aspect of the Moon – the bright, benevolent and chaste aspect. Arduina incorporated the dark side of the Moon as well, and, in this capacity, was portrayed as a Black Madonna. One of the centres of her cult was the town of Lunéville ('City of the Moon'), where a large statue of her was situated. In the 6th century, this statue was destroyed by a zealous Christian missionary. Nevertheless, the cult of Arduina persisted. As late as 1304, the Church was still issuing vehement edicts against it.

Pagan predecessors

When Christianity first spread to Europe, it was a rigorously patriarchal creed. This rendered it unpalatable to the populace at large, who sought in it an equivalent of their ancient Mother Goddesses and could not find any. In order to establish a foothold, Christianity had to adapt itself, had to render itself more acceptable to its potential converts. Thus, the cult of the Virgin Mary was introduced and made to harmonise in as many respects as possible with previous beliefs. Mary's Assumption, for example, was officially celebrated on 15 August – the date of the chief festival to Diana.

For the same reason Mary, in the popular mind at least if not in that of the theologian, came to be associated with the Moon. European peasants would refer to her as 'Our Moon', 'Perfect and Eternal Moon' and 'Moon of the Church'. Alternatively, the Moon itself was often called 'Notre Dame'. Confronted by this popular identification the Church was obliged to make certain concessions. Pope Innocent III sanctioned the association of Mary and the Moon thus:

Towards the moon it is that he who is buried in the shadow of sin should gaze. Having lost divine grace, the day disappears, the sun no longer shines for him, but the moon is still on the horizon. Let him speak to Mary; under her guidance many every day find their way to God.

Identification with the Moon was not the only respect in which Mary came to take on attributes of the old Mother Goddesses. By the Middle Ages, as we have seen, she had acquired Astarte's former title, 'Queen of Heaven'. She had also acquired from Astarte the title 'Stella Maris', 'Star of the Sea'.

This Mary, had precious little to do with the Virgin Mary of the Gospels or of official theology. In fact she remained an essentially pagan Mother Goddess, overlaid by a transparently thin veneer of Christianity. The people themselves did not bother to quibble about names. The goddess, for them, had once been called Belisama or Arduina or Rosemertha. Now the Church insisted that she be called Mary. But despite the new designation, she herself remained essentially unchanged.

However, the figure of Mary as propagated by the Church does not seem to have

Above: the Black Madonna of Montserrat, which was either brought to the New World from Spain or executed there from a Spanish copy. It is now in the National Museum of Colonial Art, Quito, Ecuador

Below: Pope Innocent III, who gave his official blessing to the popular association of the Virgin Mary with the Moon

Goddess was already well established in Europe even before the Roman Empire established its dominion. Certain Black Madonna sites – Chartres and Le Puy, for example – were important Druidic centres, and the Black Madonnas found there may well date from Druidic times. It is known that the Celtic tribes in pre-Roman Gaul worshipped a god named Belen, whose consort and sister was the Black Virgin Belisama. The cult possessed a sacred stone at Chartres, above the subterranean crypt where the Black Madonna was subsequently found. It is thus reasonable to assume that the Black Madonna found at Chartres originally represented not the Virgin Mary, but Belisama. Similarly, the Black Madonna found at Sion-Vaudémont in Lorraine seems to have represented the goddess Rosemertha – the local consort of the Teutonic god Wotan, from whom Vaudémont ('Wotan's Mount') derives its name.

As the Roman legions overran western Europe, the native Mother Goddesses were amalgamated with their imported Roman equivalents. Celtic and Teutonic deities were identified with the corresponding god or goddess in the Roman pantheon. Arduina, the tutelary goddess of the Ardennes, was equated with the Roman moon goddess Diana. Diana, however, represented only

to it, to propitiate it. This situation seems to have dictated a search for an alternative feminine figure within the context of established Christianity – a figure who, unlike the Virgin, *could* accommodate the darker aspects of the old Mother Goddesses.

Such a figure was readily available in the Magdalene, who represented everything the Virgin did not. Concurrent with the cult of the Virgin, there arose a cult of the Magdalene, which gained increasing status during the Middle Ages. While the Church insisted on a rigorous distinction between the Virgin and the Magdalene, the people sought a conception of the feminine which reconciled and combined the two – and thereby constituted an organic continuation and perpetuation of the Mother Goddesses. This seems to have found expression in the already ambiguous figure of the Black Madonna.

Most Black Madonnas were loosely associated, at least in part, with the Virgin. When first discovered, the pre-Christian statues were regarded as miraculous pagan precognitions of Jesus' birth. As we have seen, however, the Black Madonnas were also attributed with characteristics and powers quite divorced from the Virgin – sexuality, for example, fertility, marriage, the underworld, earthly rather than heavenly bliss, matter rather than spirit. To this extent, the Black Madonnas represent the Magdalene as much as they do the Virgin – indeed in some ways more so. In fact, there are certain Black Madonnas which, quite explicitly, are not associated with the Virgin

harmonised with her pagan predecessors as perfectly as might have been desired. As we have seen, the ancient Mother Goddesses were multi-faceted and characterised by a dual nature. They combined, in one and the same figure, diametrically opposed attributes – the conflicting attributes traditionally ascribed to the feminine principle. Christianity refused to acknowledge this ambivalence. Instead, it postulated a Virgin who was pure, immaculate, chaste, asexual, totally devoid of any negative or dark aspects – in short, an idealised and ultimately lopsided image.

To the former devotees of a complex, multi-faceted conception of the feminine, the image of Mary promulgated by the Church seems to have been oversimplified, incomplete, perhaps even 'too good to be true'. Through their own personal experience, they were already familiar with other, darker aspects of both femininity and nature – aspects which Mary, pristine and unsullied as she was, could not accommodate. To whom could they ascribe the negative aspects of their former Mother Goddesses? The Church insisted that these aspects be ascribed to the Devil; but the people themselves did not see the 'dark' side of the feminine as unequivocally evil. And in any case, evil or not, they had often of necessity to come to terms with it, to appeal

at all, but with the Magdalene. Les Saintes Maries de la Mer near Marseilles, for instance, is a major centre for the cult of the Magdalene; and the Black Madonna there is generally acknowledged to represent the Magdalene. On this basis, it might be argued that *all* Black Madonnas – at least in Christian times – were once deemed to represent Jesus' companion, rather than his mother.

Black Madonnas, lines of force, and a ship that breasts the sea of time: see page 154

Above left: the naive simplicity with which the Virgin and Child could be represented as dark-skinned is exemplified in this early 14th-century painting from Sienna

Left: the idealised image of the Virgin Mary in Renaissance and modern art owes a great deal to the studio of Botticelli. In this tondo (now in the National Gallery, London) the basic human qualities of the figures have become asexual, antiseptic abstractions

The way to the stars

An astronaut might be able to travel through a black hole to distant parts of our Universe. But how would he return? ADRIAN BERRY believes that by creating white holes astronauts will return to their point of departure – instantaneously

IN THE DISTANT future, perhaps three to six centuries from now, a fleet of 1000 interstellar bulldozers could be setting off from Earth for a point in space one light year from the Sun. Their mission: the construction of a black hole, through which astronauts could travel to other parts of our Universe.

The idea may seem fantastic, but the difficulties involved in gathering the material needed to build a black hole with a total mass of more than 3 million times the mass of Earth will not be quite as great as it might seem. Each interstellar bulldozer will be capable of generating a magnetic field some 150,000 miles (240,000 kilometres) wide; a field capable of gathering matter, mainly iron, nickel and hydrogen plasma, as soon as the bulldozer is beyond the orbits of the outer planets of our solar system. To generate this huge magnetic field, electrical energy can be supplied through a superconducting system powered by the vehicle's main engine. The iron, nickel and hydrogen plasma piling up in front of the magnetic field will form a great column of matter stretching forward for hundreds of thousands of miles. This mass will be propelled forward by the vehicle.

We can calculate that the interstellar matter will be gathered up at the rate of 35 ounces (990 grams) per second per ship; or, if a fleet of 1000 ships is at work, at a rate of 35,000 ounces (990 kilograms) per second: about 3500 tonnes per hour.

Suppose that, because of the great distances involved in their journey one light-year round the Sun, 20 years elapse between the time that the ships embark on their mission and the time that they begin to accumulate matter in significant quantities. After this

If astronauts are to travel through artificial black holes to remote parts of the Universe, vast cities in space will have to be built to act as bases for operations

period, their task will be made easier by a factor working in their favour: the accumulated matter will itself ionise fresh matter, which will in turn be caught up in the eddying forward movement.

It is not unreasonable to predict that when this process of accumulation really begins to mount, its actual rate of increase will itself increase at a rate of perhaps 1 per cent every 24 hours. Now anything that increases at 1 per cent per day will double, by compound interest, every 70 days. If such a rate of doubling can be achieved with the ships cruising at about 7 per cent of the speed of light, or 47 million mph (76 million km/h), a black hole can be constructed about 15 years after the end of the 20-year preparation period – less than 40 years from start to finish.

Gateway in space

Having constructed the black hole, what happens to an astronaut attempting to enter it? Should he just let himself go, abandoning the controls of his spacecraft to the gravitational fields, trusting that he will be safely hurled down the whirling spiral? No, for if he did this he would be sucked into the singularity and be crushed to pieces. Instead, he must remember the disc shape of the black hole. This disc (assuming that the black hole has 10 times the mass of the Sun) will have a circumference of just under 116 miles (190 kilometres) rotating at a velocity of 1000 complete revolutions per second. Each part of the disc will be revolving at a speed of 116,000 miles per second (190,000 km/s). The astronaut must match this speed precisely as he approaches the black hole. This speed, which is slightly more than 60 per cent of the speed of light, is not prohibited by any scientific law but could only be attained by some super-spacecraft of the future.

When the astronaut has matched his speed with that of the spinning disc, each in a sense will now be stationary, relative to each other. The astronaut 'looks' at the disc-edge beside him and 'sees' a long rectangular aperture with a height of about 640 yards (590 metres). This aperture is the gateway to another region in space and is the one route which passes through both event horizons (inner and outer) and avoids the crushing densities of the singularity. Diving directly into the aperture, the astronaut and his ship vanish from the sight of any outside observer. Yet they survive; they vanish only in the sense that a spectator at an airport sees an aircraft and its passengers vanish into the sky. For the astronaut and his ship will have vanished out of the immediate region of space. They will have accomplished the miracle of vanishing in one place and reappearing, a moment later, in another place which may be separated from the point of disappearance by a vast distance. How does this miracle occur? What actually happens in the region between the two event horizons?

This region is highly mysterious, but

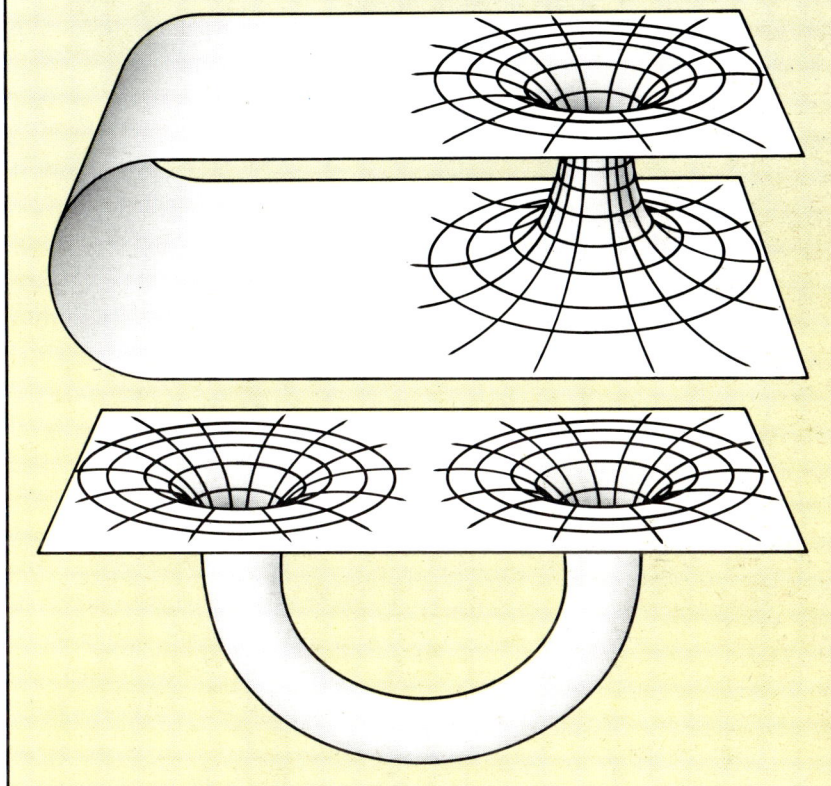

Albert Einstein and Isaac Rosen developed this simple model (top) of a static black hole – the famous Einstein–Rosen bridge. A spacecraft entering the black hole along the upper surface of spacetime will emerge on the lower surface – but where will this be? Einstein and Rosen suggested that spacetime in our Universe may be curved (centre), so the spaceship will emerge at a different time and place; but if, as astronomers now believe, spacetime in our Universe, is almost flat, the shape of the Einstein–Rosen bridge could look more like a wormhole (bottom) linking different parts of our Universe

there is one thing that can be said of it with certainty; distances within it are abridged absolutely. The word 'distance' not only loses its present meaning, it ceases to have *any* meaning. By its very act of passing through the inner event horizon of the black hole, the spaceship has begun to cross what is known as an Einstein-Rosen bridge – a timeless passage that interconnects different regions of our Universe – and, an immeasurable fraction of a second later, emerges in another and distant part of space.

But the curious feature of entering the black hole and passing along the Einstein-Rosen bridge is that the spaceship is not only flung into another part of space, but in making this journey it is propelled *backwards* in time. The Einstein-Rosen bridge is, in fact, a time machine.

It may seem that, in talking of time travel,

we are entering into complete fantasy. But this is not so, for a time machine and a distance-abolishing machine are merely two phrases to describe the same thing. Distance simply means time travelled, or to be more precise, it is the average speed of a journey multiplied by the time taken to achieve it. If, for example, a distance of 3500 miles (5630 kilometres), the distance between London and New York, was miraculously reduced to zero, you could travel this distance instantaneously, in no time at all, because zero divided by any number equals zero. Yet to make this instantaneous journey, you would be moving backwards in time *while* moving forwards in space.

Passing through the black hole, and thereby achieving an instantaneous journey to another part of the Universe, how will our astronaut ever return? Is he not lost for ever? In fact, he can return to his point of departure by way of a white hole.

A white hole is no more strange than a black hole. It is simply its opposite. A black hole is an implosion, and a white hole is an explosion. Nothing can ever escape from a black hole; everything must, sooner or later, escape from a white hole.

Do white holes exist? In theory at least, white holes should be visible from telescopes on Earth. Yet, though 'visible' they have so far proved difficult to identify. A giant white hole would, in any case, be indistinguishable from an exploding galaxy, and a relatively small one of, say, 10 solar masses, would look at a great distance like an ordinary star. J. V. Narlikar and his colleague K. M. V. Apparao of the Tata Institute of Fundamental Research in Bombay suggest that those very violent exploding galaxies known as Seyfert galaxies (after their original discoverer Carl Seyfert) could be giant white holes, presumably of many millions of solar masses, pouring back into the Universe matter that had been devoured by distant black holes. They

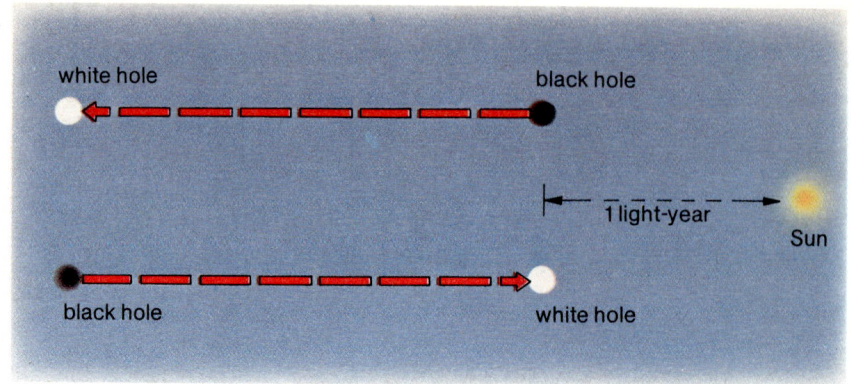

Above: travel between distant parts of our Universe will require *two* black holes, each with its corresponding white hole – one for the outward journey, the other for the return journey. The 'outward' black hole would be constructed at a convenient and safe distance – say about one light-year – from the Sun; the black holes and their corresponding white holes would be several light-years apart. The arrows indicate the only possible directions of travel

Left: Seyfert galaxies, like this one, are believed to be giant white holes pouring matter back into the Universe as fast as black holes are taking it out

Further reading
Adrian Berry, *The iron sun*, Coronet 1979
John Gribbin, *Time warps*, Dent 1979
William J. Kaufmann III, *Black holes and warped spacetime*, Freeman (San Francisco) 1979
William J. Kaufmann III, *The cosmic frontiers of general relativity*, Penguin 1979
John Taylor, *Black holes*, Fontana 1974

propose that the physical mechanism of a white hole will be identical to that of a black hole, except that everything happens in reverse. Now the nature of the Einstein-Rosen bridge, the region where forward distances are reduced to zero, predicts that the white hole will come into existence at the very same instant as its corresponding black hole. And so, if any astronaut can vanish down a black hole without himself or his ship being destroyed, then he will be able to emerge equally unscathed, a fraction of a second later, from a white hole.

If instantaneous cosmic travel is to be achieved, starting from a sort of 'cosmic railway station' one light-year from the Sun, it will not be enough simply to construct a black hole. The black hole would enable astronauts to travel instantaneously to distances of many light-years, but they would have no means of coming back, except through normal space, a journey which would take them many decades. It will be necessary to construct a *second* black hole at the distant point where they will emerge into normal space, which they will use for returning to a point no further than about one light-year from the Sun.

This second black hole, in turn, will bring into existence a second white hole. The approximate positions of the four holes, two black and two white, is shown in the diagram. Two parallel Einstein-Rosen bridges will have come into existence, with matter flowing through them in opposite directions, and each with a black hole and a white hole at their respective ends.

The construction of black holes as gateways to other universes will have answered one of the most formidable problems of future ages, the feasibility of travel to the stars. Failure to solve it could bring about the eventual stagnation and ruin of the human species. Yet if it can be solved, whether by the method outlined here or by any other, the prospect will instead be the establishment of a Galactic community, a society in which our descendants will be scattered through millions of worlds in orbits around countless stars. Humanity will be safe for ever from the threat of extinction, and there need be no limit to the flowering of human culture that this diversity will produce.

From the sea serpent to the super-otter

Besides classic sightings of sea monsters there are 'classic' hoaxes, too. But this does not mean that we should discount the existence of unknown creatures. And, as JANET and COLIN BORD show, using the techniques pioneered by the Belgian zoologist Bernard Heuvelmans the whole subject can now be studied scientifically

MANY SCIENTISTS remain sceptical about the existence of underwater monsters, yet sightings of giant sea creatures, some extremely detailed, continue to be reported around the world.

An active monster of recent years, sighted off the coast of Cornwall, England, is known as Morgawr (Cornish for 'sea giant'). This was seen quite often during 1975 and 1976, in Falmouth Bay, and on 5 March 1976 two photographs of it were published in the *Falmouth Packet*. Although these were submitted anonymously, nevertheless they do appear very convincing, showing a long-necked creature similar to that reported to be in Loch Ness.

Another strange creature has been seen in the waters of Cardigan Bay off the west coast of Wales. On 2 March 1975, six local schoolgirls were walking along the beach at dusk when 200 yards (180 metres) away a creature moved across the beach towards the sea. They described it as being 10 feet (3 metres) long with a long neck and tail and large green eyes. They were quite terrified at this spectacle and ran away to report it to the coastguard. Later they described it to their art teacher, Colin Palmer, who drew the creature. When he showed his sketch to the crew of a fishing boat, who had seen a monster when they were fishing off Bardsey Sound,

The Cornish sea monster Morgawr was sighted several times during 1975 and 1976. 'Mary F' succeeded in photographing the creature, of which 15 to 18 feet (5 to 6 metres) were visible, in February 1976 at Rosemullion Head, near Falmouth

there was 'instant recognition'.

The consequences of the publicity attached to famous sightings are twofold: there is a sudden increase in similar reports, many of which turn out to be well-authenticated, and a subsequent crop of hoaxes. Researchers are, of course, keen to expose the latter. Spurious reports are intended to bring ridicule on those who believe them, so eventually they must be revealed to make their point.

A hoax report that contained, perhaps deliberately, a clue to its true nature was published by the *Globe* in 1848, scarcely a week after *The Times* had published an account of a sea serpent seen by Peter M'Quhae, Captain of HMS *Daedalus*. The hoax was printed in the form of a

Sea monsters

Above: until the Age of Enlightenment in the 18th century, people still thought of the oceans as full of fearsome monsters. In this 16th-century engraving, the whale is depicted as a huge creature with terrible fangs and claws

Right and below right: this strange-looking carcase with its huge head and duck-like beak was washed up on the rocks at Santa Cruz, California, in 1925. Decomposition made the specimen hard to identify but, after examining the skull, the Museum of the California Academy of Sciences showed that the carcase was that of an extremely rare beaked whale

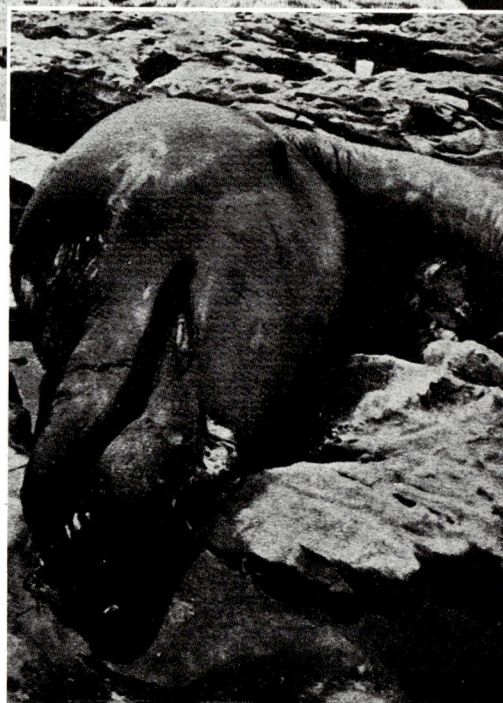

subsequent enquiries revealed that the letter was a hoax.

Over 100 years later, in March 1965, an Australian magazine published an article on 'the Great Barrier Reef monster' by a Frenchman, Robert Le Serrec. He reported that he and his family had been camping on an island on the Great Barrier Reef where they had found a sea serpent, over 80 feet (24 metres) long and lying injured in the shallow lagoon water.

After cautiously circling around the creature in their boat and taking photographs, Le Serrec and his companion, Henk de Jong, entered the water armed with a rifle and a camera. As the two men approached to within 20 feet (6 metres) and took pictures, the creature turned its massive head towards them and opened its mouth threateningly. They quickly returned to their boat and the monster swam out to sea.

The story and photographs were also offered to an American magazine, whose

letter, posted on 19 October in Glasgow and purporting to be from James Henderson, captain of the Mary Ann. He wrote that on 20 September Captain Mark Trelawny of the brig *Daphne* had seen 'a huge serpent, or snake, with a dragon's head', and the captain had loaded a gun with scrap-iron and fired at it. The 100-foot (30-metre) long monster had foamed and lashed the water and made off at 16 knots.

The Times reprinted the story and a keen-eyed correspondent wrote to ask how the *Daphne* had manged to travel from the encounter to Lisbon, where Captain Trelawny had told Captain Henderson of his experience, in only 10 days. The distance covered was 5000 miles (8000 kilometres) and would have called for an average speed of 20 knots. The correspondent drily remarked: 'Probably the serpent took the brig in tow' –

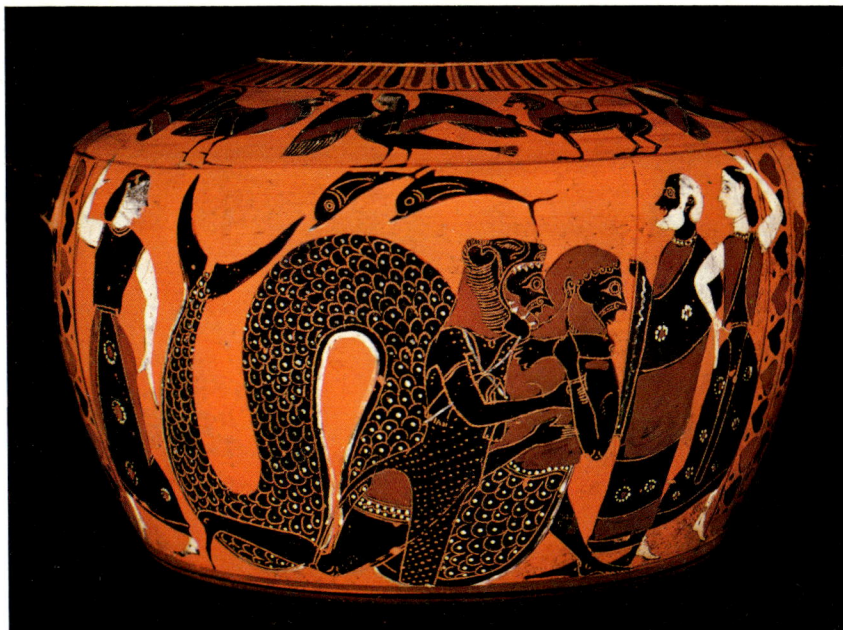

An ancient Greek vase showing Heracles struggling with the river god Achelous to win Deianira. The god is represented with the torso of a man and the body of a sea serpent

remains to examine, and periodically, strange, large carcases are washed up on remote beaches. Owing to pressure of other work and the remoteness of the locations, these are usually ignored or identified at a distance as the remains of a known sea creature, often a basking shark.

The 55-foot (17-metre) long body that was washed up on the shore of the island of Stronsay in the Orkneys in 1808, was first seen by local fishermen and farmers but, before any informed examination could be made, storms had smashed the rotting carcase to pieces. The drawing that was made from the witnesses' descriptions showed an extraordinary animal with a long neck and undulating tail and three pairs of legs, a feature hitherto unknown in a vertebrate.

The corpse was finally identified as a shark by a British surgeon, Everard Home, who had made a study of shark anatomy and was able to obtain specimens of bones that had been removed from the beast. When shark carcases are washed up on shore, the rapid decomposition of certain parts of the anatomy, namely the lower jaw, the lower tail fluke and the fins, leaves what looks like a weird creature with a long thin neck and tail.

In 1925 an unidentified carcase was cast ashore at Santa Cruz, California. It appeared to have a 30-foot (9-metre) long neck and a huge beaked head, but was eventually identified as the remains of a very rare beaked whale from the North Pacific.

The large decomposing 'glob' that was washed up on a remote beach in western Tasmania in July 1960 received little official attention until March 1962. Then scientists from Hobart located the exact spot from the air and a group went to investigate. Helicopters were used to carry away samples, and the official statement said that the object was 'a large lump of decomposing blubber, probably torn off a whale'. However, the other

editor asked Ivan T. Sanderson, the British biologist and investigator of the unexplained, his opinion of them. Le Serrec's background in France was also investigated. Here it was found that he had tried to finance his expedition by telling prospective financial backers that he would make a lot of money on the trip in a venture connected with a giant sea serpent.

Biologists who examined the photographs and descriptions were not satisfied that they portrayed a genuine animal. Its eyes were too far back on the top of its head and Le Serrec's story was not entirely consistent.

The various investigations all pointed to a hoax, probably achieved by filling a long plastic tube with air and sinking it with stones. Needless to say, the American magazine did not publish the story.

The sceptical scientist asks for physical

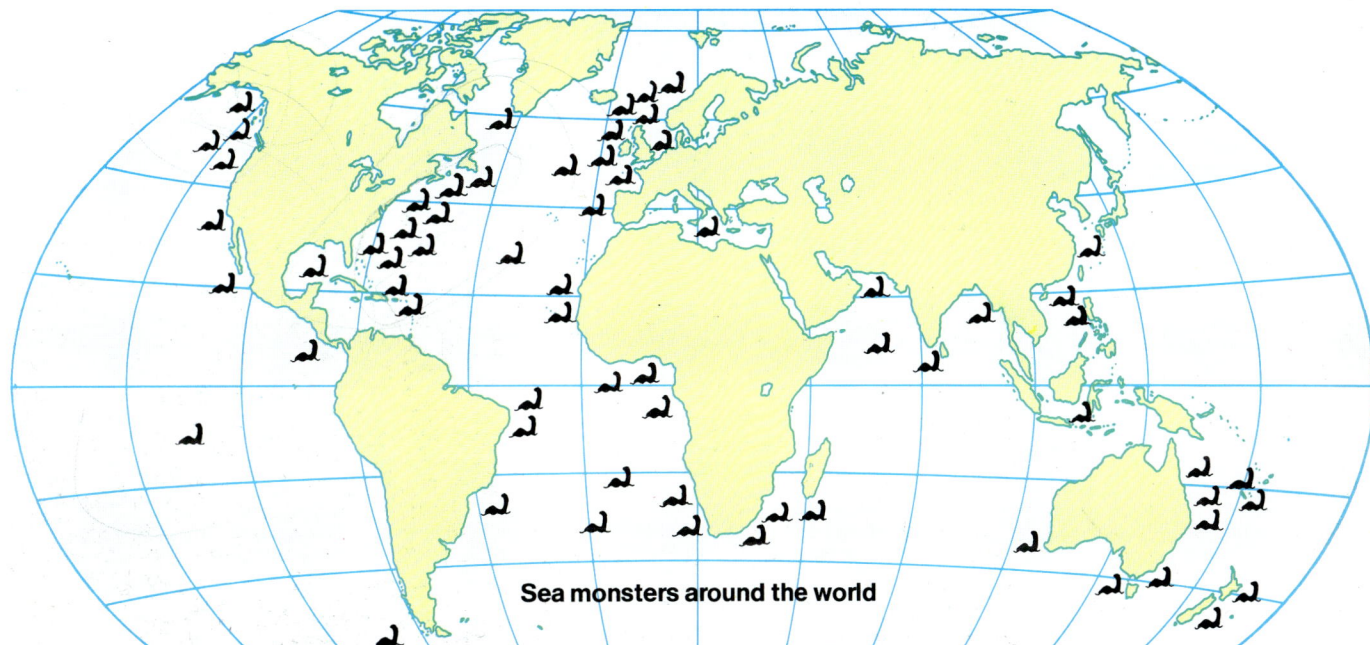

Sea monsters around the world

biologists who had been following the case thought that this was unlikely.

A more' recent find occurred on 25 April 1977, when the Japanese trawler *Zuiyo Maru* hauled up a large, partially rotted carcase 28 miles (45 kilometres) east of Christchurch, New Zealand. Concerned that it might contaminate his catch, the captain, Akira Tanaka, had it photographed and drawn, then dropped it back in the sea. The incident intrigued the world's press and a television film crew flew from Japan to cover the story. Although the ship's crew were convinced that they had seen an unknown monster, the

Right: the long-necked sea serpent appears to be the most common of the nine specific types of sea monster classified by Belgian zoologist Dr Bernard Heuvelmans. Analysis of 48 certain sightings indicate that the creature is between 15 and 65 feet (5 and 20 metres) long and moves through the water with exceptional speed for an animal of this size

Long-necked

photographs suggest a decomposed shark.

Some of the most convincing evidence for the existence of sea monsters comes from those areas where they have been sighted repeatedly over decades or even centuries. In the Strait of Georgia between Vancouver Island and British Columbia, off the west coast of Canada, the creature known locally as Cadborosaurus or Caddy was sighted by the Indians long before the arrival of the white settlers.

In this century an early sighting of Caddy was made by F. W. Kemp, a local government official. On 10 August 1932, Mr Kemp was with his wife and son when they saw it swim at terrific speed through the water. Caddy was seen frequently during the 1930s and in 1950 was sighted by Judge James Brown and his family, when it appeared as a 45-foot (14-metre) long serpent that rose out of the water several times. Mrs. R. A. Stewart, who saw it in 1963 when fishing with her husband, was terrified by its wide-open jaws.

Further south on the American west coast is San Clemente Island, a favourite area for deep-sea angling and an area where water

Above and right: a recent find that attracted worldwide attention was the carcase hauled on board the Japanese trawler *Zuiyo Maru* in 1977. Concerned that the carcase might contaminate his catch, Captain Akira Tanaka had it photographed, then threw it back in the sea. Biologists believe that the photographs show a decomposed shark and not an unknown monster

monsters have been seen frequently throughout this century. When technical fishing writer J. Charles Davis interviewed numerous independent witnesses, he found their descriptions tallied to an amazing degree. Many of the witnesses were wealthy members of the big-game fishing clubs, who knew what to expect from the sea and had no desire to lay themselves open to ridicule.

Why does the sea serpent still remain comparatively unknown? One reason might be that although more than 60 per cent of the Earth's surface is covered by water, very little of it is travelled over by commercial

Many-humped

Super-otter

Left: the many-humped sea serpent and the super-otter are about the same size – 60-100 feet (18-20 metres) long. The many-humped category has been seen chiefly along the coast of New England, USA, though the number of sightings has diminished since the beginning of this century. As there has been no sighting of the super-otter since 1848, Dr Heuvelmans believes it may now be extinct

Right: the main characteristic of the many-finned sea serpent is breath blown out of the nostrils. It grows to a length of more than 60 feet (18 metres) and has been sighted only in tropical waters. The last mammal in Heuvelmans' classification is the merhorse, which has huge eyes and a reddish mane. It has been sighted in most waters of the world, apart from the Indian Ocean and the Polar seas

shipping, which follows fixed and narrow routes. The vibrations made by engines and bow waves are sufficient to keep timid sea creatures away from these areas, in contrast to the days of sail when the silent ships relied on wind and currents and were often driven well off their routes.

The cases cited above, and the hundreds of others that can be found in the various works on the subject, point to the fact that there is not just one type of sea monster. In 1965, Belgian zoologist Dr Bernard Heuvelmans completed the most detailed and exhaustive work on the subject in recent times – *In the wake of the sea-serpents*, a book that has been of great value to all modern writers on water monsters. In it, Dr Heuvelmans describes and analyses more than 500 reports, dating from 1639 to 1964. From these reports he draws certain conclusions and here we attempt a brief summary of them.

Of the 587 sightings that Heuvelmans collected, 56 of them he considered most likely to be hoaxes. Another group were known sea creatures mistakenly reported as unknown monsters – he found 52 of these. Another 121 reports were removed from his final analysis because the details given were too vague or ambiguous for any useful classification to be made.

This left 358 sightings with various characteristics of appearance and behaviour that could be divided into nine types. These

Further reading
Rupert T. Gould, *The case for the sea serpent*, Philip Allan 1930
Bernard Heuvelmans, *In the wake of the sea-serpents*, Rupert Hart–Davis 1968
John Keel, *Strange creatures from time and space*, Sphere 1976

range from the most frequently seen 'long-necked' sea serpent, which has a cigar-shaped body, four webbed feet and is a fast swimmer, to the very infrequently seen marine saurians that look like crocodiles 50–60 feet (15–18 metres) long and have only been seen in mid-ocean tropical waters.

The other types Dr Heuvelmans names informally as merhorses, many-humped, super-otters, many-finned, super-eels, fathers-of-all-the-turtles and yellow-bellies. He has also found a group he calls 'ambiguous periscopes', which might be either long-necked monsters or super-eels. He

Many-finned

Merhorse

considers the long-necked serpent and the first four categories above to be mammals.

The super-eel is probably a fish whose normal habitat is the ocean depths and when seen on the surface is usually near death, while the marine saurian could well be a survivor from the Jurassic period that normally lives well below the surface and so has survived to the present. His yellow-belly group is somewhat more difficult to classify owing to a lack of detailed descriptions, but it could possibly be a fish, perhaps a shark.

Another interesting observation that Dr Heuvelmans has made is that the most frequent sightings during this century have been of the long-necked sea monster, which as a species may be on the increase. Conversely, there has been no sighting of the super-otter since 1848 and Heuvelmans suggests that these two are, or have been, in competition for the same ecological niche – the super-otter must be the loser and it may well now be extinct.

The world beneath the sea has still not been fully explored and, despite the sceptics, there appears to be abundant evidence for the existence of large, unknown sea creatures. Scientists believe that before long they will have a much more detailed knowledge of life in the ocean depths – indeed, new species are being discovered every year, so perhaps they will soon find the answer to the mystery of the underwater monster.

The language of the dead

Under hypnosis, people blind from birth have described how they could see in former lives. Others have broken into foreign tongues that they have never heard or read. Is this, asks DAVID CHRISTIE-MURRAY, proof of reincarnation?

GRAHAM HUXTABLE, a 'charming, soft-spoken' man from Swansea, Wales, was one of the most extraordinary cases ever encountered by Arnall Bloxham. Under hypnosis, Graham Huxtable regressed to become a 'swearing, illiterate gunner's mate with a hacking cough and an earthy chuckle' in the Royal Navy at the time of the Napoleonic Wars. His voice became deeper, his Welsh accent changed to that of rural southern English, he used archaic naval slang and his descriptions of life on board an English frigate at the turn of the 18th century were later confirmed as accurate by naval historians. But neither the ship's name, which Huxtable called the 'Aggie', or the ship's master, 'Cap'n Pearce', have been identified.

The case highlights many of the problems encountered by researchers into hypnotic

Two frigates of the Royal Navy pursue a French warship during the Napoleonic wars. Graham Huxtable (inset, right) recounted similar experiences as a gunner's mate when he was hypnotised by Arnall Bloxham (left)

regression. An illiterate sailor, unable to read his ship's name, ignorant of any information not communicable by word of mouth, whose horizons were limited by the neighbourhood in which he lived and the ship on which he served, whose social intercourse was with people as ill-educated as himself, is inevitably unable to supply the kind of information historians look for. Yet, as in other cases, Graham Huxtable adopted a persona that was able to provide information of which Huxtable himself was ignorant, vividly describe events that had happened to him and speak in a voice that was beyond any reasonable possibility of fraud. His screams of agony as he relived the experience of his leg being shot off in a naval engagement convinced even the most hardened sceptic that there was nothing false about Graham Huxtable.

Edna Greenan, a middle-aged housewife, hypnotised for over 80 hours by Joe Keeton, presents similar problems to the researcher. Under hypnosis, Mrs Greenan consistently 'became' Nell Gwyn (1650–1687), the illiterate actress and mistress of Charles II. The material she supplied through Mrs Greenan is of six kinds: historically correct, definitely incorrect, fresh information of great historical interest if it could be corroborated, half-truths, informed guesses, and small talk and gossip of the time.

It might be suggested that so much has been written and is known about Nell Gwyn that Mrs Greenan could have created her character either consciously or subconsciously. But when questioned about whether she had read anything about Nell she answered, both when conscious and under hypnosis, that she had not. Her whole manner and her speech, liberally sprinkled with nicknames and items of gossip, were entirely convincing to witnesses.

Nell Gwyn (left) was at the centre of Charles II's court in the late 17th century. Three hundred years later Joe Keeton hypnotised Mrs Edna Greenan (right) who gave an intriguing account of a former life as Charles II's mistress – none other than Nell Gwyn

Sceptics who demand historical accuracy from regressed subjects and knowledge of events that were happening at the time of a 'previous life' might listen to the conversation held in a modern bus queue or shopping centre before they condemn the simplicity, naiveté and lack of general knowledge of the common people in past centuries.

Where, then, might we find hard evidence to substantiate the claim that cases of hypnotic regression 'prove' that reincarnation takes place? One way is suggested in cases of regression with the congenitally blind, who in alleged previous lives were apparently able to see. If under hypnosis they are able to describe objects, events and experiences in the same way as a sighted person, where could they have acquired this ability other than in a previous life?

Work done by Paul Palmer and Dr James E. Parejko of Chicago State University with six blind subjects, of whom four were regressed, indicates that those born blind 'gave essentially the same life reports as sighted persons', and described events during regression as if they were sighted. Their reports may, of course, merely denote a manner of speech, as when one says 'I see' meaning 'I understand'. Alternatively they might be experiencing the kind of thing, for which there is a large body of evidence, as subjects who are able to 'see' with their elbows or some other part of the body. Or it could be a case of some other form of paranormal ability that we have yet to identify.

Whatever the cause, the blind subjects under hypnotic regression usually relied upon touch, taste and smell to describe their experiences. Only occasionally did they use expressions one would expect of a sighted person, and expressions like 'rosy cheeks that looked warm if you touched them' were common. One subject was able to describe a wooden lion's mouth, the shape of the carved teeth and how the whole thing appeared water-stained. Another subject claimed to be able to 'see' a clean-shaven man with blotches like pimples all over his cheeks and with a little tuft of whiskers growing on his throat.

Other descriptions were of a sloppy woman in a dirty blouse, windows reflected in a mirror, curtains with sunlight behind them and jewellery so dazzling in sunlight that it caused the subject to avert his eyes. Objects tended to be described three-dimensionally and at a distance – an old piano across a room, lips in a half-pout, a distant girl with red hair that was not a wig, clothes looking as though they had been slept in.

These blind subjects did not dream visually. In their regressions, however, they saw in colour and also not in colour. Like sighted people they distinguished between 'seen' objects and 'felt' objects, but the blind found that seeing objects was more of an effort than it was for those who are normally sighted. Yet they certainly spoke as if they saw and, when they returned to the same 'previous life' several times, their surroundings remained the same and more details were related. This phenomenon, which can be repeated under experimental conditions, is perhaps the best evidence there is for reincarnation.

This promising line of enquiry, however, could possibly be handicapped by lack of suitable subjects or opposed on the grounds that it is cruel to 'give sight' to someone who has never been able to see. The blind person must, of course, be given the choice of being hypnotised. But there is another line of criticism that is more damaging. It has been suggested that rather than giving an accurate description of things 'seen' the blind person is really describing things as he *imagines* a sighted person *would* describe them.

The gift of tongues

Another phenomenon that some have claimed provides proof of reincarnation is that of 'xenoglossy' or 'xenolalia'. This is the ability of some subjects, while under hypnosis, to speak a foreign language of which they are totally ignorant when conscious.

Dr Ian Stevenson relates the case of T.E., a 37-year-old American, whose doctor husband hypnotised her for therapeutic purposes. Under hypnosis she regressed to become Jensen Jacoby, speaking broken English or Swedish in a deep male voice. Jacoby, a peasant, appeared to have lived some centuries ago either in Sweden or New Sweden (present-day Philadelphia) in America. Eight scholars, seven of them Swedish-speaking, studied T.E. and her tapes, and since exhaustive research into her background showed that there was no time in her life when she could have learned Swedish or had contact with Swedish-speaking people, they agreed that it was a true case of responsive xenoglossy.

Another case investigated by Dr Stevenson is that of Dolores Jay. Hypnotised by her husband Carroll Jay in May 1970, Dolores regressed to become 'Gretchen', replying to Dr Stevenson's English in German. In 22 sessions between 1971 and 1972 Dr Stevenson, a German speaker, interviewed Gretchen in the presence of three Germans.

Gretchen responded well to Stevenson and two of the Germans but not well to the third. She gave her family name as Gottlieb, said that her father, Hermann, had been Mayor of Eberswalde, that her mother was dead and her close friend was called Frau

El Greco's painting of the Pentecost (now in the Prado, Madrid) shows the disciples of Christ receiving the gift of tongues. The miracle has been repeated in modern times, as hypnotised subjects have spoken languages that they have never been taught

Schilder. She could name no political leaders or heads of state living at the time. A Roman Catholic, Gretchen named Pope Leo and was obviously afraid of the *Bundesrat* – a word which entered Germany's political vocabulary in 1867. This was a repressive measure that discriminated against German Catholics. Gretchen died at the age of 16. Research showed that the only Eberswalde known did not have a mayor.

In the transcripts 237 German words appeared, of which 120 were spoken before any German words were spoken to her. The German spoken by Gretchen was modern, though with some archaisms. Her pronunciation was generally excellent though sometimes grossly wrong, and her grammar was sometimes faulty. In April 1971, Dolores wrote 38 words in a mixture of correct and phonetic spelling. She had not studied German nor attended a school where German was taught. Nor had she had any contact with German speakers. A lie detector confirmed her statements.

Less than a year before Gretchen manifested herself under hypnosis, she had appeared in a dream to Dolores. In 1971 and 1972, a series of nightmarish dreams and a sense of Gretchen's presence in Mrs Jay's house culminated in a brief hallucinatory flash in which she appeared. This appearance, combined with a general sense of strain, caused Mrs Jay to end the sessions.

Possessed by a spirit

A spontaneous case of either regression or possession involving xenoglossy, again investigated and reported by Dr Stevenson and a colleague, Dr Satwant Parsricha, may be included here because, though not hypnotic, it belongs to the same family of phenomena.

'Miss A', a university teacher, lived with her mother at Nagpur, Maharashtra, in India. She and her family had always lived there, speaking Marathi, with some Hindi and English. Miss A had studied Sanskrit and during her high school days had taken at most just a few lessons in reading Bengali script. Her father had Bengali friends but she had never spoken Bengali with them.

From early 1974 until 1978, a personality known as Sharada intermittently 'occupied' Miss A for periods varying from a day to seven weeks on about 30 occasions. She was quite unable to speak Marathi and spoke fluently in Bengali, contrasting markedly with the halting Swedish and German spoken by Jacoby and Gretchen. Sharada's possession of Miss A came on gradually, over a period of several hours, sometimes overnight while the latter slept, and appeared particularly on the eighth day of the waxing or waning Moon.

Sharada dressed, acted and spoke like a married Bengali woman of the early 19th century. Her speech was that spoken by Bengalis of that time. Modern Bengali contains some 20 per cent of words derived from

Right: Pope Leo XIII, who was correctly named by Dolores Jay during her regressions to a former life as a young Roman Catholic girl in 19th-century Germany

During the 1970s an Indian university teacher was possessed by the spirit of a Bengali girl. Not only did she dress like an early-19th-century Bengali woman (below) but spoke the language fluently

English. These did not appear in Sharada's conversation. Nor did she show a knowledge of modern inventions and technology.

Spending her days indoors and indulging almost exclusively in devotional activities and singing, Sharada showed a marked preference for, and unusual knowledge of, the foods of Bengal and a familiarity with its small towns, villages and rivers. She gave details of the family to which she belonged, whose present head has a genealogy that includes six of the men named by Sharada. From these details her life, which was ended by a snakebite, can be dated to the years between 1810 and 1830. Sharada remembers 'fainting' after the snakebite, but could not explain how she came to be in Nagpur, 750 miles (1200 kilometres) west of Bengal.

Reincarnation or possession are alternative explanations for all cases in which one personality appears to occupy or take on the personality of another person. The difference between 'true reincarnation' and possession cases is that, in the former, a personality *remembers* his previous life while retaining consciousness of his present life, in the same way as one remembers past events in this life: 'I am now six years old; I recall my fifth birthday last year; *and* I remember when I was grown up 10 years ago.'

The 'possessed' person is not conscious of having an identity other than the one he is aware of at that moment. He is either himself ('non-possessed'), or he is the possessed personality. Each is distinct. But the possessed person does have memories, memories of the personality he has assumed while possessed. And they have been shown to be memories of real events and situations. How knowledge of these events and situations is gained, remains a mystery.

What do psychologists make of hypnotic regression? How can it be explained? See page 174

A bird, a plane—or a UFO?

Weird lights in the night sky, strange silvery shapes flashing through the sunlight – these are the stuff of UFO reports, but they often have a perfectly rational explanation. JENNY RANDLES explains how to recognise unusual objects in the sky – including true UFOS

ON THE AFTERNOON of 7 January 1948, a strange bright light was seen to hover for several hours over Godman Airfield, Kentucky, USA. In due course, a team of F-51 aircraft appeared in the area, led by Captain Thomas Mantell. Though on a routine mission, Mantell agreed to divert his planes to investigate the glittering intruder. One by one, however, the pilots were forced down – lacking proper oxygen equipment to travel above a limited height. But Mantell himself continued climbing. At 20,000 feet (7000 metres) he reported seeing a metallic object, ahead and above him. Minutes later the wreckage of his F-51 was found scattered over a wide area. According to a report at the time, which has persisted to the present day, Mantell had been shot down by a UFO.

On 31 December 1978 two police officers in Hertfordshire, England, watched in amazement as an incredible object passed silently overhead. It had a cigar-shaped, silvery body with what looked like windows along the side. Behind trailed shimmering orange-coloured streamers. The thing moved slowly away out of sight and, alarmed by what they had seen, they radioed their headquarters.

Unknown to the policemen, hundreds of other people, including airline pilots and coastguards, had reported seeing the same thing in many parts of Britain. Many believed that it was connected with the piece of film taken by a television crew off the coast of New Zealand the day before; a film that was already receiving massive world-wide publicity. As with the first case, there was a

Above: Allan Hendry, whose study of UFO identification, *The UFO handbook*, has become a classic of its kind

Below: friction creates a blaze of light around the Apollo 11 space capsule as it re-enters the Earth's atmosphere on returning from a mission to the Moon. Debris from satellites and other space vehicles can cause similar displays – but because they are unexpected they are often mistaken for UFOS

Lights	stationary → YES
	NO ↓
	continuous motion ↓

Round, oval or irregular disc shape	stationary → YES
	NO ↓
	continuous motion ↓

Cigar, tube or cylinder shape	stationary → YES
	NO ↓
	continuous motion ↓

If you think you've seen a UFO, check the features of your sightings on the chart below. This shows the three major categories of the man-made and natural objects that are most often mistaken for UFOs and enables you to eliminate them from the investigation

widespread belief that the 'object' was a UFO.

On closer investigation many cases of UFO spotting turn out to have a perfectly ordinary explanation. Yet it seems to be fairly easy to misidentify a perfectly normal object, under certain conditions, as a UFO. Strange objects in the sky, especially when seen at night in a deserted area, can be alarming. There is the case, for example, of a woman who locked herself in her bedroom and hid under the bed

for an hour, terrified by seeing an object she believed to be a UFO, but that turned out to be a star. In America, ufologist Allan Hendry has described how one man was in such a panic after seeing a well-lit aircraft, believing it to be a UFO, that he ripped his neighbour's door off its hinges, so anxious was he to escape. These examples may sound funny, but it would be wrong to assume that such people are idiots.

Jimmy Carter, for example, when Governor of Georgia, reported seeing a brilliant light in the sky in 1973. The light, which changed colour, was seen to hover silently for 10 minutes at a height of 300 feet (90 metres) before descending to roof-top level. After performing various manoeuvres, it moved on. Twelve other people witnessed the same event, and despite the 'official' explanation – that it was in fact the planet Venus – the belief still lingers that it was a UFO. Especially since Carter, a trained scientist and former naval commander used to navigation by stars, was perfectly able to recognise Venus.

To help witnesses distinguish between what is and what is not a UFO, the term 'true UFO' is used for something that does not appear, after investigation, to be a case of mistaken identity. If the object seen turns out not to be a UFO but has a recognisable identity, then the term IFO – Identified Flying Object – is used.

Ufologists divide UFO reports into several categories. But, more often than not, the reports tend to fall into two simple classes. These are often called 'low-definition' and 'medium-definition' experiences.

Low-definition experiences – 45 per cent of all UFO reports – involve seeing a light or a highly amorphous phenomenon with no distinctive shape. The colour of the light is not of great importance. In most cases it is white, but there are many different coloured light sources that can be seen, and the presence of thin cloud or smoke in the atmosphere can subtly alter what is seen. If you see an unidentified light in the sky there are a number of things you can do.

First, note whether the light remains stationary or if it moves. If stationary, the chances are that it is a star or planet. Stars and planets are among the most common sources of UFO misidentification. Of course they are not really stationary, but their motion is so slow relative to an observer that it is not usually noticed except over a period of hours. This is an excellent tell-tale sign. If a light is visible in the night sky for over an hour or more, and hardly moves at all, then it is probably a star. You can check by looking at a map showing the positions of stars and planets in the night sky for that time of year.

Venus is a common source of misidentification. It is the brightest object in the night sky and at certain times of the year is very close to Earth. It can be seen even in daylight, as a bright white speck, if one

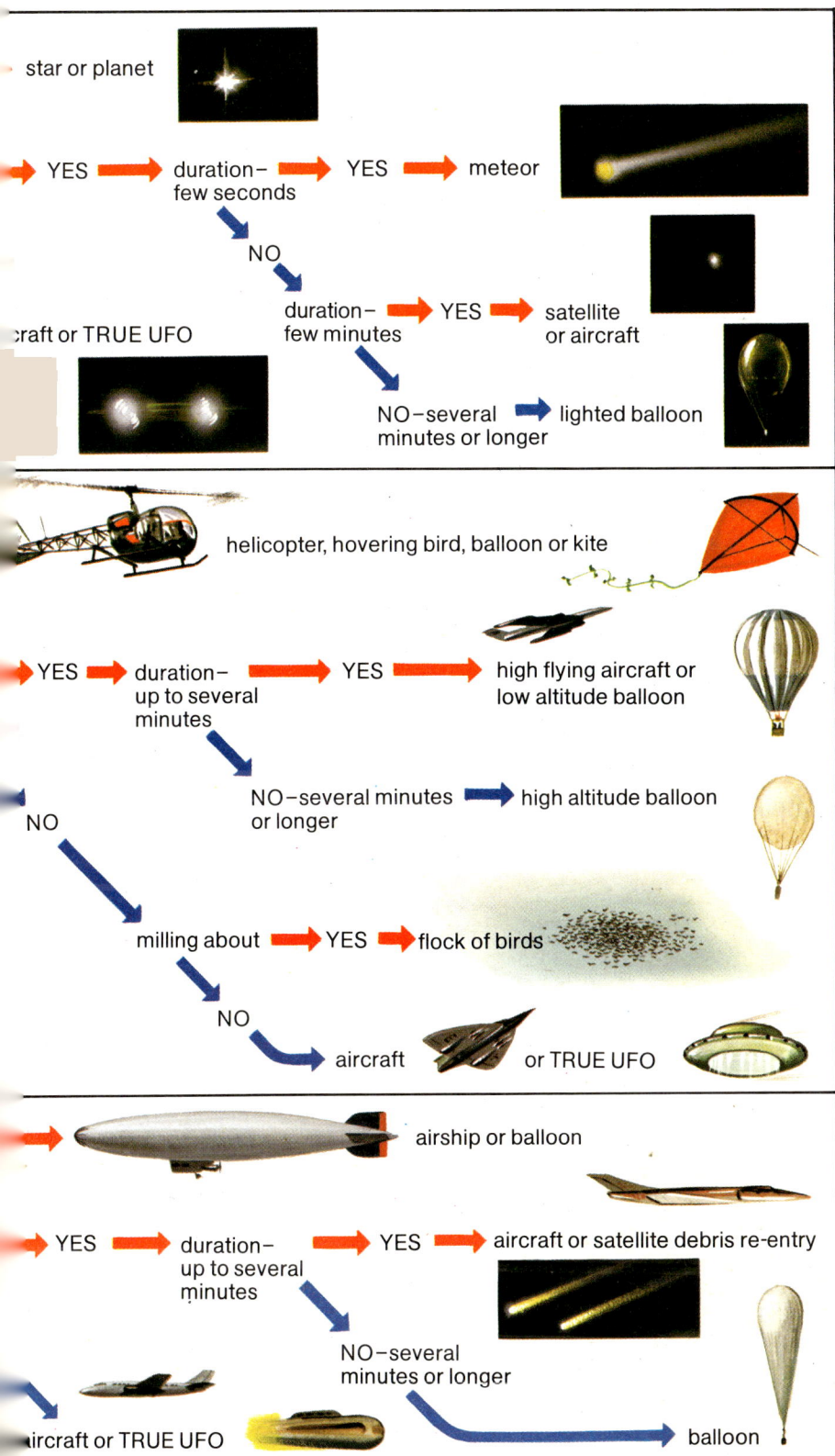

star or planet

YES ➡ duration– few seconds ➡ YES ➡ meteor

NO

duration– few minutes ➡ YES ➡ satellite or aircraft

craft or TRUE UFO

NO–several minutes or longer ➡ lighted balloon

helicopter, hovering bird, balloon or kite

YES ➡ duration– up to several minutes ➡ YES ➡ high flying aircraft or low altitude balloon

NO–several minutes or longer ➡ high altitude balloon

NO

milling about ➡ YES ➡ flock of birds

NO

aircraft or TRUE UFO

airship or balloon

YES ➡ duration– up to several minutes ➡ YES ➡ aircraft or satellite debris re-entry

NO–several minutes or longer

aircraft or TRUE UFO

balloon

computer-programmed message. The aircraft is built to fly very slowly so that the message can be read. But if the lights are seen from an angle, very weird effects can result.

Aircraft are, of course, highly manoeuvrable, and helicopters even more so. Consequently, not only might they be seen as lights on a smooth flightpath, they can also be seen to alter direction, slow down, and even stop in mid-flight. The wind can carry away the sound of an aircraft's engines, leaving only a silent light in the sky.

Most of these effects would be seen only at night. But there is one object that is often seen and misidentified as a UFO during the day – the balloon. Weather centres release balloons at regular intervals, either to test wind direction or to carry instruments high into the sky from where they radio meteorological information back to Earth. At high altitude a balloon will reflect sunlight from its shiny surface while floating across the sky.

knows where to look. But often there are good reasons why stars and planets are not immediately recognised for what they are. Optical illusion, for example, and the phenomenon known as 'autokinesis', which causes a star apparently to dart about erratically in the sky are common causes of misidentification. Since stars do not normally dart about, this effect instils the belief that the light comes not from a star but from a UFO.

If the light does appear to move, the next question is whether it follows a smooth flightpath or whether it hovers or seems to change direction dramatically. A smooth flightpath can indicate one of several things. Precisely what it is can usually be determined by the length of time the light is seen. If it is of very short duration, it could be a meteor – particles of dust or debris from space burning up as they enter the Earth's atmosphere. Meteors tend to glow for a second or two, leaving a trail of light as they streak silently through the night sky.

Occasionally, the debris is a little larger than usual and takes longer to burn up. This leads to the phenomenon known as a bolide or fireball, a brilliant light visible for up to 10 seconds and accompanied by a rumbling or whooshing sound. Fireballs have been seen in daylight too, although this is fairly rare. Usually, sightings of fireballs are so spectacular that they are witnessed by dozens of people over a wide area. They are very similar, in fact, to satellite re-entry, another common cause of UFO misidentification.

Circling the Earth are hundreds of man-made satellites. Many are too small to be seen from the ground, but others are visible at night as points of light that may take several minutes to cross the sky. As satellites re-enter the Earth's atmosphere, they can present a spectacular sight. As the pieces burn away, they glow in several colours, leaving a trail of lights through the upper atmosphere, which can take several minutes

Above left: an irregular, unearthly shape silhouetted against the sun can be very difficult to recognise as a flight of helicopters

Left: the spectacular comet Ikeya-Seki, which was seen in late 1965. A surprising number of heavenly bodies – including stars and planets – are reported as UFOs

to disappear. A few parts may even survive and reach the ground, as happened to the American Skylab, for example, which landed in Western Australia in July 1979.

But by far the most common cause of UFO misidentification is aircraft. Since aircraft possess many different types of lighting, there are plenty of opportunities for strange effects. Bright searchlights may be used in front of the plane, visible from miles away. Seen heading towards you, such a light can appear stationary for a long time before bursting into colour as the aircraft's navigation lights come into view. Strobe lights, brilliant pulsating blue-white flashes, can also be misconstrued. In many countries, aircraft are employed for advertising by using electronic lights that flash out a

every conceivable cause of misidentification. The figures issued by NUFON (the Northern UFO Network) contain 29 broad categories (see diagram) and there are known to be over 100 possible causes of misidentification that have occurred at some time or another.

Both case studies mentioned at the beginning of this article are quite typical of reported UFO sightings. Yet it is unlikely that the objects seen were UFOs. What Captain Mantell encountered was probably one of the 100-foot (30.5-metre) 'skyhook' balloons being secretly tested in the area at the time by the US Navy. These balloons were not known to Air Force officers, and although this was the probable identity of Mantell's UFO, the case has never been conclusively proven. Certainly the 'official' explanation that what observers on the ground saw was the planet Venus is not convincing.

As for the case of the Hertfordshire policemen, it was subsequently discovered that a

From the ground, the silvery dot drifting across the sky may be seen as a round or conical shape.

Medium-definition experiences are those that involve the clear perception of a shape. Though they have been seen at night, they are more commonly seen in daytime. They account for a further 35 per cent of all UFO cases and, as with low-definition experiences, the most important criterion is motion. A clearly defined shape that hovers for some time is unlikely to be an aircraft, although it could be a helicopter too distant to be heard.

Airships tend also to be a common cause of misidentification. Under certain conditions their shape could be mistaken for a cigar-shaped UFO, hovering or slowly moving across the sky. Alternatively, as already mentioned, the object could be a balloon. Kites are another possible explanation. Seen at a distance, the controlling cord of a kite may not be visible and its irregular shape could easily be taken to be a UFO.

In most cases the object believed to be a UFO is seen moving in a constant direction at varying speeds. Again, this could well be an aircraft. In strong sunlight, for example, an aeroplane's wings and tailplane can be obscured leaving just a metallic body or cylinder visible. Though really the fuselage, it can look like a UFO. Even clouds have been mistaken for UFOs. A certain type of cloud, known as lenticular, looks like a structured disc. Though uncommon, its slow movement has fooled more than one observer.

Flocks of birds have also caused confusion. In daylight, the reflective underbellies of certain species can shine in sunlight and be seen as white ovals, obscuring all other detail. At night, it is even possible for street lighting to be reflected, creating different coloured oval shapes according to the type of lighting used.

Inevitably it has not been possible to list

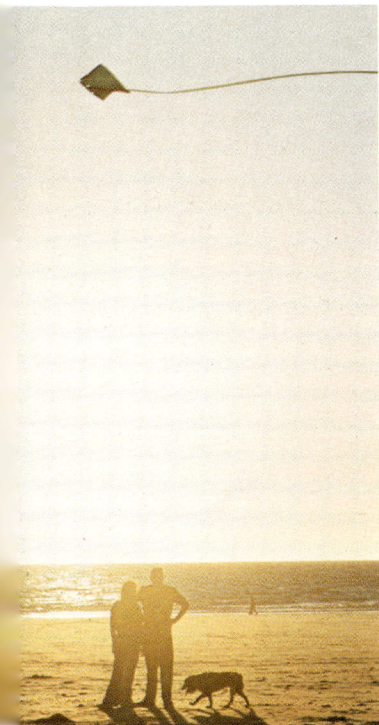

Top: the rare lenticular cloud formation, which has the characteristic shape of a 'flying saucer'

Above: a high-flying kite, glinting in the sunlight with its control wires invisible, can take on the appearance of a typical UFO

Right: this research balloon was sent up 130,000 feet (40,000 metres) to investigate cosmic rays. Even experienced airmen have failed to recognise craft like this in flight

Russian booster-rocket re-entered the Earth's atmosphere that night. Its decay orbit took it over northern Europe and it was this that many witnesses mistook for a UFO. The New Zealand film was not connected to the Hertfordshire incident at all. And while there are still those who say that what the two policemen saw was a true UFO, most accept the 'official' explanation. This, of course, is not to say that all cases of UFO spotting turn out, after investigation, to be cases of Identified Flying Objects.

If none of the explanations outlined here seem to apply to the reported sighting then it is likely that the object you have seen is a true UFO.

If you saw a UFO in the sky, whom should you tell? What should you do? See page 166

Scientific research suggests ESP is a gift we all have – if only we could 'tune in' our minds to it. How could this elusive gift be put to use? ROY STEMMAN discusses the possibilities

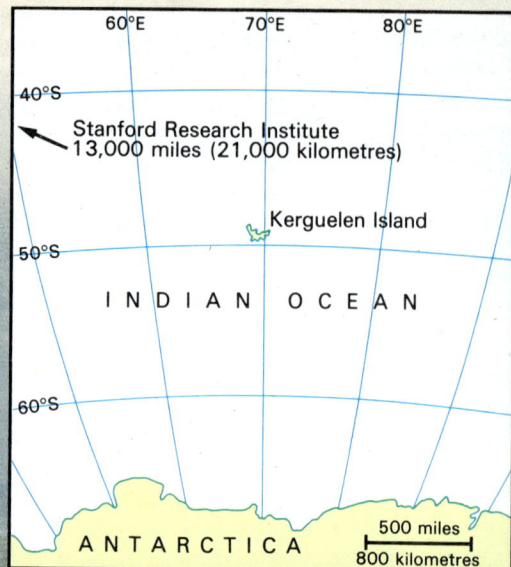

Putting the power to work

Stanford Research Institute
13,000 miles (21,000 kilometres)

Kerguelen Island

INDIAN OCEAN

ANTARCTICA

500 miles
800 kilometres

A TELEPHONE RANG in the office of Doctors Russell Targ and Harold Puthoff at Stanford Research Institute (SRI), California. A sceptical scientist who had heard about their research into extra-sensory perception was calling to issue a challenge. He had heard that Ingo Swann, one of the psychics they used in their tests, could apparently describe places given their geographical co-ordinates.

The man on the telephone asked Swann to describe what he could 'see' at 49° 20'S, 70° 14' E. Naturally, the psychic was not allowed to consult a map. But instantly he described a rocky island. The climate was cold and there were buildings, one of them orange, with a few trucks in front of them.

Swann described the coastline and continued with his description, drawing attention to specific points on the island, which he marked on a sketch map.

The psychic was absolutely right. The sceptic had come up with co-ordinates that marked the island of Kerguelen in the southern Indian Ocean. The island is administered as part of the French Southern and Antarctic lands and is a base for a joint French-Soviet research project that is studying the upper atmosphere. Many of the features described by Swann seemed to refer to Kerguelen, about which it was impossible for him to have had no prior knowledge.

This case, quoted by Puthoff and Targ in their book *Mind-reach*, is one of many that

the SRI scientists have investigated as part of their research into an aspect of ESP called 'remote viewing'. The geographical co-ordinate tests represent a variation of their normal procedure, which was to get Swann and other psychics to describe places being visited by one of the investigators.

For example, psychic Pat Price (an ex-police commissioner and vice-mayor of Burbank, California) sat talking to Targ while Puthoff left the SRI building carrying a sealed envelope that had been selected at random from a large number. Once outside the building, he opened the envelope and found instructions directing him to a particular destination. He stayed at this place for half an hour, just looking at it, while Price attempted telepathically to 'see' what Puthoff was seeing.

The psychic began describing a scene in terms that were general and rambling. But then, the scientists report, his account 'became tighter and more coherent, gradually zeroing in on a description of a tower-like structure until finally we heard "seems like it would be Hoover Tower".' Price's impressions were tape recorded and played back to Puthoff on his return to the SRI building. He then produced the envelope: the target site was, as Price had 'seen', the Hoover Tower, a well–known landmark of the Stanford University campus.

Not surprisingly, Puthoff and Targ's

In some remarkable ESP tests conducted at Stanhope Research Institute (SRI), California, psychic Ingo Swann (below) was given the co-ordinates of Kerguelen Island in the Indian Ocean (top). He immediately began to describe an island with a rocky terrain. The climate, he said, was cold, and there were buildings, one of them orange. The photograph (above) shows just how accurate his description was

134

work has excited great interest – particularly as they claim that remote viewing is an ability that most of us possess. Others have succeeded in producing similar results, but not all scientists have been able to do so. And critics claim that, for various technical reasons, the SRI scientists' results are not as impressive as they seem at first glance.

Executive ESP

If some people *can* learn to view remotely, there are all sorts of exciting possibilities. Could they eavesdrop on top secret political or commercial talks? Could they 'see' confidential plans or documents? Could they visit sensitive sites and give information about their layout and the people who work there? The very best cases of ESP suggest that such possibilities are not far-fetched; the problem is that psychic powers are notoriously unreliable. A fortune awaits the person who discovers a way of 'switching' ESP on and off at will.

Many people have searched for a key to psychic success in the hope of producing repeatable ESP experiments, but their results have been disappointing. Some of the most fascinating studies have examined personality in relation to psychic abilities: what kind of person is most likely to experience ESP? One of the first researchers to delve into the subject was Dr Gertrude Schmeidler.

In thousands of clairvoyance tests in the late 1940s and early 1950s, Dr Schmeidler, of the City University of New York, asked each person before he was tested whether he believed ESP was possible under the conditions of the experiment. The purpose was to see whether those who believed ESP was possible scored more highly than those who did not. And, indeed, Dr Schmeidler's score sheets showed such a difference: the believers scored consistently slightly above chance, whereas the scores of the non-believers were slightly below.

Another link between ESP and personality was discovered by Dr Betty Humphrey of the Duke Parapsychology Laboratory. Before testing individuals for ESP she gave them a blank sheet of paper and asked them to draw anything they liked. Bold pictures

In this SRI experiment, the subject attempted to 'see' what an agent in another part of the campus was looking at. Psychic Pat Price accurately identified the Hoover Tower of Stanford University (above)

Above right: these drawings indicate extrovert (top) and introvert (bottom) personalities. Dr Betty Humphrey of Duke University says such drawings can predict how a subject will score in ESP tests

Below: Dr Gertrude Schmeidler of City University, New York, who has shown that subjects who believe in ESP score higher in tests than those who do not

Below right: a subject in a state of sensory deprivation, or *Ganzfeld state*, which makes him receptive to ESP

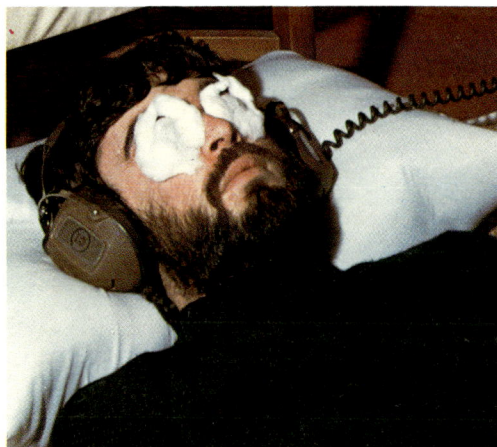

that filled most of the sheet indicated the person was an 'expansive' type; small, timid or conventional drawings showed that the person was a 'compressive'. Analysis of their ESP results showed that the expansives scored more highly than the compressives.

This work has continued into the 1980s, with different researchers using slightly different methods to gauge their subjects' personalities. The current trend is to divide people into extraverts (expansives) and introverts (compressives) using a detailed questionnaire.

The reasons for this link between extrasensory abilities and personality are still the subject of considerable conjecture, but many researchers regard it as powerful evidence for ESP. But does it mean that people who are not believers, or who are not extravert by nature, do not have ESP experiences? Not really. Research suggests that ESP can be induced by altering our state of consciousness. This may sound difficult, but, in fact, we do just that every time we fall asleep – and early researchers soon realised that dreams were a rich source of psychic experience. Numerous case histories were compiled of vivid dreams that either recorded events that were happening elsewhere at the time of dreaming, or gave the sleeper a glimpse of the future.

Modern parapsychologists use a technique that induces a state of altered consciousness easily at any time of day or night. The subject is asked to rest on a mattress. His eyes are then covered with half ping-pong balls onto which a soft coloured light is shone and his ears are covered with headphones into which 'white noise' (a gentle hissing sound) is fed. In this state of sensory deprivation the subject's mind has no visual or auditory distractions to occupy it and is, at least theoretically, more open to receiving telepathic signals from an agent some distance away, who is concentrating on a picture chosen at random. This technique induces a *Ganzfeld state* in the subject, and Dr Carl

Sargent of Cambridge University is one of the researchers who has had outstanding results with it, with average scores of 17 per cent above chance expectancy. One of his top-scoring subjects is a young computer expert, Hugh Ashton. In one session he described seeing buildings in a corner, adding:

'Keep thinking of firemen and fire station . . . Firemen definitely seen, black and white. People but not faces. I think one man at bottom in foreground: facing . . . Young face, as if photographer says, 'Oi' and only he turned round'.

The description contained much more detail. At the end of the session the agent brought into the room four pictures. They were a duplicate set of the pictures contained in the target envelope, of which only one had been selected for the test. Hugh Ashton was asked to identify the one he thought had been used for the experiment, and he was able to do so instantly. The agent had been concentrating on a picture that showed firemen playing their hoses on their special training building. They all had their backs to the camera – with the exception of one, who was looking straight at the photographer.

In another session at Cambridge University a subject was even able to name the picture being 'sent' by telepathy: William Blake's *The ancient of days*.

Another technique that has been used successfully to induce telepathy is hypnosis. Mesmerism – the variant of hypnotism that was popular two centuries ago – was used by several practitioners to produce paranormal effects in their patients. The Marquis du Puységur found that a peasant, Victor Race, could at times repeat what was going through Puységur's mind when he was deep in a mesmeric trance.

Puységur was also the discoverer of medical clairvoyance. Subjects were mesmerised and then asked to diagnose the ailments of people brought into the room who were complete strangers. Though they had no medical knowledge, their diagnoses were often astonishingly accurate.

Russian psychical researchers have been particularly keen to use hypnosis to induce ESP, and their influence was responsible for similar work carried out by the Czechoslovak Dr Milan Ryzl, who now lives and works in the USA. While still in Czechoslovakia he experimented with precognitive clairvoyance. He would hypnotise a subject and ask him or her to visualise an unpleasant event that would happen to a friend in the future so that he or she could be warned about it.

As soon as one girl, Josefka, was hypnotised she became distressed, and began describing in vivid detail a scene in which a girlfriend, who lived 50 miles (80 kilometres) away, was approached by a stranger in a restaurant. They left and drove away together on a motorcycle at high speed. Suddenly they stopped. Josefka cried: 'Oh my God! He's torn her skirt.' She described the horrific scene as her friend was savagely raped.

Next day, thinking she had foreseen a future event, Josefka telephoned her friend to warn her not to accept a lift on a motorcycle from a stranger. 'You're too late,' came the response. 'It's already happened – last night.' Josefka's hypnotic vision matched the real event in every detail.

Josefka's ESP was just as impressive in the laboratory. Dr Ryzl enclosed standard Zener cards in opaque wrappings and asked her,

Dr Carl Sargent (above) of Cambridge University has gained outstanding results in ESP tests using the *Ganzfeld* state. One of his top-scoring subjects is Hugh Ashton, who described this photograph (left), which was sent telepathically by an agent, in accurate detail

Below: Jacques de Chastenet, Marquis du Puységur (1751-1825), an early exponent of mesmerism and the discoverer of medical clairvoyance, in which clairvoyants can diagnose illnesses by means of ESP

Left: in an experiment at Cambridge University, a subject was even able to name the picture being 'sent' – William Blake's *The ancient of days*

What causes ESP?

The first scientists to study one of the aspects of ESP – telepathy – thought its mechanics would be easy to understand once enough evidence had been collected. ESP seemed to be a simple matter of the mind being somehow 'tuned in' to receive messages, like a radio.

But the reality of ESP appears to be more complex. Successful telepathy experiments have been conducted with one of the participants shielded by a Faraday cage, which prevents the penetration of radio waves and other electromagnetic radiation. Whatever carries information from one mind to another is apparently not a straightforward physical process.

Finding an explanation for ESP is made even more difficult by the strange way in which it seems, at times, to ignore the natural limits of time and space; even if we could find a 'wavelength' on which minds make contact, we would still be left with the mystery of people who use ESP to see into the past or the future.

There is another complication that has to be taken into account in studying ESP. The latest research indicates that, in Zener card experiments that were originally carried out to test ESP, the results may actually have been due to psycho-kinesis (mind over matter), with the subject somehow influencing the order of the cards. An acceptable ESP theory, then, will have to take account of psycho-kinesis.

It is possible that research into particle physics may shed new light on ESP. Sub-atomic particles appear to be able to react instantaneously to the behaviour of other particles vast distances away – to 'communicate' by no known means, and faster than the speed of light. This is impossible according to the rules of quantum mechanics. But an attempt to explain the phenomenon has been made by Professor David Bohm of London University. The way in which particles 'communicate' may be similar to ESP contact, claim some parapsychologists. Professor Bohm's theory may provide the missing link between ESP research and science.

Above: Pavel Stepanek, the 'star' of ESP experiments conducted by Dr Milan Ryzl in the 1960s. In one experiment he attained a score against odds of a billion to one

while under hypnosis, to guess what they were. Out of 250 guesses she got 121 right – chance alone would have produced only 50 correct answers. When she tried the same experiment in a normal state her score was exactly at chance level.

Dr Ryzl went on to develop a method of ESP training, for which he claimed exceptional results. His six-stage method uses hypnosis and puts a heavy emphasis on inducing visual hallucinations. His claims created something of a controversy among other researchers, but the achievements of some of his subjects are beyond question. The star was Pavel Stepanek, a Czech library clerk. During the 1960s he was the most sought-after ESP subject and was tested by many researchers, usually with exceptional results. In his first series of 2000 guesses he scored hits with 1144; the odds against such a result are a billion to one.

Psychical researcher Rosalind Heywood found that ESP frequently impinged on her own life; she called her psychical impressions 'Orders'. In her book *The infinite hive* she tells of an experience that occurred in July 1949, when she was shutting up house for a month:

Orders said that the water should be turned off at the main as a pipe in the attic bathroom was going to burst. I knew that this irrational prediction would stand little chance with my rational husband – it looked far more like fussing than ESP – and, as I expected, when I told him of it he kindly gave me the technical reasons why pipes did not burst in high summer.

At this I decided on a fatuous compromise: I would leave the water turned on as he wished and take a key to our builder for use when the pipe did burst. Although he, too, explained that pipes never burst in the summer I just had the strength of mind to press the key into his reluctant hand, thank him and fly. When the pipe did burst, as Orders had warned me, his charge for repairing the damage was £20.

Francis Kinsman, an eminent British futurologist, has attempted in a unique way to put ESP to practical use. Between March and July 1979 he interviewed 15 leading clairvoyants and psychics, asking the same simple question: 'What do you think will be the role of Britain in the world context during the 1980s?' The questioning then branched off to include politics, economics, technology and sociological developments, and the results were published in a booklet, *Future tense*. The prophecies include the collapse of the current world economic system, major earthquakes and floods, a new Middle East war, and the abdication of the Queen.

But perhaps the most fascinating aspects of the predictions concern ESP. They claim that there will be an increase in the use of psychic techniques in the field of medicine. The Russians, they say, are leaders in the field of psychic research and are secretly carrying out experiments in psychic warfare. Fear for its own safety, they predict, will lead the West to concentrate its energies and develop the extra-sensory powers that are latent in everyone.

Above: Francis Kinsman, who has conducted a series of interviews with clairvoyants about the future of Britain and the world

Further reading
Stuart Holroyd, *PSI and the consciousness explosion*, Abacus 1974
Francis Kinsman, *Future tense*, Pendulum 1980
J. B. Rhine, *The reach of the mind*, Morrow (New York) 1947
Louisa Rhine, *Mind over matter*, Macmillan (New York) 1970
R. H. Thouless, *From anecdote to experiment in psychical research*, Routledge 1972

The self-styled Count St Germain – alchemist, diplomat and adventurer – led a chequered career in the royal courts of 18th-century Europe. Some believe the enigmatic Count is still alive; FRANK SMYTH explores the myths

The man from nowhere

TOWARDS THE END of the year 1745, London was gripped by 'spy fever'. It was the year in which the Young Pretender, Prince Charles Edward Stuart, had staged his Jacobite rebellion in an attempt to regain the British throne for his father. Although the Jacobite cause had been defeated at the battle of Culloden in April, it was feared that Jacobite plotters and their French sympathisers might be in hiding in London. Foreigners, particularly Frenchmen, were prime suspects. One such man was arrested in November and accused of having pro-Stuart letters in his possession. He indignantly claimed that the correspondence had been 'planted' on him and, somewhat surprisingly, he was believed and released.

Commenting on the case in a letter to Sir Horace Mann, dated 9 December, Horace Walpole wrote:

> The other day they seized an odd man who goes by the name of Count Saint-Germain. He has been here these two years, and will not tell who he is or whence, but professes that he does not go by his right name. He sings and plays on the violin wonderfully, is mad and not very sensible.

Walpole's comment sheds a tantalising and authentic light on one of the strangest characters of 18th-century high society – a man described by Count Warnstedt as 'the completest charlatan, fool, rattle-pate, windbag and swindler', and by his last patron, Prince Charles of Hesse-Cassel, as 'perhaps one of the greatest sages who ever lived. . . .'

Dazzle of diamonds

The first of the scant historical records of Count St Germain dates from about 1740, when he began to move in fashionable Viennese circles, a handsome man who appeared to be in his thirties. His clothes attracted attention in those days of brightly coloured silks and satins, for he habitually wore black, relieved only by crisp white linen at neck and wrists. The sombreness of his clothes, however, was brilliantly set off by a dazzle of diamonds on his fingers, his fob, his snuff box and his shoe buckles; according to later accounts he also carried handfuls of loose diamonds in his pockets in lieu of money.

In Vienna he met Counts Zabor and Lobkowitz, contemporary leaders of fashion, and through them the ailing French Marshal de Belle Isle, who had been taken seriously ill while campaigning in Germany. The nature of his illness is not recorded, but according to the Marshal it was Count St Germain who

Left: the only known portrait of the man who called himself the Count St Germain, an engraving made for the Marquise d'Urfé in 1783, when the Count must have been in his late sixties, and shortly before his reported death. St Germain was arrested in London as a spy some months after the defeat of the Scottish forces at Culloden in 1745 (below). He was accused of carrying letters for the Young Pretender, Charles Edward Stuart (below left), but was soon released. He then returned to Paris, where he was introduced to Louis XV by Jeanne Antoinette de Pompadour, the king's mistress (right). Sent to the Hague by Louis, St Germain lost the friendship of Giacomo Casanova (below right), who has left us some of the most revealing descriptions of the Count

known that Christ would meet a bad end.' He had been particularly fond of Anne, the mother of the Virgin Mary, and had personally proposed her canonisation at the Council of Nicaea in AD 325.

In Paris the Count soon charmed the jaded Louis XV and his mistress, Madame de Pompadour. The truth about his two-year stay in England before his arrest in 1745 may never be known, but he could well have been engaged on a secret mission; on his return to France he carried out several delicate political errands for the King.

In 1760 Louis sent Count St Germain to the Hague as his own personal representative, ostensibly to arrange a loan with Austria to help finance the Seven Years' War against England. While in Holland, the Count fell out with his erstwhile friend Casanova, also a diplomat at the Hague, who tried hard but unsuccessfully to discredit him in public. But St Germain also made a more powerful enemy. The Duc de Choiseul, Louis's Foreign Minister, discovered that the Count had been putting out feelers with a view to arranging peace between England and France. Somehow the Duke convinced Louis that Count St Germain had betrayed him, and the Count was forced to flee, first back to England and then to Holland.

For two or three years he lived in Holland under the name Count Surmont and set about raising money to build laboratories in which he made paint and dyes and tried to perfect the techniques of alchemy, 'the ennoblement of metals'. He seems to have been successful, for records show that he disappeared from Holland with 100,000 guilders – only to turn up in Belgium, this time calling himself the Marquis de Monferrat. Here, in Tournai, he set up another laboratory before vanishing again.

Over the next few years reports of the

cured it, and in gratitude he took him to France and set him up with apartments and a well-equipped laboratory.

The bare bones of the Count's life after his arrival in Paris are well documented, but it is the long-vanished detail that provides the lasting mystery.

The legend begins shortly after the Count's arrival in Paris. One evening, according to the pseudonymous 'Countess de B. . .' in her memoirs, *Chroniques de l'oeil de boeuf*, the Count had attended a soirée given by the aged Countess von Georgy, whose late husband had been Ambassador to Venice in the 1670s. Hearing the Count announced, the Countess said she recalled the name from her days in Venice. Had the Count's father perhaps been there at that time? No, replied the Count, but *he* had been, and well remembered the Countess as a beautiful young girl. Impossible, replied the Countess. The man she had known then was 45 at least, roughly the same age as he himself was now.

'Madame,' said the Count, smiling. 'I am very old.'

'But then you must be nearly 100 years old,' exclaimed the Countess.

'That is not impossible,' the Count replied and recounted some details that convinced the Countess, who exclaimed: 'I am already convinced. You are a most extraordinary man, a devil.'

'For pity's sake!' exclaimed the Count in a thundering voice. 'No such names!' He appeared to be seized with a cramp-like trembling in every limb, and left the room immediately.

Many such stories circulated – and were believed – in fashionable French circles during the days of the Count's early fame. He hinted, for instance, that he had known the Holy Family intimately, had been present at the marriage feast at Cana, and had 'always

Count St Germain

Count's activities continued to come from various parts of Europe. In 1768 he appeared in Russia at the court of Catherine the Great. Turkey had just declared war on Russia, and it seems that his powers as a diplomat and as an insider in French politics stood him in good stead, for before long he was advising Count Alexei Orlov, head of the Russian Imperial Forces. As a reward he was made a high-ranking officer in the Russian Army, this time choosing an ironic English alias – General Welldone. At this point he could have settled down in Russia to lead an honoured and profitable life, but after the defeat of the Turks at the battle of Chesmé in 1770 he chose to go travelling again.

In 1774 he turned up in Nuremberg, seeking funds from Charles Alexander, Margrave of Brandenburg, to set up another laboratory. This time he claimed to be Prince Rákóczy, one of three brothers from Transylvania. At first the Margrave was impressed, particularly when Count Orlov visited Nuremberg on a state visit and embraced the

Following his exile from France, Count St Germain went to the court of Catherine the Great of Russia (top), where he soon achieved high standing as a diplomat and took the title of 'General Welldone'. Towards the end of his career he began to claim that he was a high-ranking Freemason. The illustration (above) shows the ceremony of the entered Apprentice, the first degree of masonry, in the 'Scottish' rite, in a Paris lodge during the 1740s. Laid on the floor is a 'tracing board', used to instruct the new member in the symbolism of masonry

Right: Prince Charles of Hesse-Cassel, the Count's last patron, in whose castle he died

'Prince' warmly. But on checking, the Margrave found that all three Rákóczys were indubitably dead, and that the 'Prince' was in fact Count St Germain. The Count made no attempt to deny these charges, but felt it prudent to move on, and did so in 1776.

The Duc de Choiseul claimed that St Germain had worked as a double agent for Frederick the Great during his period at the French court. If this were so, his old master preferred to forget the connection, for a letter from Count St Germain to Frederick begging for patronage was ignored. Undaunted, the Count went to Leipzig and presented himself before Prince Frederick Augustus of Brunswick, claiming to be a Freemason of the fourth grade.

This was a bold move, for Frederick Augustus was Grand Master of the Prussian Masonic Lodges – and, unaccountably, it was a move that went wrong. If he was a confidence trickster, Count St Germain in his prime had few equals at the game; his background stories generally stood up to close scrutiny. This time, however, they

were lame. The Prince declared he was not a Mason, while the Count feebly replied that he was, but had forgotten all the secret signs.

In 1779 Count St Germain came to his last known resting place, at Eckenförde in Schleswig, Germany. He was an old man, probably in his late sixties, although typically he claimed to be much older. Some of his surface charm had gone, and at first he failed to make much impression on Prince Charles of Hesse-Cassel – but soon, like his predecessors, the Prince was won over.

By this time St Germain, who by all accounts had previously paid at least lip service to the Catholic Church, was openly mystical in his thinking. He told Prince Charles:

Be the torch of the world. If your light is that only of a planet, you will be as nothing in the sight of God. I reserve for you a splendour, of which the solar glory is a shadow. You shall guide the course of the stars, and those who rule Empires shall be guided by you.

Parish records show that on 27 February 1784 Count St Germain died at Prince Charles's home on Eckenförde. He was buried locally, and his last patron erected a tombstone bearing the words:

He who called himself the Comte de Saint-Germain and Welldone of whom there is no other information, has been buried in this church.

But was the Count dead? There is evidence that he appeared to a number of people over the years from 1784 to 1820; some occultists believe he is still alive. The mystery has lived on and deepened in the two centuries since his supposed death.

Who was Count St Germain, and what was the nature of his strange powers? See page 141